River Road To China

MILTON OSBORNE

RIVER ROAD to CHINA

The Search for the Source of the Mekong, 1866-73

Atlantic Monthly Press
New York

First published in 1975 by Allen & Unwin, London, as River Road to China: The Mekong River Expedition 1866–1873
Published simultaneously in Canada
Printed in the United States of America

FIRST AMERICAN EDITION

Library of Congress Cataloging-in-Publication Data

Osborne, Milton E.
    River road to China : the search for the source of the Mekong,
    1866–73 / Milton Osborne.
        p.   cm.
    ISBN 0-87113-752-6
    1. Indochina—Description and travel. 2. Mekong River—Discovery
and exploration. 3. China—Description and travel.   I. Title.
    DS534.O8   1999
    915.9704'3—dc21   99-17643

Design by Joseph G. Reganit

Atlantic Monthly Press
841 Broadway
New York, NY 10003

99 00 01 02   10 9 8 7 6 5 4 3 2 1

CONTENTS

LIST OF ILLUSTRATIONS*

*With the exception of the illustration of Jean Dupuis—taken from Jules Gros, *Origines de la conquête du Tong-Kin*, Paris, 1887—all illustrations originally appeared in the *Tour du Monde*, where Garnier's journal was first published, or in Garnier's book, *Voyage d'exploration en Indochine*, or in René de Beauvais' book *Louis Delaporte, Explorateur*, Paris, 1929.

For Fiona Emily Wooton Osborne

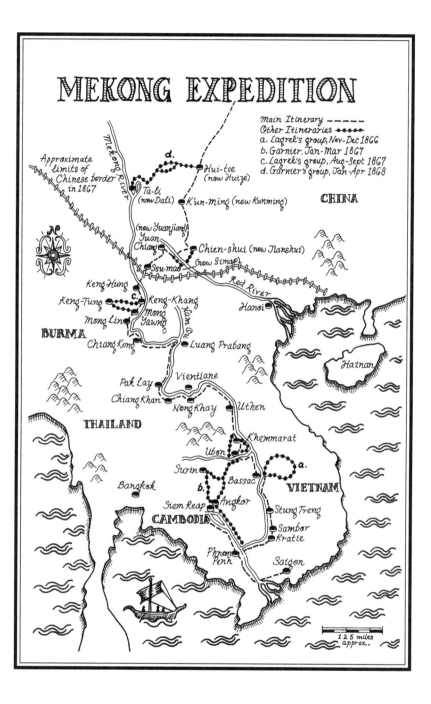

MEKONG EXPEDITION

Main Itinerary ------
Other Itineraries ••••••
a. Lagrée's group, Nov-Dec 1866
b. Garnier, Jan-Mar 1867
c. Lagrée's group, Aug-Sept 1867
d. Garnier's group, Jan-Apr 1868

CHINA

Mekong River

Approximate limits of Chinese border in 1867

Hui-tse (now Huize)

d.

Ta-li (now Dali)
K'un-ming (now Kunming)

Yuan Chiang (now Yuanjiang)
Chien-shui (now Jianshui)

Ssu-mao (now Simao)

Red River

Keng Hung
Hanoi

Keng-Tung
c.
Keng-Khang
Mong Yawng

Mong Lin

BURMA

Chiang Kong
Luang Prabang

Nam Ou

Hainan

Pak Lay
Vientiane

Chiang Khan
Nong Khay
Uthen

THAILAND

Khemmarat

Ubon

Surin
a.

Bangkok
b.
Bassac
VIETNAM

Siem Reap
Angkor

CAMBODIA
Stung Treng

Sambor
Kratie

Phnom Penh
Saigon

125 miles approx.

A NOTE ON THE SPELLING
OF GEOGRAPHIC NAMES

$\mathcal{I}$n the regions traversed by the Mekong explorers no less than five major languages are spoken today, and were spoken more than a century ago when they accomplished their journey. The languages are: Chinese, Burmese, Tai (the language not of Thailand alone, but in its various dialectal forms of millions living in Laos, Burma, China and Vietnam), Cambodian or Khmer, and Vietnamese. In addition, there are almost numberless minor languages and dialects. These many tongues are spoken in regions where political power has shifted substantially over the past hundred years. The situation makes for an author's, and a cartographer's, nightmare.

One brief example illustrates the problem. In September 1867 the Mekong explorers reached the town of Keng Hung—that, at least, for reasons of both consistency and simplicity is how I have chosen to refer to it. There are arguments to be advanced, far too long to record here, for alternative spellings. The Frenchmen in 1867 called the town Xieng Hong. Other maps show it as Chiang (or Chieng) Rung. In modern China the settlement is Yün-ching-hung.

In a search for consistency, I have in general followed the usage of *The Times Atlas of the World* (Comprehensive Edition), London, 1968. Reliance on this authority means that some relatively familiar place names are discarded in favor of more modern variants. For instance, instead of being called Yunnan-fu, the capital of Yunnan province is identified as K'un-ming.

Some reliance on old and established usage seems justified in certain cases, however. The example of Keng Hung has already been noted. And readers will find reference to the Yangtze River rather than to the Ch'ang Chiang.

Where additional cartographic guidance has been necessary I have turned to the maps published by the National Geographic Society of Washington, D.C., and to the *Atlas of South-East Asia*, London, 1964, edited by Professor D.G.E. Hall.

The existence of these authorities has not solved all my problems. Some of the locations visited by the explorers do not appear on modern, large-scale maps and I have had to rely on their own sometimes idiosyncratic transcriptions. Nonetheless, with the aid of the maps that accompany this book, a reader will have no difficulty in following the broad lines of the explorers' itineraries as they traveled slowly into China.

INTRODUCTION

I first saw the Mekong River from a noisily vibrating DC-3, a veteran of the motley but reliable fleet of Royal Air Cambodge. The airline no longer exists, and the Dakota's fate is uncertain, but the Mekong has scarcely changed. I knew little enough in 1959 about Cambodia and its capital, Phnom Penh, but of the great river spread out beneath me I knew nothing beyond its name. Most certainly, I did not realize that men had once hoped it would offer a trade route to China.

In my ignorance I was in good company, better than I realized at the time. But ignorance could not prevent an immediate awareness that here was a river of extraordinary size. Even in April, at the height of the dry season, the Mekong was a giant. Its winding course stretched endlessly through the brown, baked earth of the surrounding rice fields, disappearing into the dust-choked distance north of Phnom Penh, which sat on the river's western flank. Only later did I come to realize how great could be the transformation when the Mekong was filled with floodwaters and the wide stream of the dry months became an uncontrollable torrent, spilling over its banks to turn hundreds of square miles of dry land into a massive patchwork of temporary lakes.

Over the years I learned more about the river, traveling on it, beside and above it, in good times and bad. I react ambivalently to the experience of traversing the Mekong delta in a military helicopter. The view through the usually open side doors of a helicopter is spectacular, allowing one, however temporarily, to forget why an armed, khaki-colored machine should be the means of reaching one's destination. Traveling beside the Mekong in more peaceful days was another matter, particularly when the route ran through the remote regions of northeastern Cambodia and the extreme south of Laos. Few signs of man's presence seemed more ephemeral than the border marker between Cambodia and Laos, which I first saw in 1960. The marker stood in a savannah forest, an assertion of the values Europeans place on defining frontiers, rather than of any natural division of peoples and resources. To board a wheezing, wood-burning ferry as dawn crept over a sleepy river town was another way to come to know the Mekong. At that time of the morning it is still possible to believe that the day will be fresh and dry; until 6 A.M. the reality of the heat and humidity to come can be temporarily ignored.

As I came to know the river itself, so did I learn about its rich history. Most particularly, I found that only some ninety years before I first saw the Mekong, the Western world, and all its learned authorities, did not know the nature of the river's course. In an age that was already probing towards the moon, this seemed a remarkable business. But it was the truth. In 1866 a map of the Indochinese region could show sections of the Mekong with some measure of accuracy, but its source was unknown, and large stretches of the river were recorded only as the inaccurate guesses of imaginative cartographers.

In an attempt to solve the Mekong's mystery, six Frenchmen headed an expedition that began a survey of the river in 1866, believing their route would eventually lead them into China and so to fabled riches in that most populous of countries. My book traces the history of this expedition, which was a tragic exploration. In scope and achievement the expedition was the equal of much better remembered travels in Africa, such as those of Burton, Speke, Livingstone, and others. Death and disease took their toll, and dissension among the explorers was barely kept in check. For months at a time the French explorers moved slowly forward, never knowing what lay ahead. When the expedition ended, two long years after it had begun, the search for a navigable route to China was still incomplete.

Like many another "Anglo-Saxon," I was ignorant of the Mekong River expedition, until chance and an opportunity to live on the river's banks, in Phnom Penh, brought the story to my notice. Slowly, I began to find and read the principals' accounts of their travels. Only one of these, a book by Louis de Carné, has ever been translated into English, and it is a flawed, if interesting, work. The official narrative, by Francis Garnier, and Garnier's more personal unofficial account, both in French, are the major sources, and provided the essential background for this book. But these works present problems. First and foremost, they are difficult reading—not just because of the language but because of their style and approach. It is perhaps not surprising that these massive volumes of undigested information have never been translated.

There are other difficulties, scarcely less important. The printed sources are of the greatest value, but there is much more that can and should be read to supplement them. The archival sources in Paris offer details and insights lacking in the printed works. I have drawn heavily upon these archival materials in writing this book. It is only in them, for instance, that the true physical cost to the explorers is revealed. Private papers and unpublished official reports tell of the fevers and the dysentery that too often receive only the barest mention in the printed works. The nineteenth century was a stoic age.

Nor was it only a stoic era; the nineteenth century was also a time of genuine heroism, a factor making for further problems in writing about the Mekong explorers. Their heroism and unselfishness, their capacity to remain determined to pursue their goals despite the costs involved, have become the basis for unthinking adulation in some quarters. I have met Frenchmen who are still fighting the battles of one hundred years ago, when, once the expedition had ended, there was intense debate over the roles its various members had played. These are men who live with busts of the protagonists at their elbows; men who leap to defend or denounce, according to their beliefs and sympathies.

This passion may be understandable, or in any event forgivable. Some of the explorers were themselves men of passion; all were men of determination. Less forgivable is the fashion in which, over many decades, Frenchmen have chosen to write about the Mekong explorers, for they have deformed reality. The members of the Mekong expedition were men, with the faults and failings of men. The fact that they were singularly endowed with the qualities of courage and resilience should not obscure their essential humanity. In treating Doudart de Lagrée, the expedition's leader, or Francis Garnier, its second-in-command, as more than men, French eulogists have done their heroes little credit.

This, then, is the story of the Mekong expedition, which left Saigon in 1866 searching for a navigable route into southwestern China, and of the later fatal association of the expedition's most prominent member with an effort to find yet another river route into China, up the Red River of Tonkin. It is a story, but it is also a history. The emotions I have attempted to trace and recreate do not stem simply from imagination. My book is based on the explorers' own writings, and I have tried to be faithful to those writings. To the extent that any writer of history speculates, I hope this will be seen clearly for what it is, speculation and no more. When words appear within quotation marks, or when I write that such and such was said or felt, this is because these were the words and observations of the men whom I, too, have come to admire.

This book is the product of nearly ten years of intermittent reading and research, and of travel in the Indochinese region that began in 1959. Just as importantly, the book could never have been written if it had not been for the kindness and assistance that so many persons have freely offered me in various parts of the world.

In research for this book, as with other subjects that I have studied in the French Archives, the staff of the various archival *dépots* in Paris have been unfailingly kind and helpful. I tender my particular thanks to Mlle M.-A. Menier of the Archives Nationales de France, Section Outre-Mer. My thanks to the staff of the other archival offices, as well as those who work under Mlle Menier's direction, are no less sincere. In Paris, also, M. Ian Feldman has always acted as a kind guide to published sources, searching out rare items for my personal library and wisely convincing me that I should buy these items, which have now become increasingly rare. An author's debt to a knowledgeable book dealer can be great indeed.

In Vietnam and Cambodia I have debts that stretch back to 1959, when I first saw the Mekong. The current tortured circumstances of those countries inhibit certain acknowledgements that I otherwise would wish to make publicly. For Vietnam, however, I must record my sincere thanks to Senator Le Tan Buu, who was not only my host in Saigon on several occasions but, in addition, made it possible for me to travel over and by sections of the Mekong which, given the security circumstances at the time, I might not otherwise have seen.

Friends, both colleagues and students, in North America have lent their assistance in a most helpful fashion. I am particularly grateful to Ella Laffey of McGill University for allowing me to consult her valuable manuscript dealing with the events of 1873 in Tonkin. Tony Milner, at Cornell, never tired of requests that he check details or obtain photocopies of books that I was unable to locate in Washington.

None of those named, nor the many others who are unnamed, bear responsibility for the shortcomings of this book, which are mine alone. They deserve praise for their contribution to any virtues it might have.

Milton Osborne

July 1974

A BRIEF CHRONOLOGY

1866

June 5	*The expedition leaves Saigon.*
July 7	*The expedition departs Phnom Penh.*
August 13	*Departure from Stung Treng.*
September 11	*The expedition waves goodbye to Khong.*
September 16–December 25	*The expedition arrives at Bassac.*

1867

January 10	*Garnier travels to Angkor and Phnom Penh.*
January 20	*The main party departs Ubon.*
March 10	*Garnier rejoins the main party at Uthen.*
April 4	*The expedition leaves Vientiane.*
April 29–May 25	*The expedition arrives at Luang Prabang.*
June 14	*The expedition departs from Chiang Kong.*
July 1	*The expedition departs from Mong Lin.*
August 7–September 8	*The expedition at Mong Yawng.*
August 14–September 13	*Lagrée away from main party.*
September 18	*The expedition leaves Keng Khang.*
October 17	*Departure from Keng Hung.*
October 18–30	*The arrival at Ssu-mao.*
November 17–26	*The arrival at Yüan-chiang.*
December 9	*The party leaves Chien-shui.*
December 23	*The expedition arrives at K'un-ming.*

1868

January 8	*The party leaves K'un-ming.*
January 18	*The expedition arrives at Hui-tse.*
January 30–April 3	*Garnier's party travels to Ta-li.*
March 12	*Lagrée dies of amoebic dysentery in Hui-tse.*
April 3	*Garnier returns to Hui-tse.*
April 7	*The expedition departs from Hui-tse.*
May 9	*The expedition leaves I-pin.*
June 29	*The return to Saigon.*

1873

October 11	*Garnier leaves Saigon for Ton-kin.*
November 20	*Garnier captures the Hanoi citadel.*
December 21	*Garnier is killed in Hanoi.*

"The navigability of the Mekong . . . there is a task worthy of raising the passions of our century with its love for great undertakings. . . ."

ADMIRAL PAUL REVEILLÈRE

CHAPTER I

PHNOM PENH

The French explorers were men of their age: the enlightened, educated, scientific mid-nineteenth century. But as they rested in Phnom Penh their own age seemed to have lost much of its reality. The new capital of Cambodia (for the King and his court had only just vacated an earlier site a little to the north in this same year of 1866) might not have surprised their forebears of the Middle Ages. For these six men it was a place of constant, sometimes horrified fascination. Where, after all, in Europe was it still quite normal to find the heads of executed criminals rotting under a swarm of flies atop bamboo poles, grisly testimonies to the vengeance of a king against any who transgressed one of his most sacred concerns, the inviolability of his female household?

This was the era of the *mission civilisatrice*, the French concept of a civilizing mission that they alone among the countries of Europe were capable of fulfilling. Yet, in Cambodia, the role escaped them. Whatever was to happen later, as the nineteenth century drew to a close, the 1860s in Cambodia were still a time when old ways were supreme. Not that these old ways were always harsh. The traditional Cambodian legal code viewed adultery *outside* the royal family with a notable degree of tolerance. As well as the penalty requiring the adulterer to pay for his illicit pleasure in cash, the law did provide an alternative. Accepting that the act of adultery was more likely to take place in the fields about the city than elsewhere, the legal code provided that the guilty parties could absolve themselves by offering to the court the amount of grass that would be eaten in a day by the royal elephants. This "punishment" served the honor of all sides. It suggested heroic efforts on the part of those involved in the illicit liaison, but reaffirmed the vital interests of the King, whose elephants might, in even the smallest measure, have been deprived of their fodder.

In a way that is difficult for many in the late twentieth century to imagine, Cambodia in the 1860s was an unknown and sometimes barbaric land. The French colonizers who had come to the Indochinese region in 1858 had been slow to transfer their attention from the south of Vietnam to this petty kingdom. They knew it was a factious place where the man who held the title of King retained his position because of help from Thailand, and against the undisguised enmity of his two half-brothers. When, in 1863, they decided to insure that their influence was dominant in Cambodia, they were reacting more to imagined threats than verifiable facts. The perfidious British were an ever present danger in many French minds. In the Southeast Asian world they were seen as evil geniuses orchestrating the activities of the Thai court, and thus as likely to threaten the newly established French position in southern Vietnam. It is difficult to be absolutely sure, but the best evidence is that at the time in question the highest ranking British subject within the Thai court was the bandmaster.

So, with a dash of gunboat diplomacy to insure that Thai influence in Cambodia became negligible, the French government, in 1863 and 1864, established a "protectorate" over Cambodia. The expectation was that without Thai influence Cambodia would be peaceful. It was not. As French officials worked to make Cambodia a further shining jewel in Napoleon III's colonial crown, the country sank deeper into disorder and rebellion. This time the Thais, and their presumed directors, the British, could not be blamed. The problem was more fundamental and more local. It was the problem of the King, and in particular of the contrast between his apparently absolute power at court and his near lack of power in the provinces.

The Frenchmen who were about to explore the unknown course of the Mekong came to Phnom Penh well acquainted with the character of the Cambodian ruler, if not reconciled to it. The leader of the expedition, Commander Ernest-Marc-Louis de Gonzague Doudart de Lagrée, had already spent more than two years in Cambodia as the representative of the French government. It had been his task to persuade and finally to force the Cambodian King, Norodom I, to agree to the French protectorate. The other naval officers and officials in the service of the French government accompanying Lagrée knew Norodom only at second hand. Francis Garnier's experience of the East had been in Vietnam, across the cultural divide from Cambodia. This, too, was the Asian experience of Dr. Clovis Thorel, one of the two medical men included in the expedition. Dr. Lucien Joubert, the other, had never served in the Indochinese region before; his foreign service had been in Africa. Louis Delaporte was also a newcomer to the East. And so too was Louis de Carné, the youngest member of the expedition, who had gained a place through his uncle's influence, and who was to provide the one public blot on the enterprise's honor before he died, five years later, from a disease contracted on the slow journey up the Mekong.

The letters that Doudart de Lagrée sent home to France in 1864 and 1865 provide some of the most vivid pictures of the Cambodian court and its ruler. It is no wonder that the other members of the expedition, who now met Norodom for the first time, observed and spoke with him in such an interested way. If only half of Lagrée's stories were true, then here before them was a living example of an oriental despot. Doudart de Lagrée might choose to speak of Norodom as a "kinglet," but this was not the vision held of him by his subjects. Nor, assuredly, was it how Norodom thought of himself.

The man whose Cambodian titles described him as the "Great king with heavenly feet, better than all others, descendant of angels and of the god Vishnu, excellent heart, supreme earthly power as full of qualities as the sun, born to protect men, supporter of the weak, he who knows and understands, better than all others, eternally precious like the angels, victorious, great among the greatest . . ." was a little man with a pockmarked face. When he was crowned King in 1864, Norodom was twenty-eight years old. Barely five feet in height, he had no doubts as to the rights he should enjoy over his country even if these were seldom translated into reality. He had spent six years of his early life, between 1848 and 1856, in Bangkok living as a part guest and part hostage in the Thai court. During the late 1850s, in the closing years of his father's life, Norodom spent his early manhood in the Cambodian court at Oudong, twenty miles north of Phnom Penh. As the King's eldest son he could indulge his pleasures, even if he also risked occasional beating when he incurred his parent's regal rage. A European visitor to Oudong in 1859 found Norodom to be a considerate host whose English vocabulary comprised only one phrase, "Good brandy." Throughout his life he showed himself ready to match this statement of approval with unstinted consumption of the brandy itself.

But it was not his heavy drinking, nor his use of opium, that so confounded the French. In their less prejudiced moments, Frenchmen recognized his lively intelligence, but from the very beginning they could not really understand Norodom's relations with his female household. Why, they asked, when he had so many women should the infidelity of one be the cause of so many deaths and other punishments? Norodom, Lagrée once wrote, was as jealous as a tiger. It was this jealousy that explained the almost constant succession of hangings and decapitations at his court. With forty-five women to tend his pleasure, the errant behavior of one could lead, as it did one day early in 1864, to the sudden death of seven men and women judged to have infringed the ancient laws of the kingdom.

What the French failed to understand was that the women of Norodom's court were not merely part of some Cambodian equivalent of a Turkish seraglio. Many of those who shared the King's bed were also playing a political role, acting on behalf of their relatives, providing the King with advice away from the formal meetings that he disliked and distrusted. But more than this, the female household still was one area that had not passed beyond the King's absolute control. The outer provinces might be in revolt, the Thais and later the French might work their will upon Norodom to force him this way or that. But in his own household his word was absolute. When his father died, in 1860, Norodom inherited the late King's women. A deep quarrel between Norodom and his half-brother, Si Votha, over what to be done with one of these women probably explains why Si Votha withdrew into the forest and remained a rebel against the King all his life. Symbolically and practically the women of the King's establishment represented the right he had to absolute power, and Norodom did not fail to exercise that right.

This more than anything was what gave Norodom the character he had in the eyes of the French. He might be amiable with his European visitors, but he was not with his countrymen who broke the laws that said he alone had the right to his women. He even turned his considerable if erratic interest in Western technology and governmental practice to use in this regard. In the early 1870s someone told the Cambodian monarch that on occasion governments in Europe used firing squads to carry out executions. This struck Norodom as a matter of great interest. Pressing a French official for details, he listened thoughtfully while the procedure was explained. Within hours of the conversation a fusillade rang out to bring death to yet more erring members of his household. Later in the century, as he grew older and his female establishment grew larger, the problem of maintaining fidelity grew greater. The court pages, usually vigorous young men in their twenties, sometimes could not resist the blandishments of the women. Neither, always, could Norodom's rambling brood of sons. As late as 1884 it was only French pressure that prevented Norodom from punishing one of his sons for an illicit liaison with a member of the female household by having him dragged to his death behind horses through the streets of Phnom Penh. The angry King had to be content with confining his son, loaded down with heavy chains.

If such spectacles did not greet the French explorers, there was much to interest and even fascinate them as they paused in Phnom Penh to make their last major supply arrangements before heading into unknown regions. They had left Saigon nearly a month before, on June 5, 1866, and had passed most of the intervening period making the first detailed appraisal of the mighty ruins of Angkor, the center of Cambodian glory between the ninth and fifteenth centuries. Now, in Phnom Penh, they added to their food supplies and, heeding the advice of local traders, bought up large stocks of copper wire for barter in the distant Laotian states.

Though it had only recently become the royal capital once again, Phnom Penh was a site rich with memories and traditions. After the Cambodians abandoned Angkor, in the fifteenth century, this had been the country's capital for a period. Later, towards the end of the sixteenth century, the city had been the scene of a savage clash between the contending groups of foreigners, including Spanish and Portuguese adventurers, who sought to profit from the weakening state of the country. In a bloody month of fighting and arson the Europeans clashed with the Chinese community and then, in turn, were attacked themselves by the Cambodians. After another century of somnolence, Phnom Penh briefly regained its capital city status in the 1830s during a bitter period of Vietnamese occupation. This led to its destruction when the Thais, as enemies of the Vietnamese, put the city to the torch in 1834. During the 1840s and 1850s the city had a backwater existence as a settlement of small traders and merchants. Now, in 1866, the French had persuaded Norodom to proclaim Phnom Penh the capital of his country once more, and to leave his father's capital Oudong, just to the north, to decay slowly as the tropical weather pattern and the insects brought down the empty, wooden palace buildings. Not, indeed, that all were empty, for some upholders of tradition remained, unready to live in proximity to the French. Foremost among these was Norodom's mother. Another was the tragic figure so often spoken of in French accounts as "the mad woman of Oudong."

This was Ang Mey, the Cambodian princess who had been placed on the powerless throne of her occupied country by the Vietnamese in 1834. Rumor was that she had been the mistress of a Vietnamese general who ruled over Cambodia at this terrible time. Others tempered their allegations of Ang Mey's wrongdoing; the once beautiful princess, they said, may have sold her country, but not her body to the Vietnamese. Whatever was the case, she had lost her reason. Pushed from the throne when the

Vietnamese retreated before the Thais, she lived with the memory of death and dishonor for over twenty years. Norodom left her in the care of old retainers when he and his court moved to Phnom Penh. At Oudong she could still believe that she had some dignity, and her servants could placate the villagers whom she assaulted when her mind was most unbalanced, or pay for the goods that she took as a right from the merchants in the markets.

The city to which Norodom brought his court in 1866 is best seen for the first time from the river. In 1866, indeed, it could not be reached in any other way during the rainy season, and this was how the explorers came. Phnom Penh in 1866 bore little relation to the city that in the early 1960s had a population of 500,000 and that had grown by 1974, as war swept over Cambodia, to a figure well in excess of one million. In 1866, Phnom Penh numbered perhaps 35,000 souls. Most were not Cambodians. There were Chinese and Vietnamese traders in the great market. Merchants from as far away as Laos sold their wares in Phnom Penh before making a slow ascent back up the Mekong. Malay fishermen cast their nets in the Mekong and its tributary the Tonle Sap and sold their catches to the city's inhabitants. Indian traders sold cloth and lent money, and by 1866 there was even a small resident European commercial community.

These varied groups were crowded into a jumble of wooden houses that straggled along the river bank. They seemed unconscious of the stench that rose from the garbage-filled streets, the primitive drains and canals that inefficiently carried away human waste matter in this city that lacked any organized sanitation. Yet not all the smells that were so characteristic of this busy market town were offensive, or certainly not to the inhabitants. Scents of incense drifted from the Chinese and Vietnamese pagodas. Curries and spices added their contribution in the kitchens behind the Indian traders' houses, as did the distinctive smell of *nuoc-mam*, the pungent fermented fish sauce that was, and is, an essential of Vietnamese cuisine. Nor was life for these merchants and coolies just a matter of philosophically accepting an existence that promised so many of them an early death from incurable disease. This was also a city of raucous gaiety, ceremony, and parade. Hawkers shouted their wares with distinctive street cries, and the brassy ring of cymbals and gongs marked the passage of Chinese processions of celebration as well as those that accompanied the rites of death and mourning. Just to the north of the city limits the muezzins called the followers of Islam to prayer. At the edge of the city itself, the bells of the Catholic mission rang for the Vietnamese converts. With the onset of the sudden tropical night the city was lit by the gaudy paper lanterns that hung outside Chinese shops, and the click and rattle of innumerable mah-jong games sounded through the streets. Yet, however much this cosmopolitan bustle and bargaining were part of Phnom Penh, there were sections of the city that were unmistakably Cambodian: the royal palace, the Buddhist temples, and the hill itself from which the city took its name.

Built at the confluence of two wide rivers, Phnom Penh sits on dead flat ground. The Phnom (hill) from which it takes its name is not large, rising only some eighty feet above the ground. It is topped by a stupa, a Buddhist monument that rises a further ninety feet above the top of the Phnom itself. In a flat land this combined height of the hill and its monument was enough for it to dominate the city. Then, as now, it was a favorite spot for fortune tellers and for Buddhist monks in their yellow robes. These monks were a constant reminder that this city existed in a different world from that which the Frenchmen had known in Saigon. There were Buddhist monks to be seen in Saigon, some even followers of the same branch of Buddhism as that practiced in Cambodia. But there was nothing like this. With the dawn of each day the monks streamed into the streets from their monasteries to beg for food from the faithful. At any Cambodian ceremony the monks would be present, their yellow robes providing a splash of color, their voices tirelessly murmuring the prayers and rituals that gain merit through constant, almost trance-like repetition. The King himself had been a monk for a time: had entered a monastery, taken the robe, and had his head shaven. One of the French explorers was later to write that Norodom mocked the Buddha at times when he felt well and happy. This was the mockery of a true believer. For the King exemplified the rule that "to be a Cambodian was to be Buddhist." Yet to be Cambodian was also to be a follower of other religions. For the peasants, animism was the dominant belief. For the royal family, Brahmanic rituals, borrowed some fifteen hundred years before from India, still played a part alongside the other Indian religion, Buddhism, that was proclaimed the faith of the state.

With their departure set for the next day, the French explorers were summoned to the royal palace to dine with Norodom on July 6. If this was no new experience for Doudart de Lagrée, the occasion fascinated the other, younger members of the party. To enter the royal palace was to come close to the most vital and mystical features of King Norodom's world. The supreme guides to court ritual were the Brahman priests. Centuries before their ancestors had been truly knowledgeable in the philosophies of India. Their nineteenth-century descendants preserved the ritual but had little understanding of the philosophy that lay beneath it. Their long hair caught up in the traditional "buns" of their Indian counterparts, these Cambodian Brahmans cast horoscopes and were the interpreters of signs and portents for the King and his family. Possibly their most solemn duty was to guard the famous sacred sword of the kingdom, the *preah khan*. This sword, that had been passed to the ruler's remote ancestors by the gods, was a symbol and a measure of the kingdom's prosperity. It was, in the words of the Cambodian coronation ceremony, "the lightning of Indra," the king of the gods. None save the Brahmans could touch it, and even they were forbidden to touch the naked blade with their bare hands. The most terrible disaster would follow if the sword were lost or captured. Should the blade grow rusty or discolored, the fate of the kingdom would be less terrible but grave nonetheless.

Norodom's palace was not grand, if judged against Versailles, the Vatican, or the residences of lesser European rulers both spiritual and temporal. But it had its own dignity, not least for the Cambodians, who saw the palace as a symbol of man's place within the universe, the earthly center of their existence that was the dwelling place of a semi-divine monarch. When the explorers came to the palace, they saw but the beginnings of what by the end of the nineteenth century was to be a vast complex of buildings within a compound surrounded by a castellated wall. Already, however, there was a throne hall, a pavilion for the royal ballet's performances, and another pavilion where the king met his officials in daily audience and received the petitions of his subjects. These were wooden buildings, richly carved along the eaves and lintels, painted and gilded, and roofed with glistening tiles of blue and yellow that shone in the tropical sun and provided a fitting completion to this architecture of fantasy. A few years later, following the opening of the Suez Canal, the Phnom Penh palace was enriched by a new French gift to the King: the prefabricated cast-iron palace that had been used by the Empress Eugénie at the opening ceremonies for De Lesseps' canal. Shipped out to Cambodia and re-erected, it became, if we may believe the repeated claims of French authors, Norodom's favorite building in the royal compound.

It was not architecture alone that made the palace a matter of interest and wonder. There was the abiding fascination provided by the members of the court: the officials, the court dancers, the royal guard and the royal orchestras, the hereditary servants who tended the royal elephants, paddled the King's barges, and daily risked death at the King's passionate whim. Norodom was not a rich ruler, by whatever standards were used to judge him, but his wealth was sufficient for a court of two thousand persons. A devoted admirer of the traditional Cambodian orchestra composed of flutes, stringed instruments, and a range of drums, gongs, and xylophones, he listened with equal pleasure to his band of Filipinos who played in the Western style. His cavalry was led by men from Thailand. His gunners were the mixed-blood descendants of Iberian adventurers who had settled in Cambodia in earlier centuries.

Guards and servants were clothed in reds and blues and wore hats that seemed to have remained unchanged in design from those shown on the low-relief sculptures of the temples at Angkor. The more elevated members of the court, both male and female, wore a rich silk sarong, a *sampot* in the Cambodian language, drawing its hem up between their legs to fasten at the back and give the impression of loose, floppy breeches rather like the loose-fitting trousers worn by Dutchmen in so many seventeenth-century paintings. Each day of the week had its own color; the *sampots* worn on a Friday, the day of the planet Venus, would be blue; those worn on Wednesday, the day of Mercury, would be green. None of this daily exoticism, however, came near to the impression created by the entertainment the explorers had been summoned to the palace to see: the special splendor of the royal troupe of dancers.

Whatever judgments nineteenth-century Frenchmen made of Norodom—and most of them were harsh—all agreed on two aspects of his character. He loved both banquets and the dancing of his court ballet that was an essential accompaniment to the feasting. There are men still alive in Cambodia who remember, from the early days of the present century, being told by their parents of the mammoth feasting that took place within the palace at Norodom's command. Royal banquets would last as long as the King's endurance. European wine and brandy flowed alongside locally distilled spirits, and course followed course in a seemingly endless profusion, served from the heavy chiseled silver dishes made by the royal silversmiths. As the banquet progressed the royal ballet provided an ever-changing backdrop.

The dancing that Lagrée and his companions witnessed was quite unknown to all but a very few in Europe. When, fifty years later, Norodom's half-brother and successor, King Sisowath, took the Cambodian ballet to France, it was a true succès *de théâtre*. The artist Rodin led Paris society in lauding the dancers' grace and beauty. Dressed in the richest silk shot through with gold and silver thread, wearing golden tiered crowns or the masks of chimerical beasts and decked with jewels, the court dancers performed a repertoire that drew on the ancient Indian epics for its subjects: the heroic deeds of Rama and the legends enshrined in the *Mahabharata*. But the dances were not Indian in form. They were slower and more measured, less sensual but no less full of meaning. Gestures with hand and finger meant as much as a sudden movement with the whole body. In some cases, as when the monkey gods joined in battle, the dances were realistic to an almost buffoonish degree. The dancers in their monkey masks struck simian poses, bent-legged with outstretched arms or thoughtfully scratching their armpits for fleas. On other occasions, the motions of individuals and groups were as intricately abstract yet as disciplined as those of a wheeling flock of birds.

The French visitors watched the dances by the soft light of candles, with the incense blown through the pavilion by the river breeze that floated from the water a bare three hundred yards away. They sat at a long table facing the floor on which the dancers performed, waited upon by palace servants who crawled along the floor so that they should remain below the level of the King. Seated at the head of the banqueting table, Norodom mixed banter with a more serious purpose. Which of the dancers, he inquired, struck the Frenchmen as the most beautiful and accomplished? They gratified their host by correctly pointing to the King's current favorite; Norodom's attentive gaze had made their choice none too difficult. More earnestly, in conversation with Lagrée, the King strove to press a bar of gold upon the group's leader for their expenses along the way. Doudart de Lagrée refused. He realized that Norodom hoped in offering them this gift, to ask in return for their further delay. For if the banqueting and dancing kept the Frenchmen from daily cares that were soon to be frequent and demanding, these diversions had a similar part to play for Norodom. As he savored his brandy and watched with a connoisseur's appreciation the steps that his dancers performed, he knew a rebellion was already under way in the eastern provinces of his kingdom which could threaten his hold on the throne.

The real world beckoned the explorers. The river was visible from the dancing pavilion, and it was why they were here. Fantasy would be in short measure in a little while, but this night's experience could not be prolonged. Norodom might stay watching the ballet, but the explorers took their leave, following the strict naval discipline that Lagrée's orders demanded that he preserve. The next day the expedition left Phnom Penh. Their route lay north up the Mekong, as the smoke from their final cannon salute drifted behind them and towards the shore.

CHAPTER II

GREAT RIVER, GREAT IDEA

Scholars still debate the meaning of the river's name. When its course was first uncertainly charted on the early maps of Southeast Asia, the cartographers used a Portuguese version of its Thai name. They called it the *Mecon*, or *Mecom*, and sometimes *Mekong*, translating this poetically if inaccurately as "The Mother of the Waters." Later travelers, confused about the river's source and knowing only a part of its great length, named it after one of the countries through which it flowed. So it was called *le Cambodge*, the Cambodia River. This was the name used by the French explorers of the mid-nineteenth century. But by the end of that century the modern name had taken firm root. As France, Britain, and Thailand haggled over their spheres of influence in the Indochinese region, the diplomats' maps agreed in showing the Mekong River. For the people of Cambodia and of Vietnam, however, the river has always borne another name. The Cambodians speak of the *Tonle Thom* and the Vietnamese of the *Song Lon*. Both names have the same meaning—the "Great River."

The Mekong is, indeed, a great river. Rising in the high plateaus of Tibet, its course runs some 2,800 miles to the South China Sea, passing through China, Laos, Cambodia, and Vietnam, and delineating the borders of Burma and Thailand. For southern Laos, Cambodia, and the delta region of southern Vietnam the Mekong is essential to existence. The river comes into flood during the wet season as the local monsoon adds its rains to the melted snow that feeds the Mekong when summer comes to Tibet. Standing on the revetted banks in the Cambodian capital of Phnom Penh, one may watch the river rise day by day, until the difference between low water and high water has become as much as forty feet. Away from the artificial revetments of the city the water spills over the land, flooding the paddy fields that have been dried by six months of relentless sun.

There is so much water at this flood time that the Mekong

causes one of nature's oddest events to occur. When the river rises to flood level at Phnom Penh, it starts to back up along its tributary, the Tonle Sap. Having flowed south for half the year, the Tonle Sap reverses itself during the wet season and runs north between June and November. As the Mekong floods it irrigates the land along its course, leaving a rich silt on the flood plains. The water forced backwards up the Tonle Sap not only replenishes the Great Lake in the heart of Cambodia; it also starts a breeding cycle for the fish that swim there. When, in November after the rains have stopped, the Tonle Sap starts to flow swiftly towards the south again, the swirling brown waters carry a mass of fish. For the Cambodian peasants the annual harvest of fish that is made at this time provides the protein that is otherwise so lacking from their diet.

Hydrographers have calculated that the vast volume of water flowing down the river carries with it enough silt to add two hundred additional feet of land each year to the coast of Vietnam near the Mekong's mouth. Modern planners have begun their efforts to control the river's flooding and to harness its power for hydroelectricity. These are the latest hopes for the river. Even if the plans finally reach fulfillment, the Mekong's vital role will still be to provide irrigation, food, and a route for travel, as it has always done, even before recorded history.

At the dawn of history ancient civilizations rose and fell near the mouth of the Mekong. This was before the great drainage efforts of the settlers who came to the region many centuries later. The land about the lower Mekong was a watery patchwork of lakes and streams. It was possible, as one early Chinese traveler put it, to "sail through Cambodia." Farther north in a land covered by primeval jungle and forest the Mekong provided a way to the south for the Khmers, the ancestors of modern Cambodians who migrated from an area in southern Laos during the seventh century. One of the earliest Khmer inscriptions stood in the river bed near the modern village of Sambor, in northeast Cambodia. There, below one of the Mekong's biggest sets of rapids, the Khmers paused to mark their passage by engraving an inscription on a great rock, affirming piety to the

Hindu god Sambhu (Siva). The prince who ordered this Sanskrit testimony to stand in the bed of the river was Chitrasena, a shadowy figure whose name is remembered today only by scholars. But his decision to honor the god Sambhu is echoed in the place name that has survived for more than fourteen hundred years and is still used today.

When the great Cambodian kingdom of Angkor was founded, at the beginning of the ninth century, its first ruler did not site his capital on the banks of the Mekong. This choice did not mean that Jayavarman II (reigned 802?–850) was unaware of the river's importance—quite the contrary. The site of Angkor, inland and near to the Great Lake, was safer than any position chosen on the Mekong proper. A city on the Mekong itself would have been much more readily vulnerable to attack from the Chams, a people of Indonesian stock whose kingdom once dominated the coast of modern central Vietnam. War between the Chams and the Angkorian Khmers was endemic. As Angkor grew to greater and greater strength, its rulers used the city of Sambhupura (Sambor) as a base from which to send expeditions against the Chams. The Chams, for their part, marched westward across the mountains to the banks of the Mekong.

More than three hundred years after the kingdom of Angkor had been founded, the Chams showed that its inland site was no longer safe from attack. Sailing their huge war canoes up the Mekong, the Chams then passed along the Tonle Sap to attack Angkor from the Great Lake. The Cham defeat of the Cambodians in 1177 A.D. was a heavy blow to the Angkorian state, and only under a quite remarkable king, Jayavarman VII (1181–1219?), did the city recover its former glory. Angkor was still the mightiest city in the southern seas in the eyes of the Chinese envoy, Chou Ta-kuan, when he visited the city in 1296. His journal tells of how he, like others, had traveled to Angkor from the sea, ascending the Mekong as far as the modern site of Phnom Penh, and then making the final stages of the journey along the Tonle Sap and across the Great Lake. This was the same route used by the Cham raiders over one hundred years before. Whether men came in peace or for war, if they wished to reach the heart of the Angkorian kingdom, the waters of the Mekong and its tributaries were vital arteries for travel and trade.

None of this was known, or at least recorded, by the Europeans of the day. Angkor's decline and fall, in the fifteenth century, was an event of profound importance, but it passed unnoticed by those in the West who had still to learn of this remote region that lay outside the experience of even Marco Polo. With the fall of Angkor the Cambodian court, reduced in wealth and power, moved south to a series of sites near the confluence of the Mekong and the Tonle Sap. It was to the Cambodian capital of Lovek, on the Tonle Sap, that the first Iberian adventurers came in the sixteenth century. They thought they would gain riches and authority, and their barely rational schemes had the zealous support of missionary priests in the Spanish Philippines. Neither the priests' prayers nor the adventurers' courage prevailed. Later, Dutch merchants established their trading stations in the same region. On the northern outskirts of modern Phnom Penh is the site of a Roman Catholic church known to Cambodians as the "Hoalong Church." Few nowadays realize that this is a name that links the site with the early trading endeavours of men from Holland.

The earliest European visitors to the lower reaches of the Mekong left accounts of their travels and of the information they gathered from the Asian traders they met. But these accounts were limited in both the information they provided and the geographical areas they covered. In the early years of the sixteenth century a remarkable Portuguese chronicler, Tomé Pires, an apothecary turned trader, writing from his base in Malacca, knew enough about the Indochinese region to record the fact that "the land of Cambodia possesses many rivers." Thirty years later, in 1555, a Portuguese missionary, Father da Cruz, could supplement this information as the result of his own visit to the decaying kingdom of Cambodia. He traveled on the Mekong itself, noted the abundance of wild animals that roamed its banks, and knew from the traders he met that men from the distant principalities of Laos descended the river to trade at the Cambodian capital of Lovek. Though Da Cruz and others who followed him related some fascinating details, these early visitors to the Indochinese region were unable to gain any real knowledge of the Mekong very far north of modern Vientiane, in Laos. They believed that the source of the river was in China, possibly in a great inland sea that fed the Menam or Chao Phraya River in Thailand, as well as the Mekong. But anything more was unsubstantiated guesswork. Even those who had traveled between the lower reaches of the river near Phnom Penh and onwards to Vientiane gave little impression of the formidable natural barriers that stood in the way of easy passage, other than to note that the Laotian traders took as long as three months to make their way back up the river from the Cambodian capital.

Men like the Dutch trader Van Wuysthof, who made this three months' journey in 1641, were no strangers to arduous travel and did not dwell on the difficulties. Concerned either with gaining wealth or souls, or both, few of these early travelers had the time or inclination to provide extended description. Though their successes and failures were spectacular for brief periods, the impact of these men was ephemeral. Priests, traders, or adventurers, they survived despite the ravages of disease and the daily discomfort of grossly unsuitable European clothes. But they were little more than parasites on the body politic of the region.

Nearly three hundred years after Father da Cruz had written of the Mekong, the state of European knowledge had advanced scarcely at all. Traders knew of Phnom Penh as a minor commercial center, and of Vientiane farther north along the river's course. But the passage of the centuries had not swept away uncertainty about the river's origin, and details even of its lower reaches remained scant. The brief heyday of the Iberian adventurers in Cambodia had ended by the turn of the sixteenth century. They had seen the mighty ruins of Angkor, but faraway Europe forgot about the temples' existence. A few European traders and missionaries continued to hope that the lower Mekong would provide a springboard for their efforts. For the traders this was a forlorn hope, and they faded away. Hope was just as forlorn for the missionaries, too, as they admitted to each other, if not to the world at large. The comment made by the French missionary bishop, Monseigneur Miche, in 1861, was an excellent summary of the situation that had confronted his predecessors throughout their labors in Cambodia. Writing in the *Lettre Commune* of his order, Miche observed that "It is certain for anyone who has lived some years in Cambodia that one can never obtain much success with Cambodians, unless it is through buying the freedom of debt slaves; but that method is long and very costly." The missionaries remained in Cambodia despite their essential failure.

In the nineteenth century, however, interest in the Mekong quickened. British commercial and political involvement now extended beyond the Indian subcontinent into Burma and the Malay archipelago, and by 1830 there was a lively discussion of the still largely unknown lands of Indochina. French, British, and American travelers had all skirted around the periphery of these territories, but extensive and scientific exploration had still not taken place. One has only to read the travelers' accounts of the period to realize how great was the lack of knowledge. Even when all the available information was brought together, the unknown factors were greater than the known and the doubt and distortions greater than the certainties. Nowhere is this better demonstrated than in Josiah Conder's engagingly titled book, *The Modern Traveller*, published in London in 1830. Here Conder drew upon the most modern, if not always the most complete, knowledge. Yet the picture he gives of Indochina bears striking similarities to that provided by Tomé Pires and Father da Cruz three hundred years before. The sixteenth-century idea of all the great rivers of Southeast Asia flowing from a single source still deserved consideration in Conder's view. And he ventured agreement with another idea of the early travelers in the region: that the Mekong and the Chao Phraya, and possibly other major Southeast Asian rivers such as the Salween in Burma, formed a huge inland lake during the flood period of the rainy season.

Inaccurate though Conder's information was, his account of the Indochinese region showed why there was a growing interest in the upper reaches of the Mekong. Europe was already set on the path of imperialist expansion. The value of the China trade had long been recognized, and ten years after Conder had written his book the First Opium War was fought to ensure that trade with China would be on terms that European merchants wanted, not on those the Chinese government desired. British traders and soldiers in Burma discussed the possibility of trade with China by an overland route—a hope that was never truly realized during the nineteenth century. For Josiah Conder, summing up the import of his information on the Indochinese region, the future seemed rosy: "Who can tell but that, in a few years," he wrote, "we may have a British factory at Touron [modern Da-Nang], steam boats plying on the Saigon River, or even ascending the unknown course of the Mei-kong, and that a joint stock company may be formed to work the gold mines of Tongkin!" Who, indeed, could tell? The irony of Conder's point of view was that the men who did come to try and trade in Indochina and to explore the Mekong were French and not British. And the double irony was that these Frenchmen were spurred on in their efforts by the quite erroneous belief that the perfidious English were poised to grab a position in Indochina when such was demonstrably not the case.

Nothing was more convincing to those who finally hoisted their country's flag over the Colony of Cochinchina and then the "Protectorate" of Cambodia than the proposition that they were the latest in a long line of Frenchmen who had forged an indestructible link between this region and France. Undeniably there were links stretching back over a long period. That these links were in some fashion indestructible and God-ordained is a less easy proposition to defend. Frenchmen were first associated, in any sustained fashion, with the Indochinese region through the work of missionaries whose names resound through the canon of colonial literature on Vietnam and Cambodia. Heading the list is the name of a Jesuit priest, Father Alexander of Rhodes. His labors in Vietnam began at the end of 1624. Over the next twenty-five years, whether in Vietnam or elsewhere, Alexander of Rhodes worked constantly to advance the cause of the Catholic Church in this distant region. Modern scholars may doubt the reliability of the numbers he claimed as converts to Christ, but none question the contribution he made to the task of developing a romanized transcription of the Vietnamese language.

Through his endeavors, Alexander of Rhodes established a pattern in which French missionaries came to look upon the Indochinese region as their special preserve. In succeeding centuries the results achieved were sparse. The names of missionaries such as Bishop Pallu are remembered for dedication rather than for evangelical success. Whatever the interest of a limited number of French priests and traders in the Indochinese region may have been through the seventeenth and eighteenth centuries, the actual accomplishments were limited. It is arguable that the most particular exception to this rule was Pigneau de Behaine, Bishop of Adran.

As a member of the French missionary order founded following Alexander of Rhodes' enthusiastic propaganda, the Société des Missions Etrangères, Pigneau de Behaine did, indeed, play an important role in the politics of late eighteenth-century Vietnam. Pigneau was as convinced a French nationalist as he was a Christian. Lending his support to one side in the major Vietnamese civil war that was raging at the time, he sought to involve his country as well for the benefit he thought would follow. In this aim he failed, not least because of the fall of the French monarchy which had been more sympathetic to his proposals than those who triumphed in the Revolution. But he was able to recruit more than three hundred Frenchmen to fight on the side of the Nguyen family, who eventually united Vietnam under their rule in 1802.

The men who responded to Pigneau de Behaine's call to assist the Nguyen were a varied lot. Many were impoverished French adventurers, ready to take employment in any enterprise that promised booty. A more limited number were trained military officers, men such as Chaigneau, Vannier, and Olivier, whose talents undoubtedly played some part in bringing the Nguyen dynasty success; just how significant the part played by the French really was remains a matter for dispute between French and Vietnamese historians. Neither the French mercenaries nor Pigneau de Behaine acted as representatives of their government, and their efforts did not lead to France's gaining any special position in Vietnam once the Nguyen dynasty was in control of the country in the first half of the nineteenth century.

After the first Nguyen ruler's death in 1820, his successors were even more reserved towards the West, and grew less and less ready to tolerate the activities of missionaries whose proselytizing they saw as a political rather than a religious threat. By ordering the deaths of a limited number of French missionaries and a much greater number of Vietnamese Christians, the Vietnamese Emperor, Ming Mang (1820–1841), and his successor, Thieu Tri (1841–1848), helped to accelerate the coalescence of French missionary and government interest in the Indochinese region. When, by the early 1850s, the hope of trade was added to the zeal of evangelism and the expectation of imperial glory, the stage was set for French intervention.

The hope for trade did not, however, reflect any clear understanding of the commercial opportunities in this remote corner of the world. France's checkered political history from the beginning of the nineteenth century had frequently left its successive governments unready to devote their energies to the promotion of distant enterprises. Once Louis Napoleon came to power after 1848, he and his ministers were more ready to listen to the advocates calling for French action in the East. The missionaries wanted protection for their priests and followers; the naval officer corps believed that French *gloire* required action equal to that of the British; and the merchants, particularly those of Lyons and Bordeaux, fretted because France did not have possessions to match Singapore and Hong Kong. Vietnam, when it was attacked in 1858, was not to be saved merely for the greater glory of God, but also for the prestige of *la patrie* and the pockets of the *commerçants*.

There was nothing hypocritical about linking these three goals in the minds of mid-nineteenth-century Frenchmen. The age of rampant imperialism was yet to come, but France's entry into Vietnam was seen by its promoters as opening many paths to glory, not least to the presumed riches of China. The question was how to reach the valuable markets of the Middle Kingdom.

This was no simple matter, for when the French attacked the Vietnamese port of Tourane (Da-Nang) in 1858, their expectation of an easy victory quickly faded away — almost as quickly as did the Vietnamese Christians, who showed that whatever their missionary leaders may have promised, they had no intention of fighting with the French troops against the forces of the Emperor. So successful was the Vietnamese resistance at Tourane, and so greatly did the combined French and Spanish expeditionary force suffer from tropical diseases, that a new invasion point was chosen farther south, at the inland port city of Saigon. Here, from 1859 onwards, the French slowly worked to consolidate a colonial position, abandoning for the moment their hopes for major commercial posts farther north and nearer to China. If trade with China was to be a chief concern of a French colony in the Far East, then the Cochinchinese region was far removed from that goal. It was in these circumstances that young and eager French officers came to think about the possibilities afforded by the Mekong River.

Even though the French were firmly established in Saigon by 1863, the Mekong remained an unknown quantity. Its course to some distance above Phnom Penh was by now quite well known. French missionaries, despite their difficulties in gaining converts, continued to live near the Cambodian court, then still at Oudong, a settlement near the Tonle Sap about twenty miles north of Phnom Penh. Here, if nothing else, they were free from the persecutions of the Vietnamese government, and they knew a little of the country to the north of the royal settlement. One Catholic missionary had even traveled to the fabled city of Angkor. Father Bouilleveaux's visit in 1850 must be counted as the first step in the modern rediscovery of the Angkor temples, even if he was strangely unimpressed by them. Certainly his concern with his evangelizing mission outweighed his interest in providing a detailed description of the remarkable buildings he saw. His travels, arduous though they were, still lay within the generally if imperfectly known area of the Indochinese region. It was left to another Frenchman, Henri Mouhot, both to proclaim the wonders of Angkor to the European world and to take the next steps in the exploration of the Mekong.

An ardent naturalist and explorer, Henri Mouhot was to some extent a prophet without honor in his own country. His interest in exploration received more encouragement in England than in France. This may well have been because of his links, through his English wife, with the famous British explorer Mungo Park. The period Mouhot spent exploring in Thailand, Cambodia, and Laos between 1858 and 1861 was relatively brief, but the importance of his efforts was considerable. His description of the temples at Angkor was not the first to come before the European public, but it surpassed all that had gone before in detail and feeling. Unencumbered by ethnocentric esthetic standards, Mouhot recognized the grandeur of the temples he found set in the deep forest. He could not believe that buildings of such magnificence were built by forebears of the Cambodians of 1860. The men and women he saw were surely the descendants of a lesser race, he argued. The greatest of all the temples, and the least damaged, was Angkor Wat, and this Mouhot considered a "rival to that of Solomon, and erected by some ancient Michelangelo . . . grander than anything left us by Greece or Rome . . . a sad contrast to the state of barbarism in which the nation is now plunged."

If Mouhot might with justice be described as the man who brought the wonders of the Angkor ruins to the attention of the Western world, his efforts to explore the Mekong were less successful and failed to resolve most of the questions of detail that puzzled the French community in Saigon. His sudden death in November 1861 prevented him from following his goal of traveling down the Mekong, from a point near Luang Prabang in Laos, to the region in Cambodia, just above Kompong Cham, that he had reached when he had gone northward from Phnom Penh in 1859. In his diary he left a vivid description of the river between Luang Prabang and Pak Lay, of its fast-flowing current rushing through high gorges with a sound like the stormy sea. He wrote, too, of the darkness of the tropical night and of the hardships he faced as a solitary explorer. His diary is strangely and movingly evocative of his determination and loneliness in the forests and jungles of Laos.

While the middle reaches of the Mekong remained unexplored, let alone those remoter sections of its course closer to China, there was a risk—or so the Saigon community feared—that Britain would steal a march on France. The force of this imperial rivalry cannot be overstated. French naval officers, in particular, looked back on their country's history since the Revolution with feelings approaching despair for the loss of colonies it had seen. In a crude distortion of the social Darwinism that was to be so influential later in the century, the young naval officers who played such an active part in seizing and then administering the new colony of Cochinchina saw imperial expansion as necessary for France's survival. The index of greatness, ran the argument of one publicist, was the acquisition of colonies. It should not be France's role to hold back and then try to benefit from the efforts of others, as the United States had done in its commercial relations with China. Previewing the arguments of the *pieds-noirs* one hundred years later, this writer argued that the fact of French expansion into Algeria did not count, for by its proximity to France and the nature of its products Algeria could not be considered a colony. Glory was to be found in the East, and "since the last distant expeditions, France can dream of not only again finding overseas the activity necessary for its commerce, for the development of its industry and the creation of outlets for the future, but also of beginning again the noble civilizing mission that has always given it such a high place in the world."

There was no cant in these views, however self-interested they appear more than a century later. But there were distinct problems associated with such hopes. Most particularly in 1864, when these words were written, there seemed little promise that Cochinchina would provide the commerce that was to speed France towards greatness. True, some individual Frenchmen might gain wealth by selling goods to their fellow countrymen in Saigon. And in Cholon, Saigon's twin city, the resident Chinese population seemed to prosper in a manner that excited French envy and admiration. But none of this disguised the basic fact:

taken as a whole, the colony was a clear financial liability on the French state. The growth of the rice trade would not be really significant for several decades, and the thought of rubber plantations was not even in the imaginings of the Frenchmen of the 1860s. The answer, it was increasingly argued by the men on the spot, lay in the commercial opportunities of the Mekong River.

The staggering *naïveté* of this view, as it appears more than one hundred years later, must not disguise the force and conviction with which it was held at the time. For both the British and the French commercial communities in the early 1860s, China remained a presumed source of boundless mercantile success. The huge population of the interior of China was cited again and again as a basis for commercial hope. It seemed indisputable that China's millions were only waiting to be given the opportunity to buy the products of Europe. As for China's own resources, these too were thought to be ready for exploitation by industrious foreigners. The British in Burma had long dwelled on these possibilities. As early as 1837 a Captain McLeod had traveled up the Salween River and then to the Chinese border before being refused permission to enter Yunnan. After McLeod other British soldiers and officials continued to speculate on the possibilities of a trade route into western China from Burma. Interest quickened at the beginning of the sixties. With the efforts of earlier explorers in mind, the Manchester Chamber of Commerce asked for government support in 1860 so that trade might be opened with western China. Two years later the British authorities in India gave an indication of new official interest in the possibilities of trading with China by way of Burma when Arthur Phayre was dispatched as an envoy to the Burmese court at Mandalay.

All this the advocates of French expansion knew and feared. Even before their hold over the area around Saigon was assured, the French in Cochinchina were preoccupied with the Mekong and its commercial and navigational potentialities. After 1863, in the words of one Frenchman in Saigon, the "idea of the Mekong was in everybody's mind." The immediate problem was to translate the "idea" into reality.

CHAPTER III

THE FIRST RAPIDS

$\mathcal{D}$eath was a close companion for the French administrators who came to Saigon in the 1860s. The colony's official newspaper, the *Courrier de Saigon*, lists a constant succession of early deaths, with few of those who died being above thirty years of age. Fever, malaria and dysentery took their continual toll. Yet the letters that have been left by those who survived give little if any sense of an atmosphere of mortality hanging heavily over the small colonial society that developed in Saigon as the French hold over southern Vietnam slowly tightened. For those who survived, the risks of tropical disease and the deaths of their friends were accepted with a forbearance that reflected experience in a Europe where many of the great medical advances were still to come. But this only partly explains the sense of confidence and impatience for activity that marked the letters the young men based in Saigon wrote to their families and friends. There was so much of importance to be done. And for many of them in the 1860s the exploration of the Mekong was the most important concern.

The great river and the riches thought to lie along its distant northern banks were discussed again and again in the evening gatherings that took place under the informal direction of Francis Garnier, the young naval officer appointed "prefect" of Cholon in 1863. A faded photograph of one of these evening meetings, held on the outskirts of Saigon, shows solemn young men, grouped about the base of a tree, eyes firmly fixed to the front, luxuriant beards only partially disguising their relative youth. It is an unfair picture, for if Garnier and his associates could be serious they were certainly not solemn. More than enough is known to be sure of this. Wine was drunk and plays acted in fancy dress. But above all there was discussion of the "great idea."

Frenchmen such as these were the last persons to live easily with the clear but bitter fact that the new colony in which they served was a commercial failure. Garnier and the other young naval officers who formed the nucleus of the colony's administration believed passionately in the worth of what they were doing and in the need to do more. France had gained a colony in Cochinchina; now they feared that foolish minds in Paris might renounce the new possession. If the colony was to be retained, it must find some commercial justification. By 1865 earlier tentative thoughts had become firm convictions. Trade should be sought with China, up the Mekong River. This was the thinking that spurred men to speak and write of exploring the upper reaches of the Mekong. Fears that the British might preempt the trade of Yunnan by a route through Burma, or that the Thais might block French efforts to trade along the Mekong, added urgency. But this was not all. For those who thought and talked about the possibility of opening trade with China by an inland route there was also the attraction of mystery. No one *knew* what lay along the river's length. This fact of mystery only encouraged speculation—which rapidly became belief—that the Mekong could make Saigon, and the colony spread about it, rich.

From the monotonously flat, humid landscape of Saigon and its twin city Cholon, Garnier wrote letters, reports and pamphlets that summoned up visions of a very different world to be found along the yet unexplored reaches of the Mekong, one of coolness and mountains, and a fresh exoticism superior to the frequently tawdry life of Saigon. From the high, unknown wastes of Tibet the Mekong River flowed down into the "chaos" of tribes and peoples who knew nothing of the Western world. If France were to penetrate into this chaotic region, Garnier argued, the Mekong could then provide a certain route for the commerce of China. Despite a total lack of positive evidence, there was no disposition, on the part either of Garnier or of others in Saigon, to doubt that riches would be found. Garnier's was only the most vocal expression of a generally assumed truth. So, he urged his countrymen to "take the measure of the unknown riches enfolded in the valleys and mountains that enclose these rivers. If one believes the travelers' tales these valleys contain active and industrious peoples who trade with the Celestial Empire. What is certain is that the Chinese province of Yunan each year sends many workers to the mines of amber, serpentine, zinc, gold, and silver that lie along the upper course of the Mekong."

The man who wrote these words in 1864 was twenty-five years old. The son of an army officer, Francis Garnier determined, from his earliest years, to enter the navy. His slight frame seemed insufficient to withstand the physical and mental demands to be made of it. In a century more attuned to the psychological implications of adolescent experience, it is hard not to see a connection between the nickname "Mademoiselle Bonaparte" that his physique caused his fellow naval cadets to give him, and his later intense determination to strive and to succeed. That Garnier was driven by strong inner compulsions is clear from his private correspondence. In his relations with his family he was surrounded by affection but at the same time beset by repeated efforts to frustrate his dearest wishes. His entry into the navy was opposed. Once this opposition was overcome and he had taken up his post in Vietnam, his new hope to explore the Mekong brought impassioned pleas from his mother that he should not by embracing this cause burden her with yet another "thorn for her cross." As with the men who climbed Everest seventy years later "because it was there," Garnier's own summary of his motives was both simple and profound. For him, he wrote in a letter to a friend, the "unknown was irresistible."

He must have been a difficult companion for many, if a dearly cherished friend for a few. Even in an age that was more accustomed to open emotion, despite its high esteem for stoic courage, Garnier's life seemed to go beyond the normally high expectations of heroic behavior. Once in the navy, he suffered a shattering fall to the deck of a training ship while engaged in showing that his slight stature was no handicap to madcap balancing on the peak of the mainmast. He recovered by force of will after jettisoning the prescribed medicines into his slop bucket, but was to continue coughing blood like a consumptive for years afterwards. In 1858 Garnier, by now a lieutenant, saved a shipmate who had fallen overboard from the *Duperré* as it sailed through the China Sea, plunging into the sea in the darkness of the tropical night without thought for the sharks that had been escorting the vessel. Impatient with authority and with the prospect of routine employment, and with a nature he himself recognized as "stormy," Garnier seems to have been a man whose great talents did not always prevent him from being a wayward subordinate in official terms, and in personal relationships somewhat self-righteous. This latter trait, not least, made it difficult for Garnier to understand those with whom he disagreed.

For people in the twentieth century to whom the inherent virtues of the French colonial occupation of Vietnam are less than self-evident, Garnier's aims and beliefs seem both prejudiced and presumptuous. "Nations without colonies," he proclaimed, "are dead." Frenchmen needed to remember that in Vietnam "we carry out the political and moral education of a people entrusted to us by Providence." His chauvinistic vision of France's colonial goals led many to embrace his ideas, but the side of Garnier's character that made a few men hold dear his friendship as opposed to his dreams may be sensed only occasionally. Fellow colonial officials such as Eliacin Luro disagreed with many of his extravagant views but responded to the warmth of his feelings and his irrepressible enthusiasm for anything that interested him. No one can read his letters to his future wife, Claire, without sensing that this passionate man could inspire love as well as exasperation. If many of Garnier's pronouncements on empire seem almost to be caricatures of an imperial age's self-image, those addressed to his wife remind us much more of a France both delighted and scandalized by the romantic life of men such as Franz Liszt.

By 1865 the desirability of exploring the Mekong was widely accepted. The colony's Governor, Admiral de La Grandière, had initially been hesitant about the proposal. His predecessor, Admiral Bonard, had been a supporter of the idea, but in this enterprise, if nothing else, La Grandière showed initial caution. Eventually, however, he joined the ranks of the enthusiasts both in

France and Cochinchina. In mid-1865, while he was on leave in Paris, La Grandière gained the approval of the Minister for the Colonies to send an expedition up the Mekong.

Garnier had played a vital part in bringing opinion to this point. Now he wished to be part of the expedition. At first La Grandière seemed disposed to deny him this wish. This, above all, was a case of like resisting like. La Grandière was no less an enthusiast than Garnier for France's role in the East. They shared the same prejudices, the same arrogant assumptions about France's "civilizing mission." In short they were far too alike to confront each other easily, not least since the Admiral found the younger man overly ready to press his views beyond the point of discretion usually expected from a junior officer. In the small, introspective world of Saigon, however, Garnier's passion for the expedition could not be easily denied because of personal animus. Moreover, La Grandière was shrewd enough to recognize both Garnier's undoubted abilities and the desirability of seeing this troublesome spirit absent from Cochinchina. When La Grandière chose the personnel for the projected expedition, in the early months of 1866, Garnier's name was on the list.

La Grandière wanted a more senior officer as leader of the expedition, however, and his choice fell on the French representative in Cambodia, Doudart de Lagrée. Age, temperament, and experience set Lagrée apart from Garnier. In 1866 Lagrée was forty-two, Garnier's senior by sixteen years. He was a graduate of France's most renowned educational institution, the Ecole Polytechnique. The two men did share one thing in common. Both were naval officers who had embraced colonial service when France invaded the Indochinese region. But before this Lagrée's much longer record of service had included distinguished participation in the Crimean campaign. Where Garnier's nature predisposed him to action, Lagrée was a much more contemplative individual. Before he came to serve in Cambodia, few periods of his life seem to have been more satisfying than an extended archeological excursion in Greece.

Beyond the convictions that he felt concerning France's role as a colonial power, Doudart de Lagrée had a practical reason for seeking a post in Indochina. Following service in the Crimea, he had been forced, in the late 1850s, to renounce a life at sea because of a chronic throat ailment, which was aggravated by winter conditions. His choice of Indochina was in part dictated by the possibility that the warmer climate would cure his ulcerated throat. As his letters show, this was never to be: and the Mekong expedition was led by a man in frequent and sometimes severe pain from an apparently incurable condition. Yet this had no effect on Lagrée's enthusiasm and determination.

Once in Indochina, Lagrée found his appointment one of the loneliest possible. As the French representative at the court of King Norodom of Cambodia from 1863, he had few European companions, yet his detailed letters to friends and relatives in France give little sense of this isolation being a burden. His personality contrasts sharply with that of his chief assistant. Where Garnier was forever restless, Lagrée's private and public character was marked by a calm acceptance of his circumstances and a general disinclination to mix emotion with duty. To be able to observe the Cambodian court and delve into the country's history was satisfying in itself.

It is perhaps one of the most notable ironies of the Mekong expedition that Lagrée was chosen to lead it when he had already seen what might be the greatest barrier to navigation up or down the river. As early as July 1863 he had traveled up the Mekong and seen the Sambor rapids. Then, he had judged the rapids to be an "uncrossable barrier." Yet the possibility of exploring further lingered in his mind. Even though the rapids seemed impassable when he saw them, there might be other periods of the year when a passage would be less difficult: a highly powered steam launch might overcome the force of the current at the high water season; or there might be a deeper channel that could be navigated in the calmer period during March or April before the river became swollen by the combined effect of the melted Tibetan snows and the monsoon rains.

But while the exploration of the Mekong was being actively canvassed in Saigon, other matters demanded Lagrée's attention. Cambodia and its "kinglet"—to use Lagrée's own term—

had to be brought under France's protection, and once this was achieved there was the daily need to persuade the Cambodian monarch that there were some courses of action that would gain French approval and others that would not. In these circumstances, the possibility of exploring the Mekong was interesting but scarcely overwhelmingly so for the French representative in Cambodia. Nothing makes this clearer than Lagrée's own reaction to La Grandière's proposal that he should lead a French party up the river. When in December 1865 the governor asked, "Would you not be the man to try and ascend the river for six or seven hundred leagues, to see what occurs in Tibet, in the interior of China?" Lagrée's response as the ultimately laconic "Why not?" And both men laughed.

After the years of debate the French Mekong expedition left Saigon on June 5, 1866. At first glance, its material needs seemed adequately provided for. For costs along the way there were gold bars, Mexican dollars, and Thai coins, to a value of 25,000 francs. Packed into one hundred and fifty cases were more than five hundred kilograms of hard rations, biscuits, and twice-baked bread. There were over three hundred kilograms of flour. And since this was a French expedition, the commissary in Saigon had provided more than seven hundred liters of wine and three hundred liters of brandy. There were fifteen cases of trade goods but only one case of scientific instruments.

These supplies were to sustain a party of six principal explorers and a secondary personnel of sixteen. Among the principals, Lagrée and Garnier, leader and second-in-command, both possessed several years of experience in the Indochinese region. This was not a qualification the other explorers, with one exception, could claim. Clovis Thorel, aged thirty-three when the expedition left Saigon, had, it is true, served as a naval doctor in Cochinchina since 1861. During this time he had shown a strong interest in botanical research, and this, in addition to his medical skills, had commended him to the expedition's planners.

The other doctor in the party, Lucien Joubert, also gained his place because of a combination of capacities. He took the place of a mining engineer previously under consideration. At thirty-four his record of long and healthy service in Senegal plus an interest in geology proved sufficient recommendation. Another regular naval officer, Louis Delaporte, an amateur musician and better-than-amateur artist, had been based in Cochinchina less than a year when he found himself assigned to the expedition and made responsible for the pictorial record of its achievements. In 1866 Delaporte was twenty-four years old.

Finally, and most controversially, there was the youngest member, Louis de Carné, Delaporte's junior by one year. Although selected to represent the French Ministry of Foreign Affairs, he clearly owed his inclusion to the fact that he was Governor La Grandière's nephew. Where Delaporte's natural exuberance acted to dissipate tensions and encourage harmony, de Carné's tautly enthusiastic personality seemed fated to give frequent offense. His mind was filled with grand plans: France's colony in the East could be the economic equivalent of the American Far West, and "Socialism" could be contained by the success of French expansion overseas. But he had little talent for friendship and found it difficult to accept the details of discipline and control in an expedition led by a military man. From the very beginning both Lagrée and Garnier made little secret of their belief that this young diplomatist had been unwisely chosen for the task that lay ahead. Indeed, at the start of the expedition, Garnier appears to have held serious doubts about all the other members except the party's leader.

And even at this early stage there was abundant evidence of inefficient planning. If supplies seemed adequate, there is little sign in the surviving records of the expedition that any serious thought was given to how these cases were to be transported, or to how any surplus was to be returned as the group's instructions required. The same lack of planning was apparent in the designation of an escort. To the already large party of six principal explorers were added three interpreters (one French, one Cambodian, and one Laotian), four French military men, two Filipino soldiers, and seven Vietnamese militiamen. Porters and boatmen were to be found along the way. Lagrée later bitterly decried the large size of the party as a heavy burden to its leader.

In addition, although the matter seemed less demanding at this early stage, the expedition prepared to leave Saigon without any certainty as to when its members might receive the necessary passports for travel into, and through, China. Satisfactory arrangements had been made for territories that fell under the authority of the Thai court, and it did not seem of great consequence that passports were not in hand from Burma; the Frenchmen doubted that the weakened Burmese kingdom could do much to hinder their progress. But China represented a different problem. The great state to the north was their final goal so that it would be foolish, at best, to try and enter China without proper authorization. This was even more true in the middle sixties when, as the explorers knew, southwestern China was the scene of a major Islamic revolt against the imperial authorities. To delay, however, did not any longer seem possible. Their hope had to be that the passports would soon reach Saigon and be sent on after them.

At Angkor the explorers found the jungle had taken over most of the ruins.

Leaving Saigon on June 5, the expedition traveled by steam-powered gunboat, first to Kompong Luong, a little north of Phnom Penh, and then, more importantly, to the great ruins of Angkor. Garnier described this as "consecration" of the expedition's scientific purpose, emphasizing the extent to which Lagrée throughout his service in Cambodia had worked to record the details of the temple ruins. Yet for all the scientific detail, and less than scientific speculation that the visit to Angkor produced, these few days between June 23 and July 1, 1866, spent among the ruins had the air of a holiday. There was even a group photograph taken of the explorers ranged along one of the broad temple entrances. Reproduced as an engraving, it is a sobering reminder that this was the last period when the expedition was not beset by almost daily problems of health and purpose.

Backtracking from Angkor, the explorers paid their visit to Phnom Penh at the beginning of July. Despite its exotic character, they, in common with other French explorers of the nineteenth century, could not believe that they saw a city ruled over by a descendant of the Angkorian monarchs. When the time came to leave Phnom Penh, the morning after Norodom's great banquet, the Cambodian interpreter, Alexis Om, refused to leave. As his first name suggests, Om was a Cambodian Christian, one of a tiny minority holding this faith in a Buddhist kingdom. Well aware that rebellion was brewing in the eastern provinces of Cambodia, he had no stomach for the adventures the Frenchmen so confidently expected would lie ahead. Despite his earlier agreement to travel with the party, he now changed his mind. But his appeals to be allowed to stay behind were ignored, and Lagrée gave orders for him to be held under guard on board the gunboat. From the leader's point of view it was essential to have the services of all three interpreters: the Frenchman Séguin for travel in Thailand, the Laotian whom they called Alévy and whose knowledge of the distant regions north of Luang Prabang would make him invaluable as they moved nearer to China, and Alexis himself for the early stages of their travels.

Leaving Phnom Penh early in the morning of July 7, the group traveled rapidly up the Mekong to Kratie, in the northeast of the kingdom. Here, at the limit of their gunboat's capabilities and nearly at the limit of the Cambodian King's domains and their own known world, exploration proper began. Strung out along the left bank of the Mekong, Kratie in the 1860s had a population of about five hundred. A century later it was still a distant, isolated place, only rarely visited by foreign travelers. When the Frenchmen saw the little town in 1866 the houses of the inhabitants were set against a background of dark tropical landscape, with their fruit trees and rice fields scattered behind them. Few who have not seen these regions can appreciate the general somberness that pervades upcountry Cambodia, where only the yellow robe of an occasional Buddhist monk or the straggling vines of bougainvillea present a touch of bright color against the darkness of the trees and distant hills. By mid-July, the season at which the expedition paused at Kratie, the rainy monsoon had set in, and the monotonous landscape was matched by a gray sky to further depress the spirits.

Even the enthusiastic Garnier was affected by the dreary atmosphere of this Cambodian outpost. Nothing, he wrote, better demonstrated the results of the despotic system by which the country was ruled. The avarice of the officials insured that there should be no spark of initiative among the population at large. But there was surely more than this to the tone of gloom that pervades the reports of the mission's stay at Kratie. For all their confident assertions of the future value of the Mekong, here, below the first known major set of rapids—those Lagrée had already seen—the explorers had to face the possibility that these hopes were unrealizable. With the expedition scarcely under way, this was more than enough to compound the gloom of the physical surroundings.

Two days were spent in transferring the expedition's supplies from the gunboat to the shore, and then in loading some of the cases onto the *pirogues* that were to carry the explorers further north. Already the impossible bulk of the stores was apparent; both men and equipment had to be accommodated aboard narrow craft, each between thirty and fifty feet in length, carved from the trunk of a single tree. Going upstream these pirogues were neither rowed nor paddled. Rather, a team of six to ten men positioned on the bamboo platforms built on top of each canoe either used long poles to punt the craft forward or employed the hook at one end of their poles to pull the boat along against the current, hugging the shore, where trees and rocks were available to assist this strange method of progression. This "painful" style of travel, as Garnier called it, was the only way to proceed when the river was already in flood and the current was running in the opposite direction to the explorers' destination.

Leaving Kratie on July 13, after a sleepless night caused by a mix of excited conversation, rain, and mosquitoes, the explorers made one final stop before they reached the rapids of Sambor. This was at the settlement of the same name, only a few miles north of Kratie, which was the residence of the last senior Cambodian official they would meet—a man whose uncertain rule extended to the mountains and uplands of the east. From these high regions came exotic forest products and slaves, the latter in sufficient quantity to make this isolated post a rewarding one for officials who were both prepared to risk fever and unconcerned by the exigencies of life in this Cambodian *Ultima Thule*. Strangely, for the French explorers were extremely curious for fact and legend, there is nothing in the records to suggest that the alien travelers were aware of Sambor's important place in Cambodian history. When they saw Sambor they could scarcely have known that it had been a Cambodian city whose distant greatness was remembered in the official and folk literature of the state. They might, on the other hand, have been expected to learn that only thirty years earlier Sambor had been a larger, more prosperous settlement before it was sacked by Thai troops. But most surprising of all is the failure of any member of the expedition to mention the stupa built over the ashes of Princess Nucheat Khatr Vorpheak. In 1834 the princess had been taken by a crocodile. Later her remains were recovered, miraculously preserved, when the crocodile was caught and killed, and after her cremation the stupa was erected over the ashes. By the 1860s this stupa had already become a site for pious pilgrimage. Nearly a century later Prince Sihanouk sought the advice of this royal ancestor, through the medium of a woman of Kratie province, when he considered matters of international import.

Beyond Sambor were the rapids, where fast-moving water dominated a world in flood. In the low-water period the river bed north of Sambor is a jumbled mass of islands set amid countless water channels, broken by a seemingly endless series of rapids. All this is transformed by the rising waters of the rainy season. With surprising speed all but the largest islands along the river's course are submerged. In mid-July when the French explorers began their slow progress along the eastern bank of the river, the water level was at least fifteen feet above low water, and rising steadily. The gray rocks forming the low-water rapids seldom showed above the water streaming south at more than five knots, and the tops of trees waved liked feathers blown in the wind as they remained just above the advancing flood. Already the Mekong had spread to more than a mile in width. In later months its spread is broader still, and the river height is so great that no sense of the rocks below is gained by a traveler whose boat, even nowadays when propelled by a powerful outboard engine, must still hug the shore to progress against the current. In flood the Mekong above Sambor is a majestic sight, not least in the closing hours of daylight when the storm clouds frame the dark, distant hills, and lightning heralds yet another downpour which will raise the river's height even further.

Ever optimistic, and still unaware of the difficulties ahead, Garnier at Sambor pronounced this region to be quite certainly navigable. Since the flooding submerged the rapids, all that was needed was a vessel with sufficiently powerful engines to overcome the force of the current. For the expedition itself, however, the means at their disposal were more primitive. Slowly their pirogues were hauled by the boatmen along the eastern bank. By July 16 the party had reached the most difficult area of the rapids. No longer were there any clearly defined banks on either shore, and the boatmen had to strain to achieve even minimal progress. Garnier's dream of the Mekong as a route for trade from China to southern Vietnam, still held only three days earlier at Sambor, "seemed from this moment gravely compromised."

There was no way of knowing where the main channels of the river lay, and the sudden alternation of depths and shallows promised little assurance that any deep water channels would persist long enough to make them navigable. To match the disappointment of the days as the explorers moved through the area of the rapids, there were the rigors of the night. Unable to land and set up camp in the evenings, the expedition remained on the pirogues, drenched by frequent rainstorms, sleeplessly watching the spectacular electrical storms that circled around the dark skies.

During these days between July 15 and 19 as the flotilla of pirogues made its slow progress up the eastern bank of the Mekong, the Frenchmen heard repeated references from their boatmen to the great rapids of Preatapang. These, they were told, lay near the western bank of the river, not far from the northern limits of the rapids they had been traversing since they left Sambor. When, just as they were entering calmer water at the northern end of the rapids, the boatmen announced that Preatapang was nearby, Garnier immediately attempted a brief reconnaissance. Using a light pirogue, he urged his Cambodian boatman towards the opposite bank. But try as he might, his boatmen adamantly refused to do more than indicate the general direction of the Preatapang rapids. Disappointed, Garnier returned to his companions as the party now passed into calmer water below Stung Treng. The fury of the rapids, stretching for more than thirty miles, was now replaced by the familiar broad sweep of calm river characteristic of the Mekong in its lower reaches.

One day later the explorers were at Stung Treng itself. By now they had passed out of the territory of the Cambodian King. In this distant northeastern area authority had shifted many times in the preceding centuries. Where once Cambodian kings had ruled, the Stung Treng region was now in vassalage to the Thai ruler in Bangkok. The nature of authority at Stung Treng was vital to the expedition, since from this point on they had to rely on local officials to provide them with transport and boatmen. Their glacially reserved reception by the Laotian Governor who represented Thai power in Stung Treng was therefore disturbing for the difficulties it might present, and also puzzling.

The explanation, as they quickly found, was simple. Yet it leaves some intriguing questions unanswered. He was less than well disposed to the expedition, the Governor said, because he and the population under his charge had only recently met another Frenchman, a trader who had penetrated into the Stung Treng region, where he abused confidence and repaid assistance with poor faith. By their own combination of threats and blandishments, Lagrée and Garnier were eventually able to overcome the mistrust that this mysterious figure had engendered. But the question remains: who was he? At a time when the region through which the official expedition was passing was quite unknown to the Western world, who was the lone French trader whose travel to Stung Treng must be regarded as just as notable, in its own solitary way, as the efforts of the well-equipped and sizable official party. Even if he did not reach Stung Treng by way of the Mekong—and nothing suggests that this was the case—the journey overland, presumably from Bangkok, was still a remarkable achievement. Yet like so many solitary travelers in isolated regions, his existence is almost all that is known of the man.

In Stung Treng, Lagrée weighed the next steps that he and his subordinates should take. Set at the confluence of the Mekong and the Se Kong Rivers, Stung Treng with its eight hundred inhabitants was an ancient commercial center. In 1866 its chief trade was in human beings: slaves who were brought out of the high country to the east and sold downstream to Cambodia. With the knowledge that there were further settlements to the east of Stung Treng, Doudart de Lagrée decided to extend the investigations of the expedition up the Se Kong. But for Garnier there was another task, one that suited his adventurous character. There was the need to travel down the Mekong towards Sambor once again, to investigate the dangers and the possibilities of the rapids at Preatapang. To leave them a mystery was unacceptable to both Lagrée and Garnier.

Still hoping to find a navigable channel between Sambor and Stung Treng, therefore, Garnier set out to travel down the right bank of the river, and so close to Preatapang. Two Cambodian boatmen had been persuaded to remain while the rest of their countrymen returned direct to Kratie. For a special payment in silver, they were to take Garnier and a member of the expedition's escort, a French sailor named Renaud, down the western bank so that a complete survey might be made of this vital section of the river.

Leaving Stung Treng on July 24, Garnier and Renaud found that the swift current carried them south at such a rate that after only half a day they were at the head of the rapids. Following a night spent in a forest clearing beside the river, the travelers began their journey again. As the speed of the current increased, they reached a point where they could hear the distant rumble of the Preatapang rapids. Garnier called for the boatmen to continue on their course, following the right bank and heading directly for the rapids. He still hoped that this would be the direction in which a navigable passage might be found. The boatmen protested. With Renaud, who had spent some years in Cambodia, acting as interpreter, they told Garnier that only a madman would attempt the passage, that the water was so agitated it seemed to be boiling and that the current was swift as lightning. Nothing was more calculated to urge Garnier onward. He would, he told the boatmen, pay double their promised wages, but they must head towards the rapids.

Seemingly they agreed, but soon Garnier realized that they were heading crosswise towards the distant left bank, away from Preatapang. Grasping his revolver, he threatened the Cambodians as he pointed again to the dangerous route they were to follow. Reluctantly they obeyed and the light pirogue once more headed towards the roar of the rapids, moving ever faster as the current gripped the fragile craft and the boatmen struggled to insure their survival. Garnier's own account of the events that followed is still the best one:

> . . . the current now ran at a speed of six or seven miles an hour, and it was too late to turn back. If I had not been preoccupied with an examination of this section of the river, the appearance of comic anguish shown by my two boatmen would have made me laugh. For

the rest, I could see from their faces that if there was danger in making this terrible passage, there was no certainty of death. . . . Our threat to take the paddles in our own hands had achieved its effect. They preferred to rely on their own skill and knowledge of the region to save themselves rather than to place their fate in the hands of audacious but uninformed Europeans.

Now I saw the nature of the rapids. . . . Angered by the sudden barrier they encountered, the muddy waves furiously attacked the banks, leaped over them, rushed into the forest, foaming about each tree and each rock, leaving only the largest trees and the heaviest outcrops of rocks standing. Debris piled up along the waves' passage. The banks were leveled, and in the middle of a broad, strikingly white sea of water, full of whirlpools and flotsam, a few forest giants and dark rocks still withstood the assault, while columns of spray rose and fell ceaselessly on their summits.

Now we were there with the speed of an arrow. Of the greatest importance was the need to avoid being drawn by the current into the submerged forest where we would have been smashed into a thousand pieces. . . . I saw this all as a vision, in a flash. The noise was deafening, the spectacle fascinating to behold. Crossing this vast area of water, moving in every direction, with the current running at a speed that I estimated could not be less than ten or eleven miles an hour, our fragile craft was dragged through the middle of rocks and trees, hidden and tossed in the spume. It would have given the least impressionable person a sense of vertigo. Renaud had the courage and skill, when I gave him the signal, to take a sounding that showed there was thirty foot of water beneath us. But he had no time to do more. A moment later we brushed against a tree trunk that caused the water to surge many feet into the air. My boatmen were bent over their paddles, pale with fear, but with speed and skill they prevented us from smashing into the tree. Little by little the sickening speed of the current diminished and we entered calmer water. The bank was once more definable and my boatmen wiped away the sweat that coursed down their foreheads.

Garnier now knew the worst. Though the channel that he had just traversed was deep enough for a powered craft, there seemed no possibility that the current could be overcome. At half past two in the afternoon of July 25 he and his exhausted boatmen reached Sambor. In a little more than twelve hours they had covered the same distance that the expedition working against the river's flow had completed only in six long days. Pausing merely for a night's rest in Sambor, Garnier and Renaud again set off to the north, reaching Stung Treng on July 30.

When Garnier returned to Stung Treng, the expedition had been in progress for less than two months, yet its fundamental *raison d'être* was already in question, if not totally destroyed. In an all too human and understandable fashion, this was something the explorers found difficult, if not impossible, to accept. In spite of what they now knew, the thought that some means might still be found to overcome the barrier of the rapids sustained them. And the tasks of exploration, as they mapped the course of the river and recorded their detailed observations on the country and people about them, served to push the unpleasant truth into the background. While Garnier had been shooting the rapids of Preatapang, Lagrée had been leading a small party up the Se Kong to chart its course and note what possibilities there were for commerce. In Stung Treng itself, Garnier and others recorded details of the population, of the Chinese merchants who had taken up residence even in this remote town, and of the forest products that filtered out of the uplands and mountains to the east. And as the necessary pirogues and boatmen were slowly assembled for the next stage of the journey, the explorers discussed the way ahead to the Khone waterfalls. This was the next great obstacle along their route, and virtually the only remaining known feature ahead of them until they reached the area well to the north of Vientiane that Henri Mouhot had visited in 1861.

In this atmosphere of hopeful preparation the first major illness struck the expedition. Garnier and Joubert were the victims. While dysentery was accepted as an almost normal, even daily hazard — Dr. Thorel had contracted a severe case at Angkor that lasted until after the expedition passed Kratie — the explorers' greatest fear was of "fever." In both his official and his unofficial accounts of the expedition Garnier passes rapidly over his illness, only briefly noting its gravity. But it was serious indeed. Whereas Joubert was well on the way to recovery within ten days of the onset of the sickness, Garnier's more acute attack left him either unconscious or delirious for eighteen days.

The nature of the fever he contracted is uncertain. As his companions tended him, becoming ever more concerned for his life, they learned from the inhabitants of Stung Treng that it was "forest fever." Dr. Thorel later gave a detailed account of the illness, but the state of medical knowledge at the time prevents certainty as to its nature. It may have been scrub typhus. As time passed, and as the likelihood of Garnier's death seemed to grow stronger, Lagrée decided that the expedition could no longer delay its journey, even though to proceed meant transporting the still unconscious second-in-command in one of the narrow pirogues carrying the explorers towards Khone.

The very day that they started north again, Garnier, left untended for a moment, tossing and turning in his delirium, plunged unwittingly into the water from the canoe in which he lay. He was rescued from the water with difficulty, but this sudden shock was followed by a marked improvement. When four days later, on August 17, the expedition paused just below the Khone waterfalls, Garnier came to his senses for the first time in eighteen days. Much of his skin was sloughing away, and he was to lose all his hair as a result of the illness. His left leg was partially paralyzed, and it was six months before it regained its strength. He could assume few duties for the expedition until the beginning of October, thirty-three days after the illness began.

That Garnier recovered at all is remarkable, and is an indication of an underlying physical capacity that matched his strength of will. For the leader of the expedition, the illnesses of those around him were not a minor matter, but neither were they a subject for extended commentary. When towards the end of October he sent an official report to the Governor of Cochinchina, his summary of the expedition's health was brief and unemotional. "Since our departure from Kratie," Doudart de Lagrée wrote on October 27, 1866, "the only serious illnesses that have occurred are the following: Monsieur Thorel, dysentery; Monsieur Garnier, typhoid fever; the sailor Mouëllo, bilious fever; the principal Annamite soldier, bilious fever with hemorrhage." As he put it in summary, "The general state of health is as good as one might desire in the conditions in which we live."

CHAPTER IV

ONE STEP BACKWARD AND ONE STEP FORWARD

*W*hat the explorers expected at Khone it is hard to know. They had heard of a waterfall, and Lagrée later confided in a letter to his sister-in-law that he had hoped to see another Niagara, a vast single fall of water, tumbling from precipitous heights. He did not explain how this would affect his repeated hopes that the Mekong might be a navigable route for trade. Instead they found a series of falls and cascades, some dropping directly more than sixty feet into the broad basin of deep water immediately below, others falling in stages, a few feet at a time. This was not Niagara, but it was a formidable obstacle nonetheless, a series of interlocking falls and cascades running some seven miles and extending from one bank to the other.

Observed from the eastern bank of the river in the closing weeks of the rainy season—the time when the explorers first saw the falls—the scene at Khone is impressive. Instead of the spectacular combination of height and flow that so marks Niagara, the sense here is of limitless power spread over a vast horizontal distance. The traveler must shout to be heard above the thunderous roar of the nearest falls, reinforced by the accumulated volume of sound rising from the rest of the river system stretching out of sight to the west. Standing and watching, one sees tree trunks thrown outward and upward by the water before splashing downwards as the Mekong surges over the top of the falls. It seems a wonder that this force has not been sufficient to level the rocks that stand in the river's path and form the multitude of islands separating fall from fall and cascade from cascade. Spume rises in the air, forming a misty cloud that catches the sun to create passagery rainbows contrasting with the muddy khaki of the river above and below the falls. A breath of wind is

The leader of the Mekong expedition,
Doudart de Lagrée.

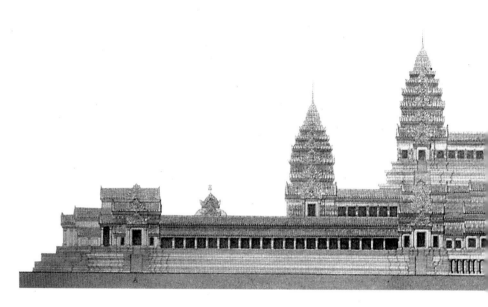

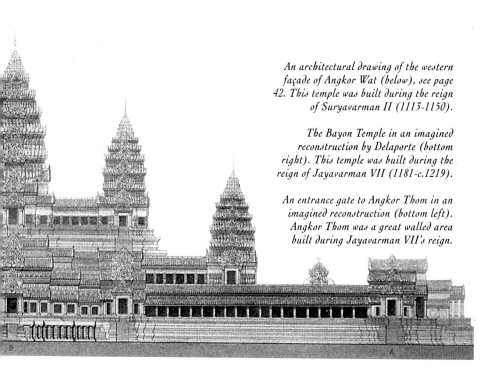

An architectural drawing of the western
façade of Angkor Wat (below), see page
42. This temple was built during the reign
of Suryavarman II (1113-1150).

The Bayon Temple in an imagined
reconstruction by Delaporte (bottom
right). This temple was built during the
reign of Jayavarman VII (1181-c.1219).

An entrance gate to Angkor Thom in an
imagined reconstruction (bottom left).
Angkor Thom was a great walled area
built during Jayavarman VII's reign.

Angkor Wat seen from the western entrance (left). Built in only 35 years, Angkor Wat is the world's largest religious monument.

The explorers entertained by King Norodom (right), see page 50.

The passage of a rapid (below). The frequent presence of rapids in the course of the Mekong doomed the explorers' hopes of using the river for large-scale navigation.

The French explorers at Angkor in June 1866. From left, Garnier, Delaporte, Joubert, Thorel, de Carné, Lagrée. See page 54.

The explorers camped before a set of rapids in Laos. Rapids continue to present major problems for navigation of the Mekong in the present day.

A view of Stung Treng, where the Se Kong River flows into the Mekong. Garnier fell seriously ill here. See pages 62-3.

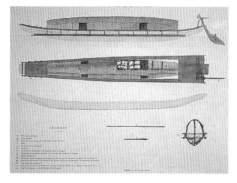

A plan of a pirogue, the boats carved out of single tree trunks that transported the explorers, their escort, and their supplies along the Mekong.

*A photograph of Delaporte, the artist of
the expedition.*

enough to carry the spray hundreds of yards to dampen the watcher downstream. In their combination of noise and power these cataracts are almost too overwhelming for the onlooker, who soon becomes exhausted—even repelled by—what he sees.

With Garnier still slowly recovering from his illness, the other members of the expedition surveyed the area from their camp below the falls. They learned that light, local craft used waterways to the extreme east and west of the main river system to bypass this great natural barrier. Lagrée's reconnaissance to the east suggested it would be the best route for the expedition. This was confirmed by Delaporte after he had examined the passage to the west where one of the highest falls was located. Although the western passage might be passable by small craft in the dry season, he reported, it was not worth considering at this time of flood. The deep water below the falls was dotted with the dead bodies of fish and alligators that had been caught in the fierce current upstream and pounded to death by the height and force of the falls. Possibly Delaporte's survey work was regarded as routine; whatever the cause, the expedition's official record makes no mention of the more unpleasant hazards Delaporte encountered. In the course of his short expeditions during the week the explorers spent below the Khone falls, he narrowly escaped death in quicksand, barely avoided a confrontation with tigers, and fell victim to a mass of leeches that gripped his flesh in their dozens. Only by climbing a tree, shedding his clothes, and then pulling off the leeches one by one did he rid himself of these loathsome creatures. Delaporte's experience was a distasteful harbinger of things to come. For the next twelve months leeches were an annoyance, and even a serious hazard, for the members of the expedition.

After a week camped below the falls, the explorers made their way up the eastern passage, leaving at midday on August 25. The difficulties of maneuvering even their light craft through the fast-flowing water slowed their progress. To cover only the few miles separating them from their next destination, the island of Khong above the falls, took until the late afternoon of the following day. There, at long last, the river had a single course once more. Ever since Kratie—even in the calmest stretches near Stung Treng—the Mekong had been a river of divided channels, running on either side of large and small islands. Here, northwards from the island of Khong, the river was formed by one great stream, over a mile wide. They found a sense of peace in the village at Khong and a prosperous population numbering perhaps ten thousand inhabitants on the island. Authority was exercised by a friendly octogenarian governor who responded to the gifts the Frenchmen gave him by remarking that he now realized that the Buddha must have been born in France; how else could the visitors be so munificent? He sent the explorers the gift of a bullock in return. Nothing could have been more welcome as they ate fresh beef for the first time since leaving Phnom Penh two months before.

The temptation to remain at Khong was strong. In this unknown region the party needed a base for exploration to the east and west of the Mekong, while they awaited passports for China. Despite their expectation that these would reach them soon after leaving Phnom Penh, the documents were still not in hand. Lagrée was left with difficult choices. Should he travel forward or wait? And what was the explanation for this unexpected delay in the arrival of the documents? For the moment Lagrée was reluctant to proceed further without the passports, so he planned a program that combined local exploration with some rest while they awaited the papers. For surely it could not be much longer before the French authorities in Phnom Penh would send them by local Cambodian and Laotian messengers. Lagrée's choice of a base was not Khong but Bassac, the chief political center for this area of southern Laos, five days' river travel further north. Early on September 11, 1866, the expedition landed there, never thinking that this was to be their base for over two months.

Quite without foreknowledge, Lagrée's choice proved excellent. Bassac was scenically striking, set on the western bank of the river with a large, cultivated island before the settlement, and dominated to the rear and west of the long, winding settlement following the river's bank by a series of dramatic mountains. As the explorers also soon found, there was a major temple ruin (Wat Phu) nearby to attract their interest. But before this could be investigated, or any survey made of the country to the east or west, they had to wait until the end of the rains. Other than exchanging courtesies with the local ruler, the "king" of Bassac, there was little the French party could do but sit restlessly in their quarters. At the end of the rainy season the monsoon clouds sometimes seem to make one final major effort to flood the land below, and this was what the Frenchmen now experienced. For eight days the rain fell almost without interruption. It was September 20 before the members of the expedition could move freely about their tasks.

Eagerly they undertook the duties that Lagrée assigned to them. A climb three-quarters of the way up one of the mountain peaks directly behind Bassac showed Garnier, Thorel, and Delaporte the magnificent vista of the Mekong winding its way past forest and mountain with only the most limited areas along the banks cultivated by man. At the beginning of October Garnier and Thorel, accompanied by Renaud from the escort party, set off to survey the Se Don River, a tributary of the Mekong that joined the major stream a little above Bassac. Traveling by canoe, by elephant, and on foot, they penetrated up the Se Don valley to an area where the inhabitants were no longer the Buddhist Laotians of the lowland regions, but scantily clad hill tribesmen living on the fringes of society. The Frenchmen searched unsuccessfully for the silver mines that rumor placed in these hills; but none were to be found. They were sure that native cunning had triumphed over the frankness of their European inquiries.

In Bassac itself the explorers watched and recorded the busy life that went on about them. After the lassitudes of the long wet season the population prepared to engage in the busy occupations of the dry months that would last until April. Like so many Western observers before and after them, the Frenchmen wrote almost simultaneously of the "laziness" of the Laotians and of the way in which the population hastened to fish in the falling waters of the Mekong or spent long hours in the paddy fields building shelters in preparation for the weeks of labor that would occupy them during the rice harvest.

How does one explain this curious double standard? Possibly it stemmed in this case from a form of selective memory. In the course of the explorers' stay at Bassac they saw one of the great festivals of the year, the water festival or festival of the boats: a great calendrical event, a blend of fertility rite and pre-Lenten festivity, sometimes almost saturnalian. All along the Mekong, whether at Bassac, Vientiane, or Phnom Penh, the rites associated with the festival have a fundamental similarity. Canoe races are held to celebrate the end of the rains and the swift fall of the river's level; giant pirogues, as long as ninety feet, manned by as many as sixty men, compete in races before the local ruler and the assembled population. On the shore, each night, there is feasting and unrestrained search for pleasure in drinking and sex. Transvestites appear in great numbers, so that this element of Indochinese sexuality becomes suddenly apparent to Europeans whose awareness of local mores is usually of the more obvious male-female relationships.

The events of the festival took place before the fascinated eyes of the French exploratory mission. Indeed, its members became part of some, at least, of the celebrations. In Bassac the festival included a ritual swearing of allegiance by the vassal "king" of the region to the throne of Bangkok. Lagrée attended with his personnel, and, to lend luster to the occasion, escorted by his tiny guard bearing fixed bayonets. It added, Garnier noted, "not a little to the splendor of the affair." So too did the fact that the "king" of Bassac found he was the father of a new son during the course of the festival. The ruler's joy in the daytime, the Europeans recorded, became drunkenness in the evening.

The great pirogue races climaxed the third day's events. Bearing the colors of particular villages and pagodas, the slim shallow craft, with scarcely any freeboard, sped down the river, fifty or sixty paddles flashing in the sun before dipping in unison to push the craft faster than the foreign observers thought possible. In the middle of each craft stood a masked buffoon, balancing, gesturing, urging the boatmen on and shouting ribald commentary. The watching Frenchmen knew that the commentary was "lascivious," but they did not record more. They may have been uncertain of what was being said; more probably they felt that although they might laugh at what they heard, this was not what they should record for posterity. One hundred years later observers were less influenced by this type of judgment. When the same kind of race, with the same kind of buffoons, took place in Phnom Penh, the chants from the pirogues were probably little different from those the explorers heard in Bassac:

> It has rained a great deal this year, the river has broken its banks. There will be much rice and joy. All the women are pregnant, either by their husbands or by their lovers. It doesn't really matter. Aya!

or:

> Oh you women, lift up your sarongs so that I can tell who amongst you pleases me the most. Aya!

Then, finally, on October 28, the festival ended with a floating fireworks display as bamboo frames were set upon the water to drift with the current past the watching crowd. It was a gay and uninhibited affair.

But the end of the festival signaled the true beginning of the dry season, for the explorers as well as for the local population. This was the best time of the year for travel; but still the French party was in Bassac, six weeks after leaving the Khone falls, and four months after their departure from Saigon. Their passports for China had not arrived, and already there were hints of indiscipline in the escort which were later to become overt and challenging problems. The essential need was to begin traveling north once more; yet, without the passports, to press on might only lead to great disappointment. The solution was for Garnier to travel downstream to Stung Treng, where they now confidently expected the much desired documents would be waiting for collection.

On November 2, still not in full health but with the best of spirits, Garnier set off for the south, accompanied by Renaud (his escort from their earlier passage of the Preatapang rapids), a Vietnamese militiaman, and the Cambodian interpreter, Alexis Om, who was again refusing to remain with the explorers. Only six days later the little party was in Stung Treng—where Garnier found that their hopes for the passports were illusory. In the period of a little more than two months since the expedition left Stung Treng, much had changed in the border lands of Cambodia and Laos. The rebellion against the King of Cambodia, that had seemed a minor matter when the Frenchmen sat with Norodom watching the palace dancers in Phnom Penh at the beginning of July, was now an affair of consequence. The rebel leader, Pou Kombo, a pretender to the throne without any justification for this claim other than his forceful personality, had gathered a mass of peasants about him. To the south, in the area about Kratie, the rebels held sway, having killed the Governor at Sambor, the last Cambodian official the expedition had seen before beginning their ascent of the Sambor rapids. Any thought that, by depending on the swiftness of the current, Garnier might pass unnoticed down the river to Phnom Penh was negated by the realization that he was almost certain to be captured on his return voyage by the insurgents who held the banks on either side of the Mekong.

For Garnier the problem was insoluble. Each day that he spent in Stung Treng gave greater confirmation to the reports he had received. There was nothing he could do. Travel to Phnom Penh, or even to Kratie, was out of the question. The Laotian Governor of Stung Treng was suffering from a fever that Garnier alleviated through the use of quinine, but nothing improved the French officer's spirits. The sight of a caravan of slaves being brought into Stung Treng from the eastern highlands, the men seemingly indifferent but the women deeply moved and clutching their children in desperate efforts of protection, depressed him further. He could only return to Bassac, leaving the interpreter Alexis Om at Stung Treng in the hope that, being a Cambodian, he might be able to pass undetected down the river to alert the French in Phnom Penh to the plight of the expedition. Leaving Stung Treng on November 12, Garnier again started north; this time, in contrast to the period almost exactly two months before, fully conscious of all that he saw. Once past the Khone falls he traveled along the right bank of the river, stopping where the onset of each night found him, showing already his willingness to travel through unknown regions with a minimum of companionship.

The camp to which Garnier returned on November 23 was not a happy place. Delaporte had found Bassac enchanting, and his journal is full of enthusiasm for the time he spent there. The inhabitants readily sat as subjects for his sketches, not least a young woman whose parents, so the young officer believed, hoped he might marry their daughter. The local ruler prevailed on him to build an armchair, having learned that this was how men of Europe chose to be seated. Then, in the evenings, Dela-

Listening to Laotian music.

porte played his violin to the enjoyment of the local population, trading an excerpt from "Orpheus in the Underworld" or "La Belle Hélène" in return for the opportunity to hear the local musicians perform their own airs. But this type of entertainment had not been sufficient for the French military men in the escort, or for Séguin, the expedition's European interpreter whose conduct had hovered near insubordination for weeks. They wanted liquor and they wanted women. These were natural enough desires, and ones that neither officers nor rankers denied themselves in Phnom Penh or Saigon in the 1860s. Writing with a trembling hand in the early 1870s, the French Apostolic Vicar of Saigon vehemently condemned the almost universal practice by French officials of keeping Vietnamese concubines. But an expedition, for the officers, was a different thing—a time when physical desires should be sublimated to the greater good of confronting hardship in the name of France. The same standards had little attraction for the personnel of the escort.

In Bassac the escort lived a life of enforced idleness. Their lack of contact with the outside world was total. Just occasionally an indication of the sexual frustrations endured by the party as a whole emerges obliquely in Garnier's own record of events. He noted his mildly embarrassed realization that the women of Laos had come to seem gracious and "even pretty." Whether this was the result of his long stay in Cochinchina or because Laotian and European women shared certain physical characteristics, he could not decide. In the account of his return from Stung Treng to Bassac he refers, almost with the vicarious pleasure of a voyeur, to his belief that a young Cambodian girl who had drunk deeply from his supply of brandy was afterwards an easy conquest for a youth of the village. But, he continues after this observation, "I will be as discreet as the tamarind trees that lent their shadowy silence to the two lovers."

Vicarious enjoyment was not enough for the secondary personnel. Upon his return to Bassac, Garnier found one member of the French escort in chains, under guard by the local ruler's men. There had been heavy drinking and a chase after women. The interpreter Séguin had threatened one of the French soldiers with a knife. A general fracas had ensued, and when it was quelled Delaporte, in charge while both Lagrée and Garnier were absent, had clapped one of the men in irons—not Séguin, curiously, but a soldier named Rande who, initially at least, had been incited to violence by the French interpreter.

Other concerns played on the minds of the principal explorers. For all of them the failure of the colonial government in Saigon to find some way to send the passports for China was a matter for increasingly bitter feelings. Garnier, indeed, came close to believing that the delay might stem from the earlier antagonism that had marked his relations with Admiral de La Grandière. Lagrée fretted at the delay and dwelled upon the error that had been made in burdening him with an excessively large party. De Carné, well aware that his inclusion in the expedition had not been welcomed by either Lagrée or Garnier, lived resentfully with the fact that the party's leader acted as if he were commanding a ship at sea. Monsieur de Carné, Lagrée insisted, did not have the right to communicate directly with the Ministry of Foreign Affairs, nor as they traveled could he decide what matters required his personal investigation. If Garnier's private correspondence at this time is any guide, the tensions between the explorers had become open and troublesome.

The frequent need to divide the party into smaller groups did little to add a sense of solidarity. Beset by uncertainty, yet seeking to find useful ways of occupying their time until the passports should arrive, sections of the party set off on their separate ways. While Garnier was making his abortive trip to Stung Treng, Lagrée undertook a major reconnaissance of the Bolovens Plateau, to the east of the Mekong. Accompanied by Joubert and de Carné, he went up the Se Don River as far as Saravan and then marched south to the commercial center of Attopeu, on the headwaters of the Se Kong, traveling some of the way on elephants. This was the river the explorers had already encountered at Stung Treng, where the Se Kong flows into the Mekong. At Attopeu, as at the other isolated commercial centers they had visited previously, the chief business seemed to be in slaves, though they also learned that gold was dredged from alluvial deposits nearby. The isolation of the little town and the reputation it had as an unhealthy area meant that Attopeu was a rare exception among centers of any size in the Indochinese region: a place where there were no Chinese residents. Yet it, too, had its cosmopolitan element. Here, in a location as distant from the known world as any the Frenchmen had yet encountered, there was a small colony of Burmese traders, dealing in gemstones and European trade goods.

The party soon found how well Attopeu deserved its reputation for being unhealthy. Doudart de Lagrée suddenly fell seriously ill. Just before leaving Bassac he had written to his brother's wife, mocking in gentle terms the vision of Laos that such men as Mouhot had provided in the past. "I do not know," he wrote on November 1, "the origin of these tales of fever and frightful sickness in Laos." This was a bold and curiously thoughtless observation for a man like Lagrée. Mouhot, as he well knew, had died from fever in northern Laos. Garnier and Joubert had been seriously ill with fever in Stung Treng. Now it was Lagrée's turn. He was stricken with fever in Attopeu, and his companions, especially Joubert with his medical training, came close to despairing of his life. In the course of the illness Lagrée lost the use of his limbs as they became cold and rigid. Characteristically, his next letter to his sister-in-law, written after the party had returned to Bassac on December 4, made light of the whole affair. They had all been affected by fever to some extent, he remarked; but although he now had to admit that the infamous fevers of Laos were no "myth," he could reassure her with the knowledge that "heavy doses of quinine easily cured us."

This was a brave but fundamentally foolhardy assessment. Just as Lagrée and the rest of the expedition were reluctant to admit that the Mekong was an unlikely route for significant trade between southern Vietnam and the regions to the north, so did their remarkable standards of courage and fortitude lead them to discount the heavy toll that tropical disease might take of their ability to survive the travails that still lay ahead. They were modern men, but modernity in the 1860s still did not imply an understanding of the cause of disease. It would not be long before the dangers of drinking unboiled water in a tropical setting would be widely known, but this was not knowledge the explorers possessed.

In early December 1866 the overwhelming need to press on was apparent to all. The expedition's experience of river travel during the height of the rainy season had been discouraging. Now, with the end of the year drawing near, they knew that within five, and possibly only four months, the Mekong would again be rising to its flood level, making progress along it a slow, perhaps impossible affair. Henri Mouhot's description of the river near Luang Prabang, in upper Laos, suggested that the experience of the Sambor rapids might, at the very least, be repeated there. Adding urgency to the situation was the failure of the Cambodian interpreter Alexis Om to travel south from Stung Treng to Phnom Penh. Ever since Garnier had left him at Stung Treng, the explorers had been able to hope that he had bypassed the rebel bands and gone on to alert the French authorities to their desperate need for the passports to China. As long as it seemed possible that Alexis had made the trip to Phnom Penh, there was an added element of indecision. When, unexpectedly in early December, Alexis reappeared at the Bassac camp, having found the way down the Mekong still barred by the rebels, hopes were dashed and action could be delayed no longer.

Lagrée and Garnier agreed on a new plan that would solve several problems simultaneously. The expedition as a whole would leave Bassac, travel a short stage up the Mekong, and then ascend the Se Moun River to Ubon in the northeast of Thailand. Lagrée believed that, because of its presumed political importance, this sizable settlement should be visited before the expedition embarked on its definitive route to the north. At the same time he accepted the proposal that Ubon should provide a jumping off point for yet another effort by Garnier to penetrate Cambodia and gain news of the missing passports. With Garnier would travel three of the expedition's secondary personnel who were now a clear liability to the party's progress. As a final if dubious precaution, Alexis Om would be left at Bassac in the hope that he might still make his way overland to Angkor and Phnom Penh and alert the French representatives as to how matters stood. He was to ask that the passports now be sent to Angkor, where Garnier might collect them.

Despite the courageous prose that flowed from the explorers' pens in the official and private accounts of their situation at this time, an air of something very near to desperation is easily discerned. Typically, both Lagrée and Garnier continued to discuss the possibility that the Mekong was, after all, navigable. But the tone of their recommendations had begun to change. Lagrée, always more cautious and restrained than his younger second-in-command, admitted that there was no longer any reason for thinking that a steam-powered vessel could pass beyond the Khone falls. Even to reach that far, passing through the Sambor rapids, would be a *tour de force*. The issue was not so clear for Garnier; he thought further investigation was necessary. The falls at Khone might be a barrier in themselves, but some means might be found to bypass them. In the circumstances of such apparent failure as now surrounded the French party, hope, however unjustified, was the only way to ward off despair.

On Christmas Day 1866 the explorers left Bassac with few regrets. The weather was fresh, even cold for men accustomed to the overpowering heat of Cochinchina. To be on the move again was exhilarating in itself, and it is striking that none of the records left behind by the explorers give any further sense of difficulties caused by those men of the escort who were now to return to Cambodia. They—Sergeant Charbonnier, Renaud, and Rande—had the prospect before them of resuming a pattern of life that, however difficult it might be, was something they understood.

The journey to Ubon was one of familiar difficulties. Shortly after the expedition began ascending the Se Moun they encountered rapids. The first came only a mile and a half after the party's pirogues turned out of the Mekong into the tributary. During the afternoon of December 31 in a series of slow portages the expedition covered less than a mile. New Year's Day was little better, except that Delaporte succeeded in shooting a hare which seemed a feast to the meat-hungry travelers.

By January 2, 1867, however, progress was no longer impeded by rapids, and the French party moved on easily, reaching Ubon on January 7. The settlement was in Garnier's terse description, "too large for a village and yet still not a town." But it was strikingly more lively than any population center the group had seen since leaving Phnom Penh six months before. There was more than one street, and two of the settlement's pagodas were built in brick rather than wood. In moving west of the Mekong the explorers found that the importance of Bangkok took on a new dimension. Stung Treng, Bassac, and even Attopeu were vassal areas to the Bangkok court, but now they were in a settlement that was linked economically as well as politically with the Thai capital. The local ruler, again a "king," was affable and ready to help them.

Once more the time had come for the expedition to split up, with Garnier now facing the longest and loneliest path. He would have had the three French military men and a Vietnamese soldier as his traveling companions as far as Angkor, or even Phnom Penh if Alexis Om had not completed his journey; but he could only look forward to returning with the one, non-French assist-

For much of the time the expedition members had to negotiate vegetation as dense as this.

ant. The main party was to divide into two groups. One, led by Lagrée, would continue north by land towards Khemmarat, another important settlement on the Mekong. Finally, since the necessity to survey all of the Mekong remained a paramount duty, Delaporte was detailed to travel down the Se Moun to the Mekong and thence to ascend the great river and rejoin the main party at Khemmarat. Garnier with his party was the first to set off once more into the unknown, leaving Ubon on January 10 to begin a grueling journey through unexplored territory that was to last for two months before he saw his companions again.

CHAPTER V

PASSPORTS FOR CHINA

*W*ith Garnier gone in search of the passports, the rest of the expedition was ready to resume its slow passage north. Before leaving Ubon, however, they watched the coronation of the local ruler, recording the event in terms of mixed interest and deprecation. They found impressive the sight of the "king" dressed in rich green velvet and borne to the ceremony on an elephant of great size, followed by twenty-two more of these huge creatures and by cavalrymen and foot soldiers bearing banners. But the band that preceded the procession played in a "deafening" fashion, and the calm of the long night after the coronation ceremony was "disturbed" by the sound of singing and the music of strange instruments. In the brevity and matter-of-fact style used to describe this affair, there is already a strong sense that the exotic had become an everyday matter for these travelers.

Delaporte was the next to leave Ubon, departing on January 15. After traveling back down the Se Moun, he started up the Mekong. Once more the great river gave Delaporte little reason to hope that it might ever provide a navigable route to China. Where the Mekong's course was not broken by rapids the current flowed lazily south, the water level as much as fifty feet below the high point reached during flood time. But each stretch of calm water was followed by the seemingly inevitable barrier of rapids. On occasion, eight boatmen paddling furiously were unable to force Delaporte's light pirogue upstream against the current, and to proceed he had to resort to portage or have his men haul the craft by ropes through the shallows at the edges of the rapids. Meticulously charting the river's course, and sketching the countryside about him, he made his way to the small political and commercial post of Khemmarat, arriving there on

January 26, 1867, ahead of the main party.

Lagrée's group had remained a further five days in Ubon before setting off on January 20. Their overland route took them almost directly north for some eighty miles. After traveling through cultivated regions, their path then passed through a dry and deserted area of northeastern Thailand. Still preserving many cases of their vast stocks of stores and supplies, the explorers headed a caravan of six elephants, fifteen ox carts, and more than fifty porters. At Amnat, half way along their route, the roads used by the ox carts came to an end. Nine more elephants and a hundred porters now bore the expedition's supplies towards Khemmarat, with beasts and men kicking up a choking pall of dust from the dry ground. The strength of the sun was still not at its maximum, but the combination of dust and heat was enervating. Dr. Joubert was carrying his pet dog, Fox, when the group reunited with Delaporte in Khemmarat on January 30. The scene is captured in a charming engraving; flanked by the other explorers, Lagrée and Delaporte eagerly grasp hands against a background of elephants, palm trees, and fascinated villagers.

This was a place of warm welcome. The Frenchmen with their servants and charts were seen as men of deep astrological knowledge and their opinion was sought on matters of consequence: when, they were asked, should an official of the settlement depart for Bangkok so as to be in harmony with the heavens' wishes? They were invited to watch all aspects of life in the village. So they saw a man and a woman judged for adultery. The fines levied were small, but before the judgment was made the guilty lovers had been punished in a local version of the pillory. They were tied to a large length of bamboo, facing each other, and made to beat upon it to draw attention to their plight.

For thirteen days Khemmarat was also a base camp for surveys of the surrounding area. Although the explorers' accounts of this activity are curiously reticent, the intent seems to have been political intelligence. Was there any significant Vietnamese influence near the east bank of the Mekong? If this could be discovered, then future French policy might be able to capital-

Lagrée and Delaporte clasp hands at Khemmarat.

ize upon it to prevent any further expansion of Thai power. The surveys, however, were indecisive, and again the expedition took to the river, heading north on February 13, 1867.

For two days rapids again succeeded rapids, enforcing a slow pace on the party. Then, in its apparently unpredictable fashion, the Mekong's course became wide and free of barriers. The expedition moved steadily up the river, stopping to inspect any pagoda which seemed of special interest, seeking information from whatever local authorities they encountered. By February 22 they were at Nakhon Phanom, the site of a famous stupa, a Buddhist shrine, or *that* in Laotian. The importance of the monument was soon made clear to the French members of the party. Alévy, the Laotian interpreter who joined the expedition in Phnom Penh, had during his varied life once been a Buddhist monk. But he had abandoned his saffron robe to marry. Confronted by this sacred place, his desertion from the monkhood suddenly became a matter for concern and expiation. While the others rested at Nakhon Phanom, Alévy spent the days in prayer. Contemplating the errors of his worldly life, he made a gesture of atonement to the Buddha by cutting off the top joint of his left index finger. Neither Alévy's portrait engraving, nor the brief and skeptical references to his character in the various accounts of the expedition, suggest a man of devout faith. Yet, on this occasion at least, the spiritual power of That Phanom caused Alévy to reflect with shame on his past.

Beyond Nakhon Phanom, as the Mekong pursued its northwesterly course, was Thakhek, and beyond that again Uthen — each reached in easy stages along the river. By March 6 the party was at Uthen, a provincial center which served as an outlet for lead mined a short distance from the river, and the expedition halted for a reconnaissance of its production. While the rest of the group remained by the river, Lagrée and Joubert set off for the mines. In their absence the main party was finally rejoined on March 10 by Garnier, still alert and eager after two months of almost constant travel.

When Garnier left Ubon on January 10, 1867, he knew neither

how long his journey would take nor the nature of the route ahead. For companions he had the three French military men who were being sent back to regular duties—Charbonnier, Rande, and Renaud—and a Vietnamese orderly, Tei. He had, too, his pet bitch Dragonne, whose presence with the expedition is only at this point suddenly and emotionally noted in Garnier's record of his travels. His pet since her birth on a gunboat of the same name in 1860, she was not to be with him much longer. Dragonne had fretted ever since the party left Saigon, and her removal now from the company of her one canine companion, Joubert's Fox, was too much. Two days after Garnier and his little group left Ubon, Dragonne disappeared during the night and plunged into the Se Moun, whose course the party still followed westward. Garnier felt inconsolable. Like other travelers in distant regions, not least the unfortunate Henri Mouhot, Garnier found that his pet dog filled a vital emotional gap in his life.

By January 14, the party was at Sisaket. River travel was no longer of any value after this point, as the main course of the Se Moun swung back to the north whereas Garnier's route lay almost due south. In place of pirogues they now traveled in light ox carts through the dry countryside. The rains had ended little more than two months before, but sixty days of unrelieved sunshine left the earth parched and dusty. The villages, grouped about small, weed-filled lakes and surrounded by sugar palms and fruit trees, seemed like oases in the desert. For the rest, Garnier noted, the countryside seemed "sterilized by fire." Thirty miles farther south the surroundings changed, and Garnier's small caravan of ox carts entered an area of forest. The flowering trees and the cool of the shadows cast by the thick vegetation were almost a compensation for the red dust that rose constantly from the hooves of the oxen trotting before their carts.

Forty miles south of Sisaket they came to Khu Kan. As was the case with settlements farther to the north, they were still within the territories of the King of Thailand, but here at Khu Kan the cultural ambience was Cambodian. The area had passed under Thai control in the seventeenth century, but the language spoken by the inhabitants was still Cambodian. One of the first inquiries Garnier made on reaching Khu Kan concerned the interpreter Alexis Om. Had he visited the settlement? When the expedition left Alexis at Bassac, the intention was that he should travel to Angkor through this region. Nothing was known of him at Khu Kan, however, which made Garnier's trip in search of the passports the more urgent.

From Khu Kan the party traveled in a largely westerly direction to Sangkeak, a distance of some forty miles. The problems of what route to follow and which direction to take now loomed large in Garnier's mind. His destination was to the south, yet all of the information he could glean from his local informants suggested that the best way to reach Cambodia was by continuing farther to the west. He was handicapped by language. He spoke Vietnamese but not Cambodian and had to rely on the uncertain translations provided by Renaud, whose service in Cambodia had given him some limited ability in the language. Garnier's concern became more acute after speaking with the Governor of Sangkeak, who claimed that the route the French party should follow lay through Surin, a town he described as being to the west. More disturbing still was the Governor's insistence that a southerly route would lead them to mountains that would surely bar their way. In an apparently dead flat landscape this warning seemed meaningless. Nonetheless, dependent as he was on local authorities for the provision of ox carts, Garnier agreed to travel to Surin with the hope that he might there gain information to clarify the situation.

To his almost immediate distress, he found that the route to Surin was as much to the north as to the west, taking him ever farther from his goal. Worse still, when the party reached Surin the local Governor was absent and his subordinate staff showed the greatest reluctance to associate in any way with the Frenchmen. Only after Garnier stormed and shouted, and following a day's infuriating delay, were carts found to take them south again. Now, to complicate matters further, the ox carts were being provided on a relay basis. Each village became a staging post where it was necessary to convince the village headman of the urgency of their need. There was no meeting of minds. The Frenchmen wanted to travel as fast as possible. The villagers could not understand either such haste in this increasingly hot period of the year, or Garnier's refusal to wait the four or five days it would take to furnish the travelers with new ox carts, better suited to their route.

And still there was talk of mountains. Late in the evening of January 22 the five men reached the village of Soukrom, having noted during the afternoon that the plain they were crossing was beginning to slope upward to the south. The information they received at Soukrom was just as puzzling as before. The village chief warned of mountains and precipices, but where these were and how they might affect the group's plans was beyond the Frenchmen's understanding. The headman wanted to assemble more men to travel with them, to assist the ox drivers they now had. But arranging this would take time, and, in any case, Garnier saw no need for more men. His account of the circumstances is remarkably frank. "I was accustomed to having the natives predict difficulties and then never encountering them. I thus did not take any objection seriously."

He did not have to wait long to discover how wrong he had been in doubting the good faith of his informants. Early on January 23 the party set off with three ox carts reluctantly provided by the village. Traveling through a forest, the track ran slowly upward, crossing a series of small streams. At one of these an ox cart driver asked them to stop, asserting that this was the last water they would encounter. Garnier did not believe him. It was early in the day and he saw this request as merely another "ruse" and confirming his view that the native population was both lazy and untrustworthy. He insisted that they should move on, and gave the lead by walking ahead at the front of the small group. To emphasize their determination, the three Frenchmen with Garnier took the reins of the oxen and urged the beasts forward. One by one the ox cart drivers slipped away until Garnier suddenly realized that the five of them were on their own. At almost the same moment the ox carts emerged from the shadowy world of the forest into the light and the Frenchmen found that their path had vanished. They stood at the edge of a high cliff more than six hundred feet above a vast plain that stretched away to the southern horizon. What they had been told was the truth after all. Garnier had known from barometric readings that there was a difference of some six hundred feet between the altitudes of Ubon and Angkor. What he had not anticipated was that this difference was contained in a single physical feature.

Standing at the edge of the cliff, Garnier saw that it might still be possible to go on. Zigzagging down to the plain below were rough tracks that clearly were used by men and beasts from time to time. They too would use these; and he gave the necessary orders to his men. They would not go back, for too much time had been lost already. Instead they would unload their ox carts, then they would dismantle the carts themselves and carry them, and their supplies, to the foot of the cliff. The decision was typical of Garnier but remarkable nonetheless. Commencing their work at midday, when the sun was at its hottest, they were without water or resources beyond their own. The rocks over which they had to climb and walk were burning hot from the sun, and the combined effect of heat and physical effort began to take its toll.

By the middle of the afternoon both the four Frenchmen and the one Vietnamese were close to heat exhaustion, dehydrated and without apparent access to water. And the greater part of their task still remained to be done. Activity ceased and the men slumped down to rest, unable to go on. They were too exhausted even to speak. Then, and only then, Garnier found a source of fresh cool water, a pool at the base of a now dry waterfall. Refreshed, they could continue. By ten o'clock at night they were at the base of the cliff with their carts again assembled and loaded. Detailed though it is, Garnier's account only hints at the worst hardships of the undertaking. For five men to carry their stores and three dismantled carts down a steep cliff, as Tei led the unwilling oxen behind him, under a burning tropical sun, and to accomplish the whole task in some ten hours suggests powers of endurance beyond easy metaphor.

They camped for the night at the base of the cliff, sleeping with a great fire burning to ward off the tigers that they heard making their characteristic coughing calls in the enveloping darkness about them. Sunk in exhausted sleep, the party was roused before dawn by a band of men from the village where they had stopped the night before. The villagers had come to help and were amazed to find the five travelers already at the base of the cliff.

The route to Angkor was now clear of any major obstruction and the party made good time. They passed through well cultivated landscapes, finding ever more frequent reminders of the great Angkorian period in Cambodian history along their way: a mighty bridge, built more than six hundred years before, still spanning a river, and the ruins of temples and sanctuaries. Garnier's enthusiastic description of all that he saw reflects his conviction that every step brought him closer to the passports. But this was not the only reason to take pleasure in the sights they saw. After the austere landscape they had witnessed in northeastern Thailand, the land through which they traveled now seemed rich and bountiful. The harvest was in progress and the stubble in the paddy fields was golden brown in color, reminiscent of the final summer weeks in Europe.

Late in the afternoon of January 29, nineteen days after leaving Ubon, they saw the citadel of Angkor in the distance. It rose before them with the setting sun outlining the battlements and giving grim emphasis to the rotting head of an executed criminal impaled upon a tall bamboo pole. The party had reached its primary destination.

Only a few minutes were necessary for Garnier to learn that his mission was still incomplete. Alexis, the interpreter, upon whose devotion to duty they had unwisely pinned their hopes, had still not reached Angkor. Worse still, the insurgency led by Pou Kombo had grown rather than diminished. The Governor had warned Garnier that it would be folly to attempt a passage to Phnom Penh in the unsettled conditions that prevailed. But to have come this far and failed would have been unendurable for Garnier, and he insisted on making the last leg of the long voyage. He engaged a Vietnamese fishing boat to complete the journey to Phnom Penh, estimating that such a craft would be of little interest to the rebels who held the banks of the lake and the Tonle Sap that lay between Angkor and the Cambodian capital. Leaving the Angkor region on February 2, they traveled south, at one stage sighting a band of rebels but passing by them without incident, and arrived at Phnom Penh shortly before midnight on February 5. In less than a month, under difficult conditions, they had covered a distance little short of four hundred miles. And, to Garnier's great joy, the passports were at last available.

Yet, if the essential travel documents were finally available, there were other disappointments. Ever since leaving Saigon the previous June the expedition had been acutely aware of the inadequacy of their scientific equipment. But the extra instruments they had supposed would be forwarded with the passports were still, it seemed, in Saigon. So, too, were the private letters that the explorers awaited. Garnier was briefly torn between traveling to Saigon to collect these items and returning to the expedition's main party with the least delay. But his journey had already lasted much longer than either he or Lagrée had hoped, and thus on reflection the decision seemed clear.

Without any sure knowledge of the progress made by the main party since he had left it at Ubon, and aware of the importance of the passports that he carried, Garnier rested for the minimum of time in Phnom Penh. For the three French soldiers who had accompanied him this was almost the end of their travels. They were to return to Saigon and pass, with the exception of Charbonnier, from our knowledge. Sergeant Charbonnier is the exception because he became the expedition's first fatality. He returned to the more familiar setting of Saigon already ill with dysentery and never recovered. As for Garnier, having paid a brief courtesy visit to the Cambodian King on February 7 and now accompanied only by his Vietnamese orderly, Tei, his path lay north once more. Passing unscathed through rebel areas a second time, they reached Angkor on February 13.

Speed being the most vital concern, Garnier decided to seek a more direct route than the one he and his companions had followed previously. Warned that to travel due north would take him through uninhabited territory, he still did not hesitate. Engaging an ox cart and a few Cambodian porters, he and Tei struck out to the north. The statement that this was uninhabited territory proved correct, and the rough cart tracks they followed through the forest were overgrown with shrubs and creepers which had to be cleared away in order for the cart to move forward. At one point, as they labored to clear a path, they were forced to pause by the presence of a herd of wild elephants. Ever impetuous, Garnier would have fired on the leader had not his more knowledgeable Cambodian assistants warned him that to do so risked a stampede that would surely kill them all. At length, on February 18, they emerged from the forest. Their route had been direct but slow. In covering forty miles they had not seen a single other human being. The next day Garnier decided that speed required him to abandon the use of an ox cart to carry their supplies. From this point they would rely on porters alone.

By the evening of February 19 Garnier and Tei were at the foot of the vast cliff face that had cost them such efforts nearly four weeks before. Now, with a minimum of supplies, the task of ascending the cliff was simple in comparison to their earlier experience. A "game" was what Garnier called it. Two days later, having traveled rather more to the west than they intended, he and Tei found themselves back in Khu Kan. For the first time there was news of the interpreter, Alexis Om. To his chagrin, Garnier learned that Alexis had finally passed through Khu Kan, headed towards Phnom Penh only a few days earlier. When the expedition left him at Bassac, in December 1866, Alexis had promised to do everything possible to make his way to Angkor in search of the missing passports. Instead, Garnier learned, he had remained in Bassac to marry a Laotian woman and spent a month in sweet dalliance before remembering the task with which he was charged. The Governor of Khu Kan laughed until there were tears in his eyes as he recounted the story. Even Garnier, finally, seems to have seen the lighter side of the tale as he reflected on the fickle Alexis, a member of the Catholic Church, awaited by his wife in Phnom Penh, who had now left a second wife in distant Bassac.

From Khu Kan to Ubon, Garnier followed the route he already knew, arriving at the settlement on the banks of the Se Moun on February 26, more than a month after the main expedition had left Ubon for Khemmarat. He had no way of knowing how much farther along the Mekong the French party had traveled. In these circumstances he decided that speed was even more vital than before. On February 27 he and Tei set forth, therefore, on foot, heading due north towards Ban Mouk, a settlement on the Mekong some miles north of Khemmarat. In many ways this final leg of Garnier's journey was the most remarkable. Apart from the briefest of pauses at Phnom Penh, they had been traveling almost constantly since January 10. The stages he and Tei undertook after leaving Ubon were the most demanding yet. Aided by bands of porters that changed regularly through the day, the French explorer and his Vietnamese orderly walked an average of twenty-two miles each day for a week, under a sun now approaching the full heat of the dry season. Tei's feet were painfully blistered and swollen by the arduous effort, and both men were pushing their endurance to the limit.

There were, however, moments of relief. At one point during their forced marches they had as porters a dozen young Laotian women, for the men were busy in the fields with the harvest. At each stream they passed, the women stripped and bathed themselves. They felt no embarrassment about Garnier's presence, it appeared, for by his beard they judged him to be an ancient of at least one hundred years whose thoughts had long since passed beyond the pleasures of the flesh. As for Tei, they rejected his amorous advances with laughter.

More dramatic was their encounter with a tiger. Towards the end of one long day's march they came upon the outskirts of a village surrounded by forest. Suddenly the evening calm was broken by cries of fear and alarm. As Garnier and his small band halted to take their bearings a tiger bounded past them, only yards away, carrying a screaming child in his powerful jaws. Reacting almost instantly, Garnier drew his revolver and fired at the tiger, then dashed in pursuit of the beast. In a moment they found the child, whom the tiger had dropped, profoundly shocked but physically unhurt. There was nothing the villagers were not prepared to offer Garnier if only he would stay as their protector. The next day, however, he and Tei were once more marching north.

At last, on March 4, they reached Ban Mouk, and saw the Mekong once again—for the first time since late December. The main party, they learned, had passed north a dozen days before, but now Garnier felt close behind his leader. Using a small craft, they headed up the river, sacrificing all to speed, and on March 10 Garnier saw the tricolor waving in the middle of a clump of palm trees at Uthen. His heart, he later wrote, beat a little faster.

Two months had passed since Garnier had left the main party at Ubon. During his travels to and from Phnom Penh he had covered a total distance of a thousand miles, much of it on foot and under the most trying conditions. Between Ubon and Angkor the area over which he had traveled, in both directions, was totally unexplored by Europeans. During his entire return journey he was a month without a single occasion on which he could speak his native language. Possibly most striking of all, yet this is not a point to which he refers himself, he began his journey only three months after recovering from the grave fever contracted in Stung Treng. If he was inconvenienced by the lack of full strength in his left leg, he did not make this a matter for commentary. To have done so would not have sat well with the stoic standards he so admired.

Now what was important was the future of the expedition as a whole. Together as a party for the first time in two months, they possessed the passports that should ensure their passage into China. But how and when they would reach this goal remained unknown.

CHAPTER VI

MIDDLE PASSAGE

*T*he "great idea" supposed the Mekong would run wide and free for most of its course, with untapped sources of commercial wealth set along its upper reaches. For Frenchmen in Saigon in the early 1860s, populous China, to the far north, loomed as an oriental El Dorado, still holding something of the golden prom- ise found in Marco Polo's chronicle. Linked together, the mys- tery of the Mekong and the supposed opportunities for trade in rich and exotic commodities had been a heady incentive to ac- tion. Now, in March 1867, with the entire French expedition reassembled at Uthen, their passports for China finally in hand, few of the original expectations seemed to be matched by real- ity. It was clear, even to the constantly optimistic Garnier, that hopes for easy navigation along the river were illusory.

In the official instructions given to Lagrée in Saigon, the French Governor of Cochinchina had written of the explorers penetrating into lands known to be rich and prosperous in former times and linking them in profitable trade with the newly founded colony near the Mekong's mouth. Whatever the stress on the value of pure scientific inquiry to be found later in the instruc- tions, the desire for commercial advantage was dominant. This was made clear in the heavy emphasis given to the need for speed and the disinclination of the officials in Saigon to provide the explorers with adequate scientific equipment. Now, nine months after the expedition had left Saigon, the record of progress to- wards the principal goal was limited indeed. The members of the mission had shown abundant courage and determination. Their capacity to endure and recover from disease seems remark- able in a later century that has adjusted to the medical revolu- tion of wonder drugs and antibiotics. The Frenchmen had charted the great river over a course that was unknown to the West. But in terms of the high hopes held at the beginning of the enterprise, the best that could be said was that the future might offer more than the past.

Despite a multitude of causes for disappointment, the explorers were sustained by the sense that they were seeing and recording the existence of a world that had not been visited by any European traveler for more than two hundred years. Ahead lay the once notable city of Vientiane. In 1641 the Dutchman Van Wuysthoff had found it to be a bustling commercial center when he journeyed there on behalf of the Dutch East India Company. Beyond Vientiane was the capital of one of the largest Laotian principalities, Luang Prabang, close to the spot where their countryman, Henri Mouhot, had died, and the point at which they would, for a brief time, enter a known and charted segment of the Indochinese world. Yet even with the continuing fascination of the unknown, the rewards of exploration often seemed meager. The explorers had seen evidence of gold in the mountains to the east of the Mekong, but there had been more commerce in slaves than in the precious metal. Dr. Joubert, acting as the mission's geologist, had pursued every suggestion provided by the local populations of the existence of lodes of this or that mineral, but to little avail. Typically disappointing was the experience in the mountains behind Uthen. There, Lagrée and Joubert had found a straggling settlement whose inhabitants were locked into a mortal system of lead mining. Without any understanding of the reasons for the illnesses and deaths that went with their exploitation of the mines, other than the blame they placed upon evil spirits, the miners and their families were victims of chronic lead poisoning. Suffering from skin diseases and internal illnesses, the wretched miners, and the even more frequently afflicted men who crudely refined the ore, tried to stave off further deaths, when one of their number died, by week-long ceremonies of propitiation. Just as uselessly they banned the wearing of white and red cloth in the mines, colors they believed offensive to the spirits. The high cost in lives extracted by the mines was not, however, a gauge of the opportunities for later profitable French exploitation of the region.

Nonetheless, the explorers continued with their allotted tasks as they moved along the river, recording linguistic data, searching for minerals and medicinal plants, and noting the characteristics of Buddhism. The records made during the expedition were sufficient to fill a folio volume of more than five hundred pages, quite separate from the equally lengthy narrative of the expedition. Dated and sometimes notably inaccurate as these records may seem one hundred years later, the achievement involved in compiling them was one the explorers themselves could appreciate and find sustaining. In private correspondence, Garnier was to complain that his leader made excessive demands in requiring him to prepare two copies of all his maps and charts. Clearly, however, he prided himself on the accuracy of his cartographic work and knew in full measure the satisfaction of recording a previously unknown area of the globe. As for Delaporte, the most junior of the naval officers and without doubt themost light-hearted, even the monotony of the scenery he and his

One of the French explorers peacock hunting.

companions frequently encountered in their slow passage was transformed by an artist's eye. He gloried in the light of the brilliant tropical days as it sparkled on the river and flooded over the dark green of the foliage until, in his own words, he and his companions were dazzled. Delaporte's contribution to the records of the expedition consisted of many hundreds of sketches of pencil, pen, and water color; transformed into wood engravings, these later formed a vital part of the mission's report. Delaporte's illustrations, ranging from detailed architectural drawings to sketches of people and places the Frenchmen encountered, make the record of the Mekong mission one of the most pictorially complete from the exploration of Indochina in the nineteenth century.

Leaving Uthen on March 13, 1867, the six French explorers and their escort moved steadily along the river, which still ran in a largely north-south direction. A little more than seventy miles beyond Uthen, however, there was new cause for concern. The Frenchmen were certain that the Mekong had its origins somewhere in Tibet. Yet suddenly the great river was no longer flowing from the north; following its course as it turned sharply, the explorers found themselves traveling first west and then, even worse, southwest. They could not believe that all of their assumptions were incorrect, not least because they knew of Van Wuysthoff's travels up the Mekong to Vientiane in the seventeenth century. But the pirogues in which they traveled were now set on a course that was contrary to all expectation, and, to add further gloom, the countryside through which they passed became tiringly unchanging. Garnier later reflected on his own psychological reaction to the situation. He recognized that novelty was an essential in an explorer's experience. Without it, the actual fact of progress along the route was not enough; "a day without a new emotional experience," he wrote, "is a disappointment."

This honest and perceptive admission related to a period when there was cause for further somber anticipation. Somewhere ahead lay the once important city of Vientiane. The Frenchmen knew that it had been sacked some forty years before, when the

Thai king had taken terrible vengeance on the city's ruler, Chao-Anou, for daring to renounce his position as a vassal of Bangkok. That some trace might remain of the rich commercial market reported by Van Wuysthoff over two hundred years before seemed just possible. Vientiane was, after all, set in unknown territory, outside the area explored by Mouhot between 1859 and 1861. Only four years in advance of the expedition's formation, two of the most erudite geographers in France, Cortambert and de Rosny, pillars of the Ethnographic Society, had suggested that Laos might hide riches beneath its soil that could make it another California. The explorers by this stage hoped for rather less, yet even for their more modest commercial hopes the sight of an almost deserted river that greeted them as they drew nearer to Vientiane was depressing. There was little reason to expect the bustling scene that Van Wuysthoff had described, in which "Moors" traded with merchants from Thailand, exchanging rich silk cloth and dealing in rare forest products, such as benzoin and lacquer, and that most prized of metals, gold. Yet they had hoped for more than they found.

A little downstream from Vientiane the expedition came to the Thai town of Nong Khay, a trading center of some size that had gained a measure of importance following the destruction of the older city in the 1820s. In terms of the trade and commerce that had once existed in this area, however, there was nothing remarkable about the town, except that it was of sufficient size to have its own separate quarter for the Chinese merchants and craftsmen who lived there. Here Doudart de Lagrée found an opportunity to rid himself of the troublesome Séguin, the interpreter whose undisciplined conduct had been a matter for earlier complaint. The Thai Governor at Nong Khay was ready to arrange for Séguin's travel, under escort, to Bangkok, where he could be left in the custody of the French Consul. A minor character in the drama of exploration, Séguin receives scant mention in the published and private accounts of the expedition, apart from those incidents of insubordination and drunkenness in which he played a role. He had lived in Thailand since childhood. But this experience had led to more than fluency in the

Thai language. It brought in addition, to use de Carné's censorious words, "the love of adventures, the love of money, and the craving for debauchery." There seemed to be no limit to the "abysses of such a degraded nature."

Yet he survived, and, in an infuriatingly brief reference in a later publication, Garnier notes that he and Séguin met again in France after the expedition was over. Séguin had made the long journey overland from Nong Khay to Bangkok and returned to France (whether to punishment or not, Garnier does not say). Having traveled over a route similar to that followed earlier by Mouhot, Séguin, Garnier noted tersely, "provided some useful information on the region he passed through." With the departure of Séguin, the mission included only one French subordinate, the sailor Mouëllo. None of the records gives any indication of Mouëllo's feelings at the departure of the one man with whom it would have been possible for him to have an easy relationship, unaffected by the protocol of rank and status.

On April 2, 1867, the expedition reached Vientiane. They quickly saw how thorough the Thai destruction had been. Vientiane's ruler had been singularly unwise in choosing to rebel against King Rama III of Thailand. This Thai monarch matched austerity with a determination to ensure that his kingdom would never again be a prey to the attacks and invasions that had been such a feature of the eighteenth century. When his trusted and favored vassal rebelled, Rama III did not offer half-measures in response. Vientiane was occupied in 1827 and the destruction began. Religious monuments were left standing, but the temporal buildings of the city were razed. Inhabitants who had not been killed in battle or chosen for slavery were driven into great bamboo structures and burned to death. When Chou-Anou, the defeated ruler of Vientiane, was captured a year later, he was sent to Bangkok, where he was immediately displayed in a cage to reap a bitter harvest of taunts and abuse. Within a few years — experts disagree on just how many — he was dead, though whether through disease or secret assassination is unknown.

Despite the destruction and depopulation of Vientiane, such vestiges as the French explorers found of the city's former greatness impressed them. The royal Buddhist pagoda, Wat Pha Keo, still preserved its basic form, with delicately carved wooden panels, rich gold leaf on the pillars supporting the roof, and decorative chips of glass that glistened in the sun like some gigantic setting of diamond brilliants. This was the pagoda that had once sheltered the famed "Emerald Buddha," whose origins are lost in legend and mystery and which may now be seen in the royal palace in Bangkok. Supposedly first discovered in the Thai city of Chiang Rai in the fifteenth century, the Emerald Buddha is carved out of green jasper, a quartz-like precious stone. More than three feet in height, it was one of the most treasured possessions of Laotian princes before it was taken to Thonburi, near Bangkok, in 1779 during another Thai campaign against Vientiane. But this fabled statue was only a memory to be evoked as the explorers left the overgrown pagoda to search for other relics of the past.

Finding the Wat Si Saket virtually untouched by time or the advancing forest, the Frenchmen saw that piety here was manifest in row upon row of Buddha images. These statues, of varying heights, set in niches along the walls, reminded the men who saw them of the vast monument of Borobudur in Java with its seemingly endless rows of stone Buddhas. From the library of the Si Saket pagoda the explorers carried away specimens of sacred books, recognizing that this would be regarded as sacrilege by the local population but justifying their action in the name of scientific interest. Finally, walking through the forest that had replaced the houses and streets of the devastated city, the Frenchmen came to That Luang, the most famous monument in Vientiane and one of the most revered in all of the Laotian states. Founded in the late sixteenth century, the great Buddhist stupa had only recently been restored when the explorers saw it. The central pyramid was covered with gold leaf, giving the Frenchmen some sense of the wonder expressed by Van Wuysthoff, who had described the central stupa as being covered with gold plates when he saw it in 1641. More than a century after Lagrée, Garnier, and the others had seen the continuing respect paid to the monument by Thais and Laotians alike, That Luang remains a potent symbol of some form, however inchoate, of Laotian identity. On the bank notes circulated in the early 1970s by the Pathet Lao, the left-wing political and military group in contemporary Laos, a picture of That Luang is set on one side, aligning the traditional past with such decidedly recent and delicately engraved scenes as Pathet Lao antiaircraft weapons operating on the war-torn Plain of Jars.

However much the atmosphere of Buddhist piety amid decay appealed to the explorers' romantic spirit, their stay in Vientiane could not be prolonged, for once again they faced the prospect of the rainy season. On April 4 they were back on the river and traveling, as Garnier recorded proudly, over a region that had previously known no association whatever with Europeans. Van Wuysthoff and a sole Jesuit priest, Father Leria, had seen Vientiane in the seventeenth century. Henri Mouhot had traveled beside the Mekong from Pak Lay to Luang Prabang. But between Vientiane and Pak Lay, nearly a hundred miles along the river, there had been no precursor to the French party.

The unknown section of the river quickly turned a grim face to the expedition. Only a few miles above Vientiane the wide valley or plains that had spread out from the river's course for most of the distance between Khone and Vientiane were replaced by increasingly forbidding hills. And with the narrowing of the river's width came the familiar barrier of successive rapids. The floor of the gorge enclosing the Mekong was now, in Garnier's words, like some giant mosaic as different colored rocks projected unevenly above the dark waters of the river. Navigation through this region of rapids would have been impossible later in the year, when the full flood swept down through the narrowing gorges. This was not very far below the area that Mouhot had visited in June 1861, with the Mekong in flood, when he expressed wonder that even the gorges were able to contain the river's torrential force. In April navigation was still possible, but at the cost of painfully slow progress. Portage became necessary so the pirogues were unloaded and pulled with heavy ropes through the most difficult rapids. In three days, between April 5 and 8, 1867, the expedition advanced only a dozen miles. To the necessity of ascending the rapids and of changing boatmen when they refused to risk their craft through some of the worst sections, the explorers had to add a further painful handicap; their supplies of boots and shoes were exhausted, torn apart in the repeated treks over the river's rocky banks. From this point onwards most in the party were reduced to walking barefoot over whatever path lay in their way. In April by the rapids it was a way filled with bruising and cutting stones. In later months the bare feet of the explorers were to traverse grass and mud that swarmed with voracious leeches.

With the course of the river still running in its unexpected direction, the Frenchmen came to Chiang Khan, the southern limit of the principality of Luang Prabang and a town where they were soon alerted to the possibility of political difficulties ahead. First, they feared they would find British representatives already active in the region of northern Laos, preempting any presumed commercial advantages and robbing the Frenchmen of their right to claim the first scientific survey of the upper Mekong. That they were already close to the British possessions in Burma was borne in upon them by the presence of Burmese traders in Chiang Khan. And they knew that in terms of distance the region they had now reached was considerably closer to Moulmein, in British Burma, than to any other major trading city. Worse information now came to them from the Deputy Governor of Chiang Khan. British timber companies seeking to exploit the teak forests around the nearby semi-independent state of Chiang Mai had come into conflict with the ruler of that region. The Thai court, the Deputy Governor reported, had decided to back British interests against those of its northern vassal. As a result, the explorers were told, some forty British officers were on their way down the Mekong to bolster their countrymen's position.

The verb Garnier used to describe his group's reaction was *accabler*, a word which has its English equivalent but which, lacking a cognate form, loses its force in any single-word translation. To understand just how dreadful was the news the French expedition received, one must realize that they were affected, in the term chosen by the group's most famous member, in a fashion that overwhelmed, overcame, and, at least metaphorically, prostrated them. Whatever their limited successes up to their arrival in Chiang Khan, all would be ashes in their mouths if it proved that the rival, if not actually hated, British had already accomplished the task of surveying the territory they had believed uncharted, and had planted the first tentative foot of political power in a region that the French dearly wished to see fall eventually under their control. Lagrée sought to rally his associates with the thought that there was still the possibility that they could make their mark, and better their rivals, by surveying the Mekong to its ultimate source in Tibet, something he felt sure the British would not have done. Even in the account written by Garnier three years after the event, however, the hollowness of Lagrée's brave words rings loud.

Secondly, and as it was to prove later more seriously, from this region of the northern Laotian states onwards the explorers were entering a political framework that had little if any similarity with the nation-state system by then established in Europe. Until and after the expedition had passed through Vientiane the local authorities they encountered were linked firmly with one or another major ruler. Cambodian writ had run as far as Sambor. Then, despite the readiness of the Frenchmen to describe the local petty rulers as "kings," they were on the fringe of the possessions of the court of Bangkok. Once within the ambit of the principality of the Luang Prabang, however, the local rulers, upon whom they depended for passports and the provision of men, supplies, and transport, were not so clearly the vassals of any single distant suzerain. This was already partly apparent in the news they heard of events in Chiang Mai. The princes of that state were the vassals of the King of Thailand, but they were capable of surprising shows of independence and were under pressure from Englishmen who claimed, in some juridically curious fashion, the rights that had one been held by Burmese monarchs in an area that was geographically peripheral but political important to their state's concerns.

Only a little of this was clear at Chiang Khan. If there were forebodings for the future in terms of the political complications that might be encountered, they were eclipsed by the dreadful possibility that a British party might already have accomplished the work the French explorers dearly wished to be theirs alone. Leaving Chiang Khan behind them on April 14, the party moved on. Two days later they rounded the great bend in the Mekong that set them firmly to the north once more. It was then, on the morning of April 16, that the expedition heard the worst. Laotians traveling in advance of a foreign party told the depressed Frenchmen that they would soon meet the British. Hurriedly completing their reports and charts, the explorers awaited the moment of truth and disillusion. In terms of what they expected, the moment never came. The "forty British officers" became, in reality, a small survey mission sent out by the King of Thailand that included one naturalized Frenchman of Dutch descent and two men of mixed European ancestry whose role was that of minor employees.

Their fellow French citizen was named Duyshart. Once employed in the colony of Cochinchina himself, Duyshart had left to become the King of Thailand's geographer. He had indeed been engaged in surveying a part of the Mekong that the French mission sought to chart in a scientific fashion for the first time — the section running south and east from Chiang Kong in the North to Luang Prabang—but he had not completed the task and in the face of threatened grave illness and stormy weather was postponing much of his work until the following year. Ironically, while the French mission was waiting apprehensively for the arrival of the non-existent British, Duyshart had been prey to an equally misleading rumor. His informants had warned him of the likely arrival of a group of Frenchmen at the head of an unruly band of Cambodian troops. The explanation of this rumor, it seemed, was to be found in a deformed account of both the actual French expedition and the revolt mounted by the Cambodian rebel Pou Kombo, whose efforts had so inconvenienced Garnier when he was attempting to obtain the passports for China. Neither Duyshart nor Lagrée and his group knew that by this stage Pou Kombo was under mounting pressure from

French and Cambodian forces; before the end of the year he would be dead.

Little that Duyshart could tell Lagrée and his men about the territory ahead was comforting. As an employee of the Thai King, he had been well received at Luang Prabang. Farther north the picture he presented was less cheerful. Chiang Kong was the limit of the King of Thailand's suzerainty, and beyond that point Duyshart had not ventured. He reported that the petty states to the north were warring, and he made no secret of his judgment that the twin dangers of political instability and the ever-feared Laotian fevers were sufficient to bring a tragic end to the French explorers' efforts.

It was a meeting that evoked conflicting feelings. The French party could press on without having to act out the pantomime of courtesy and military compliments that they had readied themselves to offer their presumed British "colleagues." Yet they were uncomfortably aware that from now on their lack of knowledge of the political circumstances facing them beyond Luang Prabang was likely to bring the frustration of delay, which had come close to sapping their enthusiasm previously. If this encounter with Duyshart lacked the drama and pathos of Stanley's with Livingstone, there is every reason to accept Garnier's observation that, long after the disappearance of Duyshart's raft down the river, he and his companions discussed their unexpected meeting with a fellow European in the essentially unknown regions of central Laos.

By the evening of the day after the encounter with Duyshart the expedition was at Pak Lay, the limit of Mouhot's rough reconnaissance of the Mekong south from Luang Prabang. They could still see near the river's bank the traces of a once much-used road that had served for commerce between China and these obscure Laotian regions before the Muslim rebellion in Yunnan had put an end to easy trade between north and south during the 1850s. The countryside through which they passed had changed; the climate seemed more temperate, and the river continued to narrow, breaking into several courses split by rocky outcrops or giant sandbanks that would later be submerged by the floods that followed the melting of the distant Tibetan snows. The population of the region no longer clustered in settlements near the river banks, and the explorers pressed on, sleeping in their pirogues for want of shelter in villages along the way.

On April 23 the boatmen warned the explorers that a great rapid would soon be reached, and as if in confirmation a corpse floated by, a presumed victim of the dangers that were soon to be faced. Once more, as they had done so many times before, the expedition unloaded their craft and slowly and painfully pulled them through the rapids, only to find at the end of the day that a further and equally imposing rapid lay ahead. As they progressed, however slowly, it was of some comfort to know that their hard-earned progress forward would be impossible a month later. The river was already rising and would, at its highest point, be fifty feet higher than it was at this time. The high-water marks on the gorges through which they passed gave eloquent evidence of the transformation that would shortly take place.

Gradually, as the expedition pressed farther north, the countryside became less forbidding, the river ran between hills that no longer rose directly from the waterline, and there was evidence once again of human settlement on the slopes to either side of the water course. They were coming closer to Luang Prabang, and when they camped for the night of April 28 their boatmen told them they would be in the city the next day. The explorers were determined to make a brave show as they entered this important center, where they judged much might be done to aid or hinder the next part of their journey.

Now questions of form became important. Despite their lack of footwear, the Frenchmen drew their best clothes from the valises; even more remarkably, given the circumstances, the escort could still be dressed as if manning an admiral's barge. They donned white shirts and trousers, sailors' collars and straw hats each bearing a ribbon with the word "Mekong" printed in gold. Only then did they prepare to enter the city where their compatriot Mouhot had been so well received six years before.

They came to Luang Prabang around a bend in the river and

found before them the largest settlement they had seen since leaving Phnom Penh more than nine months previously. Built on the eastern bank below the dark slopes of hills and mountains that retreated in successively higher waves, the city offered a sharp contrast with the straggling settlements of the river banks to which the explorers had long been accustomed and where, with rare exceptions, even the village pagoda lacked artistic interest. Now they saw a city that was growing in size and commercial importance. Garnier and Delaporte recorded the majority view when they described the princely town in approving terms. De Carné, in contrast, was not impressed. Where the others felt that Luang Prabang showed a fair face to travelers, he found its visage "mean."

Established as a political center of some importance by a dissident Lao prince in the early eighteenth century, Luang Prabang had benefited both from the destruction of Vientiane in the 1820s and from the fact that its status as a vassal of both Thailand and Vietnam was tempered by its distance from Bangkok and Hue. Dominated by a *that* on the top of a hill covered in dark foliage, Luang Prabang was a pleasing mixture of pagodas with glistening red roof tiles and whitewashed walls, a vast palace compound, and the houses of a population of some sixteen thousand. Perhaps most pleasing of all to the Frenchmen was not the happy scenic combination of an architecturally exotic city in a setting of natural beauty but, rather, the fact that there was much evidence of trade in Luang Prabang. As Garnier noted in his journal, "This was the first time since leaving Phnom Penh that we found a market, in the sense that one normally gives to the word."

A market there certainly was, operating under the control of local officials each day. There was, in addition, a long line of open-air traders to be found beside the river. Yet it required eyes suffused by hope to envisage in what Garnier saw a future major center for international trade. In terms of the principality, and even for regions beyond, Luang Prabang could with accuracy be described as an important commercial location. The goods that were sold, however, were hardly a basis for the colonial trade that men such as Lagrée and Garnier, and La Grandière back in Saigon, had hoped might flow down the Mekong. Mixed with flowers and fruits on the merchants' stalls were cottons and silks, hardware and the distinctive lacquer of Chiang Mai. In short, the stalls the explorers saw were little different from those a traveler would find in northern Thailand or parts of Laos today, a hundred years later. As such, the merchandise had an out-of-the-way charm, more particularly because it did not suffer from the debasement of form and technique that came later, with the growth of a small but artistically disruptive European community in Laos in the twentieth century. If large-scale commerce or the evidence of untapped sources of valuable raw materials was what the French party sought, they would not find it in Luang Prabang.

They did, after a hesitant and uncertain beginning, find amiable hospitality and a remarkable acceptance among the local population and its leaders. The first encounter with the ruler of Luang Prabang was frosty, with both the French and the Laotians unwilling to concede relaxation on the points that each held to be important in the practice of ceremonies and the usage of protocol. Relations rapidly improved, however, and the explorers were free to map the city or make short journeys into the surrounding countryside to record the botany and geology of the region. In this more relaxed atmosphere, Lagrée sought the ruler's permission to construct a monument over Henri Mouhot's grave. Without hesitation agreement was given, and Mouhot received the posthumous honor of a monument at the place of his death from representatives of a country that had been so unconcerned with his labors while he was alive.

Garnier described the memory that Mouhot had left behind him in Luang Prabang in emotional terms. Laotians remembered the French naturalist and brought specimens of insects to the expedition, assuming that the latest foreign visitors would also welcome and recompense the bearers of these offerings. Mouhot had died only a short distance from Luang Prabang on the banks of the Nam Kan, one of the Mekong's tributaries. The site of his grave was less than a day's journey away from the city, but it had been the most deserted place in the world when Mouhot died there in November 1861. The final entries in his diary were written with the universal despair of men dying of dread diseases in deserted places. On October 19, 1861, he had managed to write, "I have been struck down by the fever." Ten days later his next and last diary entry read, "Have pity on me, Oh my God!" On November 10, after three final and terrible days of coma and delirium, he died. A final episode of pathos for the Frenchmen paying honor to Mouhot came with their discovery that the naturalist's dog Tine-Tine was still alive. Taken in by a Laotian family living in Luang Prabang, the dog no longer recalled that his first master had had a white skin, and he bared his teeth at the Frenchmen's friendly advances.

In carrying out their "pious duty" to Mouhot's memory the explorers acted out, quite without pretense, the standards of their age. With death so close to all of those who served in the then remote areas of Southeast Asia, it was right and appropriate to pay tribute to those who had died before them. Sudden illness leading to an equally sudden death was a possibility that they all knew might confront them personally. Indeed, of the six French principals on the expedition, three would be dead within six years of the day they stood solemnly beside their countryman's neglected grave.

In Luang Prabang itself solemnity was scarcely possible; the Frenchmen found that they had become an object of the greatest interest for the young women of the local prince's household. Once again, in Garnier's description of this interest, there is an only lightly disguised indication of the sublimated sexual drives that he and the other members of the party experienced. They watched and appraised the bare-breasted young women who came to visit their encampment, among them a niece of the ruler, who is immortalized in a drawing by Delaporte. For the young women the soap used by the members of the expedition became the most sought-after gift, for, if Garnier's account is correct, they believed that soap was the secret of the Frenchmen's light skin coloring. Whether genuinely concerned or not, the Frenchmen questioned their most frequent female visitor about the propriety of her spending so much time in their presence. Her reaction was the same as that of the young female porters of northeastern Thailand who had transported Garnier's supplies during his march back from Phnom Penh. With their long beards, she told the explorers, they could not be less than eighty years old, long past the age when it was unsafe or unwise for a young woman to spend time with them unescorted by a chaperone.

For much of the time that the French party was in Luang Prabang, the city was *en fête*. With the heavy rains of the wet season close to hand the population seized the remaining dry nights as an opportunity for dancing and gossip. The period just before the rains coincided with the celebrations marking the birth, enlightenment, and death of the Buddha. The ceremonies for this occasion took place alongside others that had little to do with the austere philosophy of the Buddha himself. The young men of Luang Prabang, their heads crowned with flowers, danced before their chosen partners, serenaded them, and disappeared with them into the night.

If Garnier and his fellows took some delight in this rustic mating that did not seem too distant from the idealized, spontaneous world of the "noble savage" eulogized by eighteenth-century *philosophes*, they did not have to look far to see that Luang Prabang was no earthly paradise. Many of the young women who were otherwise so graceful were already afflicted with goiters that disfigured their necks. Among old women these goiters were of proportions that amazed the French observers, who could not understand why the physical deformity did not embarrass those who bore it. And if the sexual mores of the young Laotians whom the explorers observed did not call for censure, the readiness of the population, young and old, to indulge in gambling did. Throughout the nineteenth century there was a consistent readiness on the part of French official observers in the Indochinese region to level sharp, even bitter criticism against the inclination of the local populations to engage in protracted gambling. The reason is not entirely clear. Answers that offer psychological explanations may be partly right. Gambling was scarcely unknown in French society, at all levels. So, the argument might run, the criticism of what was done by others was a defensive reaction that absolved the critic from his own countrymen's vices. But more seems to have been involved. The supposed depravity represented by the presence of gambling as an accepted part of local life, whether in Vietnam, Cambodia, or the Laotian states, provided one irrefutable justification for the *mission civilisatrice*. To dismiss this attitude as mere rationalization would be to fail to understand how deeply the early colonialists, of whom Lagrée and Garnier were such notable examples, believed in the role they chose to play.

In Luang Prabang, however, the civilizing mission was a possibility for the future, one that could only be accomplished after the explorers had carried out their task and followed the Mekong to the borders of China, and possibly beyond. With the weeks slipping by in Luang Prabang, the question of how the next stage of the journey was to be achieved became a matter of growing concern. The four weeks spent in the northern Laotian capital had offered the explorers an almost Arcadian interlude, but they were faced there with choices they were ill-equipped to evaluate. To go on was a simple, if onerous, decision. They knew that their next three or four months' journeying would be through the worst of the year's weather, but there was no question that go on they must. The real, and for a period irresolvable, problem was to decide where they should go. For the first time during their travels this became a matter of real indecision. For as they relaxed and drew strength from the sojourn in Luang Prabang and observed with largely tolerant eyes the life that went on about them, the political intelligence they were obtaining grew more and more disturbing. At best the path ahead looked uncertain. At worst it seemed possible that to follow the Mekong into China was no longer an option open to them.

CHAPTER VII

BEFORE THE GATES OF CHINA

*B*ack of adequate information runs as a constant and dominant thread through the fabric of the French explorers' public and private accounts of their travels. Not knowing what lay ahead was the justification and the attraction of exploration. Yet this spur to action was also a cause for uncertainty, irritation, even despondency. And to their lack of knowledge of what lay ahead of them, whether in geographical or political terms, was added the almost total isolation from news of Europe, or even Saigon, that the explorers had experienced ever since Garnier had made his remarkable journey to Phnom Penh four months earlier.

What little the members of the expedition did know about the territories ahead was far from encouraging. When they had received their instructions in Saigon, almost exactly a year before, Admiral La Grandière had made no attempt to hide the uncertainties that existed about the lands that lay to the north of Luang Prabang but below the borders of China. "The ideas that we have of these upper regions," he noted in the instructions given to Lagrée, "are too uncertain for it to be useful to provide you with any particular instructions concerning these areas." Lagrée was to take "inspiration" from his general instructions and act "according to circumstances."

The immediate difficulty was to know what the "circumstances" were. Well to the north, in the southwestern Chinese province of Yunnan, the Frenchmen knew that an Islamic revolt had been in progress since 1855. The causes and the course of this revolt were complex, and without fresh information the explorers could only guess at the importance it might have for their own progress when they reached Chinese territory. Since the passports they possessed for travel through China were issued by the imperial government in Peking, there was clearly need to avoid any action that might place the party in jeopardy by antagonizing either of the contending Chinese sides.

Before the possible difficulties of China were encountered, however, a way had to be found to that country which, for all the members of the expedition, still remained a presumed if untested source of countless riches. The problems to be overcome were compounded by the political circumstances of a frontier zone that had little if any recognizable similarities with the European pattern of state relations familiar to the explorers. For their ancestors, living five or six hundred years previously in a world of suzerains and vassals, the political configuration of the northern Laotian and Burmese Shan states might have posed few problems of understanding. To Frenchmen in the second half of the nineteenth century the situation was at best confusing. Viewed from Luang Prabang, the area that now forms part of northern Laos and north-eastern Burma was, in 1867, a curiously jumbled region of petty kingdoms or principalities, none of which possessed the power or the prestige to act without some reliance and dependence upon their stronger neighbors, the Burmese, the Chinese, and, for the region directly west of Luang Prabang, the Thai monarch in Bangkok. What made the situation even more uncertain was that most of these petty rulers were in vassalage to more than one greater power.

In these circumstances of instability the fact and memory of war often seemed dominant. The Burmese rulers distrusted the Shan peoples in the Northeast of their kingdom, seeing them as old opponents and ethnic affiliates of their longtime Thai enemies whose power center lay in the lower Chao Phraya (Menam) valley. The Thai conceded Burman interest in the more northerly Shan states but disputed it in such areas as Chiang Mai. As for China, these regions immediately to her south seemed to illustrate all too well the validity of the traditional assumption that the peoples of thoses areas outside direct Chinese control were incapable of governing themselves without advice and direction.

Adding further to such problems of understanding and comprehension was the ethnic confusion of the region ahead. Lagrée and his subordinates were well aware that the Laotions and Shans they encountered were members of the great Tai-speaking people whose most successful political achievement had been the establishment of the Kingdom of Thailand with its capital in Bangkok. Springing from an ethnic base somewhere in southern China, probably as early as the eleventh century, Tai ruling groups had slowly imposed their power over an extraordinary range of what is now modern China and Southeast Asia. Despite the great distances involved, and the different names adopted by various groups, they all spoke (and still speak) Tai dialects of considerable, indeed essential, similarity. But Laotians and Shans were not the only inhabitants of the unknown "upper regions." A modern ethnolinguistic map of the area only tends to heighten the sense of confusion. Intermingled with the Tai-speaking Laotians and Shans are representatives of half a dozen other ethnic groups, some living in close association with the dominant Tai-speaking peoples of the river valleys, others remaining in essential, if not complete, isolation in the upland regions.

Even to state matters in these terms is to give a misleading impression of the problems that worried Doudart de Lagrée as he reviewed the various possibilities open to his party. With the benefit of hindsight and the accumulation of ethnological and political knowledge, a modern writer can summarize the situation and so diminish, even unconsciously, the confusion and uncertainty. What may now be summarized was known at best imperfectly in May of 1867, and by men who were already paying a heavy physical cost for their prolonged exposure to the dangers of tropical disease. When he wrote to his sister-in-law from Luang Prabang, Lagrée acknowledged his tiredness. At forty-three, he wrote of how age weighed him down. If the doctors who accompanied the expedition had been of a later generation, they would possibly have already diagnosed the disease from which Lagrée was suffering by this time, a disease that sapped his energy and required him to make supreme efforts in order to play his role as leader.

The explorers progress up the
Se Moun River. See page 78.

A river scene sketched on April 22, 1867,
just before the expedition's arrival in
Luang Prabang. See page 100.

The ruins of the Wat Pha Keo pagoda in Vientiane.
The famous Emerald Buddha, now in Bangkok, was once
housed here. See page 98.

Previous pages. The explorers watch as the 'king' of Bassac receives oaths of loyalty from his senior officials. See pages 66-72.

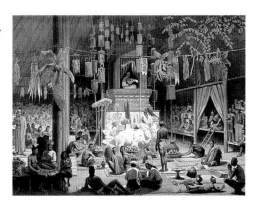

A festival in a pagoda (right) in the Thai riverside town of Nong Khay. See page 96.

The fireworks at Bassac (below). The French explorers were in Bassac at the time of the Water Festival, one of the great events of the year.

A plan of the course of the waters of the Khone falls. See pages 64-5.

The town of Luang Prabang (below). The explorers spent nearly a month in this scenically attractive city. See pages 112-16.

The That Luang stupa, the most famous monument in Vientiane, which remains revered in contemporary Laos. See page 98.

*One of Delaporte's botanical studies. This
one concentrates on epiphytic orchids
of Laos.*

Nothing more surely reveals Lagrée's already diminished physical and mental reserves than the fact that at Luang Prabang he sought his companions' opinion on the next step the mission should take. In the bickering and even bitter dispute that emerged after the expedition was over, its leader dead, the question of who made what decision, and in concert with whom, became important points about which to construct hypothetical assertions concerning the role of this or that participant. Garnier's partisans, who remain the most vocal a century later, see their hero in one role. In the 1870s and 1880s there were those, not least Louis de Carné, who promoted a cult of Lagrée and sought to denigrate his second-in-command. More than a century after the events that kindled such bitter debate judgment can be more balanced, even if the desirability of such balance would have been rejected by those who engaged in the original controversy.

Until the mission reached Luang Prabang Doudart de Lagrée's position as its leader was largely unaffected by health problems. From that period, in April and May of 1867, he was the victim of progressive debilitation. Rather than the "fevers" that had brought him low in southern Laos five months before, or the chronic problems resulting from his persistent throat infection, he began to suffer the effects of amoebic dysentery. With the reticence of the mid-nineteenth century, the chroniclers of the expedition give us little detail on the course of Lagrée's disease. But after his death, the final comments on his abscessed liver and his "unmistakable" symptoms, which can only have been the passing of a bloody flux through the bowels, leave no real doubt as to the nature of his complaint. And the picture we have of periods of remission that permitted Lagrée to act with something of his former dynamism supports this diagnosis. All these symptoms are consistent with a modern understanding of the nature of amoebic dysentery. What might set Lagrée's case apart is the staggering level of physical achievement he managed to maintain before, finally, and six months of travel beyond Luang Prabang, he was forced to admit that he could march no further.

This ultimate physical defeat was still many months distant

as Lagrée chose to discuss the future with his associates. Three courses seemed open to them, though not equally desirable. They could strike off to the northeast, abandoning the valley of the Mekong and passing along China's southern borders by way of the extreme north of Vietnam. Despite the hostility that existed between the ruler of Luang Prabang and the Vietnamese court at Hue, there was good reason to believe that this route would involve the least danger. Travel along such a route would have the additional and undeniable attraction that it would be through totally unknown territory. But in terms of the expedition's instructions it would have been an abandonment of the original goal—exploration of the Mekong valley as a route into China.

There were two other alternatives. First, the expedition could continue along the Mekong itself, risking the difficulties that seemed likely to emerge because of continuing clashes between local forces backed by either the Burmese or the Thai court. Second, the Frenchmen could adopt a compromise. Without following the Mekong itself, they could journey into China up the course of another major river, the Nam Ou, a tributary that joined the Mekong near Luang Prabang. All the information available to the explorers suggested that this would be a more direct route. The fact that such a route would bypass those territories that were in vassalage to the Burmese authorities was a further attraction. The Frenchmen had passports for territories whose rulers accepted the Thai ruler as suzerain, and for those that were vassals of the Emperor of China. They did not have authority for travel through areas that acknowledged the power of the Burmese ruler at Mandalay.

Lagrée was in favor of the last alternative. He was conscious of his own weakness and probably recognized the tiredness of the others. Garnier, on the other hand, was vigorous in advocating the Mekong route. Later he was to admit the overriding force of his "monomanie du Mékong," his single-minded mania to travel as far as possible along the great river that had dominated their journey up to this point. For a period, as the explorers still rested in Luang Prabang, the question of the route remained unresolved. Then, just after the middle of May, Lagrée made up his mind. The expedition would continue along the Mekong after all. The political intelligence that had filtered into Luang Prabang suggested that some at least of the suspected dangers along the Mekong route had now disappeared. There had been a pause in the recurrent conflicts between the petty states that had such tenuous existence at the outer reaches of their suzerains' interest. In addition, and even more important, it appeared that the Chinese Government in Peking had achieved some success in bringing rebellious areas of Yunnan province once more under its control, and that as a result a general calm reigned in the regions to the north of Luang Prabang.

Between May 18 and 25 the members of the expedition bustled to prepare once again for protracted travel. With prospects before them so uncertain they decided to reduce their baggage to a bare minimum. The collections and specimens were to be sent to Bangkok rather than carried with the mission, as they had been up to this point. Each individual was, from now on, to make do with a single bag for all his possessions. Even the common stores of the party were affected by the decision. Surplus ammunition and trade objects were considered less important than the ability to move swiftly through the poor weather and worse topographical conditions that were believed to lie ahead. Despite the annoyance of having to leave behind these objects and supplies, the explorers had only one insistent and immediately obvious concern at this time. They were acutely aware that they might run short of money. The expedition had now been traveling for nearly a year, and progress had been much slower than was ever expected at the outset. The cost of hiring boatmen had proved higher than anticipated, and the Frenchmen had dire, and as it proved correct, fears that prolonged land porterage would be even more expensive.

From the time the expedition left Luang Prabang, on May 25, 1867, until they reached the first major settlement in China, the town of Ssu-mao, nearly five months later on October 18, the travelers underwent the most physically and emotionally exhausting experiences they had yet encountered. There is small wonder in the fact that neither the official reports, nor the published and unpublished materials left behind, notably by Garnier and de Carné, make easy reading. The men who left Luang Prabang thinking they were in relatively good health were in fact prime targets for tropical disease, and all succumbed to some degree. As for the political difficulties that they believed had been diminished by recent developments along the Mekong itself and in China, these were to plague them in a fashion beyond their worst imaginings.

The early days of renewed travel were uneventful. The ruler of Luang Prabang's authority extended nearly as far as their first major stopping place, the settlement of Chiang Kong lying on the Mekong and to the west of their recent temporary base. To reach Chiang Kong was a simple matter of following the course of the Mekong, uninterrupted over this section by rapids or cataracts. Once in Chiang Kong, on June 5, political difficulties replaced the more familiar physical obstructions to which the party was so accustomed. The settlement was part of the once powerful principality of Nan, which, while it retained some vestiges of independence, was a vassal of the Thai King in Bangkok. Lying near the extreme north of territory firmly linked with Bangkok, Chiang Kong was administered by a timid Governor who hesitated to act beyond the strict letter of the law. The passports the explorers carried, he observed, gave them the right to free passage through the King of Thailand's dominions. There was no reference, however, to the expedition leaving these dominions and crossing into alien territory.

This was the briefest foretaste of what was to come. The Governor of Chiang Kong's objections were quickly overcome, an understanding being achieved that he would provide boats to carry the explorers to the limits of those regions which acknowledged the King of Thailand's suzerainty. Once there, farther along the Mekong, and in the middle of the forest, as the Governor pointed out with some concern, the explorers would be at the borders of Keng Tung, the largest of all the Shan states whose rulers acknowledged the Burmese King at Mandalay as their master. Despite the brusqueness with which Lagrée had treated the hesitant Governor in order to gain his agreement for the party to proceed, the now certain knowledge that there were Burmese authorities to be considered, and possibly placated, was disturbing. For all their earlier concern to ensure that they possessed passports for China, the explorers had attached less importance to the need for similar papers from the Burmese King at Mandalay. They had tried to obtain passports through the good offices of a French missionary bishop, but these efforts had been made fruitless by a brief but disruptive rebellion that broke out against King Mindon's rule in 1866. In the period of turbulence that followed, the question of passports for an unknown set of alien travelers was temporarily forgotten.

Doudart de Lagrée's decision in these circumstances was to send letters on ahead to the ruler of Keng Tung, arguing that the Burmese court knew of the explorers' intentions (by now a dubious assertion) and requesting permission to pass through the ruler's territory towards the final goal of Yunnan. With the letters the French party's leader sent a collection of minor gifts, scarcely realizing, as Garnier later admitted, that even in such a distant state as Keng Tung, the existence of regular trading arrangements with those areas of Burma that had fallen under British control made their offerings seem notably unimpressive. What was worse, they were to find later, was their failure to include separate gifts for the Burmese agent attached to Keng Tung. The Frenchmen did not know of his existence. They were to pay a heavy cost for this ignorance in the long weeks of despair that followed.

With their letters sent ahead, the party left Chiang Kong on June 14, 1867. One year earlier they had been in Phnom Penh, eager and confident. As they left Chiang Kong they were no less eager to continue, but they had come to learn that confidence was frequently misplaced. When Francis Garnier, always the most optimistic member of the party, had written from Luang Prabang to his close friend Eliacin Luro in Saigon, a few weeks previously, even he had admitted his misgivings. He was forced to acknowledge that it was "very doubtful" if the party could make its way to China. Yet there was no thought of turning back.

Moreover, even at moments of deep despondency there was always a point of some interest to be recorded: the ruined sites of once important settlements, the presence of another unrecorded tribal group. Less scientific but just as diverting were the seemingly endless encounters with wild animals, from deer to tigers and elephants, and even the rare rhinoceros.

Four days after leaving Chiang Kong the explorers were at the edge of the King of Burma's dominions. Eight miles from the spot on the river bank where the party first halted was the settlement of Mong Lin, one of the possessions of the ruler of Keng Tung. Still waiting for a reply from Keng Tung, the Frenchmen obtained permission to travel to Mong Lin, which they found to be a sizable village, big enough for a market to be held every five days. Some of the merchandise sold at this market was a cause for bitter reflection on the contrast between British commercial acumen and French disdain for the Asian market. Here, in such a notably isolated corner of the globe, it was possible to buy English cotton goods, printed in the preferred colors of the local purchasers and bearing Buddhist emblems. Not only that, Garnier recorded with grudging admiration, the length and width of these pieces of cloth were the same as the standard product of the local weavers.

Another feature of the local market arrangements provided more immediate cause for concern. It was no longer possible to pay for goods or services in Thai coin. From this point on the custom of the country was to pay in silver, valued against weights at a varying rate of exchange. Melting down their silver coin into bars, the explorers soon found that their payments for such essential items as rice and fowls were extremely high. The concern they had felt over the adequacy of their funds a month earlier as they prepared to leave Luang Prabang seemed all too justified. As Garnier was to record with undisguised annoyance and resentment three years later, the realization that it would be necessary to make sacrifices even in terms of their food supplies came at a time when the party's physical condition was such as to make an ample diet most necessary. Already two of the Frenchmen were seriously ill again. Thorel was suffering from a "digestive infection," presumably bacillary dysentery. Delaporte was unable to walk, his feet being swollen and ulcerated as the result of walking barefoot over sodden ground and being attacked by countless leeches. And still there was no word from Keng Tung.

Finally, on June 28, there was a favorable response. The ruler of Keng Tung gave the expedition authority to proceed, but only along the valley of the Mekong itself. If the French party should wish to travel to the capital of Keng Tung, further authorization would be necessary. The bearer of this welcome news explained the reasons for delay. Although the ruler of Keng Tung had been ready enough to permit the Frenchmen to proceed, the Burmese agent at his court had opposed this view. He was apparently angered at the failure of the French to send him a gift and made every effort to reverse the ruler's decision. With the agent's opposition overcome, and the news brought back to Mong Lin, the members of the expedition could consider their next step. They knew their next major destination, if virtually nothing of the problems they might encounter along the way. An uncertain but considerable distance to the north was the town of Keng Hung (Yünching-hung in modern China). This was the birthplace of their interpreter Alévy, and a center known to the European world as the result of a visit there in 1837 by the British explorer Captain McLeod. McLeod had traveled there from Bhamo in northeast Burma, with six elephants, during an earlier attempt to find a commercial route into China. Lagrée and his men sought to make it their next important stopping place with a growing consciousness of their weakness, and the immediate problems of finding transportation for Delaporte. While the inhabitants of Mong Lin were ready to act as porters for the expedition's supplies, at very high rates, they would under no circumstances carry the hammock on which Delaporte was to travel. He therefore was to be the responsibility of the party's escort.

Without regret the Frenchmen left Mong Lin on July 1. Their pleasure at moving forward was soon qualified by the experience of traveling with the incapacitated Delaporte and by the exactions of the porters. Villagers encountered along the way were reluctant to allow such a demonstrably ill man as Delaporte to travel through their settlements: he might be an omen of death or grave sickness for their village. Only through threats of violence backed by the brandishing of weapons were the explorers able to prevail over this repugnance. As for the charges exacted by the porters, no more than two days after leaving Mong Lin the Frenchmen decided to reduce their baggage once again. They could not continue to pay the prices demanded. As they had done in Luang Prabang, once more they took stock of their possessions, this time ridding themselves of all but the barest essentials, even their mattress pads. When they reached Siemlap, a week after leaving Mong Lin, the explorers were in a pitiful state. Garnier described their circumstances in the following terms:

> The state of health of the expedition was deplorable. The last stages that we had just completed, as often in the forests as in the rice fields, where the soil, soaked through by the first major rains, gave off dangerous miasmas and concealed countless leeches, had brought on attacks of fever and led to ulcerations of the feet that meant that half of our personnel were unable to move from their beds.

The village of Siemlap lay on the western side of the Mekong, within the general dominance of the Burmese court but under the control of yet another petty ruler, the "king" of Keng Khang, whose residence was still some distance to the north. The authorities at Siemlap were ready to send on Lagrée's request for passage through the territory of the Keng Khang ruler, but they would not permit him or his party to travel further without express approval. With his companions suffering from illness and fatigue there was little Lagrée could do to counter this refusal. What the next step should be was further complicated by the arrival in Siemlap, on July 16, of a letter addressed to the expedition's leader from the ruler of Keng Tung who, reversing his earlier position, now called on the mission to travel to his capital. Judging this to be merely an invitation of courtesy, Lagrée declined, and only two days later approval came for passage through the territories of Keng Khang.

To receive approval was one thing, to take advantage another. When the main party left Siemlap on July 23, they left behind them Joubert and Delaporte. The latter's feet were still not entirely healed, and Joubert was once again suffering from a combination of the "typhoid" fever, that had struck him down near Stung Treng nine months earlier, and some intestinal infection. For the main party the next two days of travel were a welcome change from the period of enforced inactivity in Siemlap but a renewed drain on their physical resources. They marched at first over an upland route, for the normal path beside the river was now submerged beneath floodwaters. Their bare feet were lacerated by the rough surface, and Garnier's left knee, which had been affected by his dangerous bout of fever earlier in the expedition, caused him severe pain with every step. At the end of the second day the party reached the tiny settlement of Sop Yong. Here in a broken-down pagoda beside the Mekong the party made its base for the next few days. By the time Delaporte and Joubert rejoined them on July 30 the explorers' overall situation had deteriorated. Lagrée was incapacitated with a swollen groin, the result of an infected bite by a leech. Like the other members of the expedition, Lagrée had, for the most part, given up pulling leeches from his body while marching through the day. Only in the evening was a thorough check made to find where the creatures had lodged. The results of this exercise in stoicism were clear in Delaporte's infected feet and now the leader's painfully affected groin.

Although they had rejoined the main party, Delaporte and Joubert were far from strong, and as the rains continued to fall the problem of finding porters became more and more difficult. It was even questionable whether their rough and uncomfortable quarters in the riverside village were safe from a sudden rise in the Mekong's level. As it had so many times before, the party split into two sections. Leaving Lagrée, Joubert, and Delaporte behind at Sop Yong, Garnier went ahead with the others, marching along a muddy path that seemed paved with leeches. On August 1 Garnier's group was at the settlement of Ban Passang, and four days later the others joined them.

Moving north as they were, the expedition had temporarily left behind the territory of the ruler of Keng Khang, returning once more to a region under the control of the ruler of Keng Tung. They were in the province of Mong Yawng, whose capital of the same name lay a little to the north. The French party's arrival had not gone unnoticed, and on the same day that Lagrée rejoined Garnier and his advance group two Burmese soldiers appeared at the explorers' camp. They were the servants of the Burmese agent for the province, and they required information on the party's intentions, indicating their superior's expectation that the French mission would present themselves before him at Mong Yawng.

The explorers pay their respects to the hereditary chief of Mong Yawng.

There was no alternative but to obey what was clearly an order. On August 7 the expedition crossed over the moat surrounding the once-important settlement of Mong Yawng. Within twenty-four hours the fears of serious obstruction that had been growing in the explorers' minds ever since they left Luang Prabang over two months before became a concrete reality. The hereditary chief of Mong Yawng was a weak reed, almost totally dominated by the Burmese court's representative in the settlement. Whether the Burmese agent had already been in correspondence with his senior counterpart in Keng Tung was unclear, but he knew that the Frenchmen had received and declined an invitation to travel to the capital of the territories within which Mong Yawng lay. After a series of cat and mouse exchanges lasting several days, a letter arrived from the authorities of Keng Khang withdrawing the permission that had earlier been granted for the explorers to continue their travels north through that petty principality's territories. The Frenchmen suspected that this refusal had been engineered by the Burmese agent at Mong Yawng. At the same time the weak chief of Mong Yawng, although he acted with personal goodwill towards the expedition, was unready to allow them to travel farther without approval from his master. If the expedition was ever to move forward again, and to avoid the failure that would be involved in returning to Saigon, a new initiative had to be taken. Choosing Thorel, the interpreter Alévy, and two members of the escort to accompany him, Lagrée set off on August 14 for Keng Tung, by now at least a week's travel to the west.

A dreary period of inaction followed Lagrée's departure, during which the remaining explorers fell ill one by one with "fever." The men blamed this sickness on the foul airs rising from the ground of the forests and marshes they had traversed, but the accounts that remain give few clues as to the actual disease that exacted its cost in fevers and delirium. This was still an age that did not understand the connection between mosquitoes and malaria, but whether this disease alone was the cause of the outbreak of fever that Garnier describes in such restrained terms must remain a mystery. The modern reader of these nineteenth-century journals can only be amazed at the apparent speed with which already debilitated men recovered sufficiently from their bouts of disease to begin, yet again, the arduous travels their mission required. After days of delirium, when one or more of the explorers wandered aimlessly and uncomprehendingly through the rain-sodden streets of Mong Yawng, these same men devoted their energies to recording the history of the region in which they found themselves, nursed their companions, and waited for news of their leader. What depressed them more than anything else, more even than the illnesses to which they succumbed, was the need to wait and the prospect that the end of it all would be an inglorious return along the route they had traveled to this point.

After six anxious days Garnier received a letter from Lagrée. Written before Lagrée had reached his goal, the letter gave an account of the territory through which he had traveled but could offer no certainty on how he would be received once at Keng Tung. After six further days of sickness and waiting, on August 26 another courier brought news to the Frenchmen. The Burmese agent in Mong Yawng summoned Garnier, to inform him that permission had been given for the party to proceed to Keng Hung. This was welcome news but puzzling nonetheless, for there still was no confirmation from Lagrée, who should, by this point, have been in Keng Tung. Days passed with no news other than increasingly disturbing reports of a murderous attack upon a band of opium merchants who were in the ruler of Keng Tung's employ. If bandits could kill twenty-three of the ruler's merchants, what might have happened to two Frenchmen traveling with so little protection?

Not until September 6, more than three weeks after Lagrée's departure, was there a rumor that contained anything like positive news. The leader of the French party, according to the report that filtered into Mong Yawng, had left Keng Tung with permission to travel to Keng Khang and was going there directly. This was welcome but still unsupported news for the party in Mong Yawng. It was enough, however, for Garnier to decide to move on. With their preparations made and departure set for September 8, a letter finally arrived from Lagrée. It was undated, a small but significant indication of the physical and mental toll under which the normally precise leader of the party labored; but dated or not its news was good. The ruler of Keng Tung had received Lagrée on August 25 with the best of will. He was the son of the ruler who, thirty years before, had been visited by the British traveler McLeod. Fortunately, the memory that McLeod had left behind him was a happy one—among other things, he was admiringly remembered for his awesome appetite that led him to eat three times as much at a single meal as one of his Keng Tung hosts would consume in an entire day. But the main point was that the ruler was ready to help rather than hinder the Frenchmen. Even the Burmese agent at Keng Tung, after an initial frosty encounter with Lagrée and Thorel and continuing evidence of undisguised greed for further presents, ceded to the requests of the ruler and gave his authorization for the party to proceed to Keng Khang. On September 13 the whole mission was together again. The absence of Lagrée and Thorel, which had been expected to last no more than three weeks, had lasted nearer to five. Their detour to Keng Tung had involved nearly three hundred miles of hard travel, most of it over steep mountain tracks.

The days spent in Keng Khang were a happy contrast with the period of anxious uncertainty in Mong Yawng. The ruler and his advisers were amiable. The Burmese agent, though clearly less than well disposed to the French party, could not question the validity of the passports issued by the ruler of Keng Tung and the Burmese agent in that capital. With all the members of the party apparently restored to good health, time passed rapidly as the customary ceremonial visits were exchanged and the explorers admired the evidence of substantial prosperity that seemed so much a feature of Keng Khang. The ruler's palace was "vast" and its construction testified to the presence of highly competent craftsmen. Senior officials wore rich silk robes, and the explorers were served from silver plates and bowls. Out of the hearing of the Burmese agent, the ruler confided to them that his territories were rich in minerals, even gold, but this had to remain a secret from the Burmese, who would, if they learned of these resources, require the population to mine them and render up a tenth of the value to the Burmese court. Information of this kind, even if it was unverified, was the stuff that Garnier's dreams were made of. Here was a memory to be guarded as a justification for yet another attempt to find a route to the upper Mekong and southwestern China. Brief though the period in Keng Khang was, it recaptured something of the idyll that the explorers had enjoyed in Luang Prabang.

The party's sense of satisfaction was not to last much longer. One day after leaving Keng Khang on September 18, messengers brought word south that they must not proceed onwards to Keng Hung, the last major center before China. The news came to the expedition when their hopes were highest. They had reached the settlement of Mong Long, to be delighted by the evidence they saw there of their proximity to China, the "promised land," as Garnier did not hesitate to call it. There was a bridge built in the vaulted Chinese manner at the entrance to Mong Long, and within the settlement they came upon two old Chinese women whose grotesquely small feet emphasized how close they were to the land where foot-binding remained a necessary preparation for crippled adherence to a particular view of beauty. But even as the party prepared to leave Mong Long the letter of interdiction arrived from Keng Hung and was handed to the local authorities. The Frenchmen were not to proceed but were to return along the route they had followed. Then, to add ironic confirmation to the French party's awareness of the proximity of China, the letter concluded, "Keng Hung is not only a dependency of Burma, but also of China."

For another four days the explorers had to wait in Mong Long while their case was carried to the authorities by the interpreter Alévy. Uncertain as to the real reason for the refusal to let them proceed, they staked all on the capacity of a subordinate whose talents and probity had, in the less demanding months at the beginning of the expedition, often been a matter for jest. If Alévy's own account of his efforts on the party's behalf is to be believed, at this critical juncture he more than justified his place as a member of the expedition. Whether his report of bluster and cajoling before the council determining affairs in Keng Hung was accurate or exaggerated, Alévy succeeded in gaining agreement for the expedition to proceed that far. The news was received on September 25 and by September 29 the group was in Keng Hung.

Whatever their concern for the reception they would be accorded at Keng Hung, the route the explorers now traveled was a welcome relief from the painfully slow passages they had made in the preceding three months. Instead of the half-made tracks, churned to mud by a single traveler's progress, that they had followed through rain-sodden forests, they now walked over paths that were even provided with bridges across streams. The land in the valleys was highly cultivated, and picturesque hamlets and villages clustered beneath the heavily wooded hills that more and more came to dominate the scenery. As they drew nearer to Keng Hung the valleys became narrower and narrower. Given the Frenchmen's hopes for commercial discoveries, the oxen carrying lead, cotton, tobacco, and tea that passed by them, heading south from Keng Hung, were a cheering sight.

The town the explorers entered was of very recent construction, but it was the latest manifestation of Keng Hung's longstanding political importance. The Frenchmen had now reached the capital of the fabled Sip Song Panna, a political unit of significance probably as early as the eleventh century and of some continuing importance even today when most of the region has been absorbed within the borders of the Chinese People's Republic. The dominant ethnic group within Sip Song Panna was yet another representative of the Tai-speaking peoples who then, as now, spread so widely across eastern and southeastern Asia.

After more than a century's Western interest in the area, there is still uncertainty as to the exact meaning of the name Sip Song Panna. Garnier thought it meant the number of registered inhabitants in each of the twelve divisions making up the ancient state whose glory had once been immeasurably greater than it was in 1867. Probably the correct literal translation of the name is "Twelve Principalities," reflecting the fact that under the loose authority of the ruler at Keng Hung there were eleven other territorial divisions spread across what is today China and northern Laos. When Lagrée, Garnier, and the others came to Keng Hung, a bare ten years had elapsed since the old town of that name had been destroyed during the battles and campaigns of the 1850s that had seen local rivalries once more bringing a confrontation between the Burmese and the Thais. Yet despite the relative poverty of the town, the ruler of Keng Hung's council had the vital power of decision over the French expedition's fate. It alone could decide whether the party might move on to China. Even though its first proscription against the expedition coming to Keng Hung had been overcome, the question of moving farther north still remained to be settled.

Garnier was later to write of this situation in terms suggesting that he and his companions were reasonably confident of a successful outcome. This seems, however, very much a case of selective memory. The French party was indeed allowed to proceed, but the necessary authorization was given only after complex maneuvering. In the uncertain circumstances, Lagrée took the offensive. Without revealing the nature of the travel papers he was carrying, he notified the council of Keng Hung that there were only two choices open to its members. They could present him with a written refusal of permission to proceed, and he would make such use of it as he saw fit, or they could provide the French party with the means to travel on to Ssu-mao, the first major Chinese town to their north.

When Lagrée confronted the council of Keng Hung on October 3, he found in it an institutional reflection of the Sip Song Panna's geographical and political character. Presided over by a senior official, a fat old man with white hair, the council had twelve members, the four most important of them being representatives of the divisions of the Sip Song Panna that bordered on the neighboring states. In addition, however, there were places for the agents of the Burmese and Chinese governments. The Burmese agent was present, seated to the left and a little behind the presiding official. The place usually occupied by the Chinese agent was vacant.

The opening exchanges recalled the difficulties the mission had encountered so many times before. Showing the council the passports they had received from the ruler of Keng Tung and the Burmese agent at that court, the Frenchmen were first accorded a negative response by the Burmese accredited to Keng Hung. The passports were all very well, the Burmese official argued, but there was nothing in them relating to passage from

Keng Hung into China. If the Frenchmen's judgment was correct, this almost routine expression of opposition helped rather than hindered their case. No less than in the other Tai-language regions through which the explorers had passed, the Burmese agent at Keng Hung was disliked by those whom he advised.

More disturbing was the lack of positive reaction when Lagrée proceeded to show the passports the party had received from Peking. There was uncertainty and even confusion among the council members: they did not recognize the signature on the passports; the documents had not come from the usual authority. Then the icily reserved Lagrée acted. Striving for maximum effect, he slowly drew from an envelope the letter written on the expedition's behalf by one of the most powerful men in China, Prince Kung, the brother of the Emperor Hsien Feng, who had died in 1861.

The result was all that could be wished and more. Silence fell as Lagrée passed Prince Kung's letter to the Chinese functionary representing his country's interests in the absence of the agent. The Chinese official read the letter with amazement and informed the council of its contents. This, indeed, was a letter from Peking, written by a prince of the Chinese Empire. Those who had brought it were men of high rank and should be received with honor and courtesy. The atmosphere of the meeting was transformed. The members of the council prostrated themselves before the letter and those who had borne it to Keng Hung.

The question of whether the party would be free to move on was no longer at issue. The matter was consecrated through a ceremonial audience with the almost powerless ruler of Keng Hung, a nineteen-year-old youth firmly in the grip of his advisers, who now received Lagrée before an assembly of some three hundred followers armed with ancient flintlocks, lances, and rusty sabers. For the Frenchmen, the silk robes of the ruler and his gilded ceremonial headdress, complete with tiny tinkling bells, left nothing more than a "bizarre" impression. With their passage assured, they could give full rein to their prejudices.

On October 7 the expedition was once more traveling north. Leaving Keng Hung the party crossed the waters of the Mekong for the last time, passing by ferry from the western bank. After four days' march they were at Keng Neua, the last settlement of any importance outside the Chinese Empire. The settlement provided little that was of visual interest to the explorers, but they recognized its political utility—if not significance. The ruler of the region in which Keng Neua was located was responsible for translating the messages that passed backward and forward between China and the chief town of the Sip Song Panna, Keng Hung.

The explorers were now moving rapidly through an upland countryside that was notably different from the leech-ridden rain forests to which they had become so accustomed. By October 16 the villages they encountered seemed totally Chinese in character. All the familiar signs were there: calligraphic writing on strips of red paper that hung about the doors of houses; chairs and tables, which the travelers welcomed with undisguised relief; and, overall, the "stamp of routine uniformity" which China's cultural system imposed on the diverse ethnic groups assimilated to its civilization.

Two days later the Frenchmen saw and entered their first Chinese town, Ssu-mao. They had been traveling all day when, at four in the afternoon, rounding the flank of a hill, they saw the unmistakable sight of a Chinese provincial town. Set in a vast plain, Ssu-mao was a fortified city whose center lay behind regular walls. Surrounding this central area were the less-ordered outer settlements, the market gardens, and dotted here and there the villas of wealthy inhabitants. Running away from the settlement were roads paved with stone and gravel, a sight they had not come upon since leaving Saigon more than fifteen months earlier. Here, whatever the disappointments of the past and their state of health in the present, was the country that Garnier had described as the "promised land." They were finally in China, the first European travelers ever to cross into this southwestern region of the Chinese Empire. The Frenchmen had succeeded where McLeod had failed thirty years previously. He had reached Keng Hung and been turned back before he could enter Yunnan. They had been able to pass on and to reach this point.

At this culmination of so many months of effort, the French explorers for a moment doubted their fitness to proceed. When they entered the city they were met by officials alerted to their coming, and by a gawking crowd. Still walking barefoot, their clothes showed only too well the long months that had passed. Among the naval officers only Lagrée wore a uniform coat, its badges of rank dull and tarnished. The explorers, as Garnier admits in his journal, felt a momentary hesitation and a passing sense of sadness for the apparent poverty of their group. But this sense of hesitancy and near shame could not last. The dominant feeling was one of success. The explorers were in China and, as Garnier noted later, possibly with some regret in view of the trials that came afterward, "everything that proved the existence of China was welcome." The Islamic rebellion and its possible effect on their travels could be temporarily forgotten, as could information of a devastating outbreak of cholera in the regions nearby. As the explorers rested in their quarters within a pagoda on the night of October 18, to be in China was enough.

CHAPTER VIII

ACROSS THE RED RIVER

$\mathcal{T}$he explorers were in China but, as they soon realized, in a very special region of that varied empire. Here, at the southern fringe of imperial territory, they found the "routine uniformity" of Chinese civilization and the continuing presence of minority tribes and peoples whose language and culture were linked to the jumbled ethnic groups of northern Burma, Laos, and Vietnam. The province of Yunnan, where they now rested, had become part of China as long ago as the thirteenth century, under the Mongol dynasty. In the succeeding centuries, however, its distance from northern China and the varied character of the region's population had brought it long periods of semi-independence.

By the middle of the nineteenth century, less than twenty years before the French party came in such sorry state to Ssu-mao, one group among Yunnan's ethnically diverse population was smoldering with resentment. This was the Islamic minority. Its members were the descendants of rough-riding Central Asian soldiers who had streamed out of the distant steppes to fight as mercenaries for Kublai Khan. Despite their martial antecedents these followers of Islam were not accorded a military role by the succeeding Chinese dynasties, who distrusted the former servants of the Mongol barbarians. By the mid-nineteenth century they were the victims of widespread discrimination. In 1855, with two remarkable charismatic leaders, Ma Te-hsing and Tu Wen-hsiu, at their head, the Muslims rose against imperial authority. As Lagrée and his men considered their present position and their future, the Islamic revolt was twelve years old, and the rebels controlled most of western Yunnan. The explorers had to decide how this situation would affect their plans.

More than ever before, the difficulty of decision was clear to Lagrée himself and to his subordinates, and with indecision there was the risk of dissent and disagreement. For Lagrée the value of exploring the Mekong to its source now seemed less important than making a commercial reconnaissance of southwestern China; to know more of the Mekong's origins was scientifically desirable but probably practically impossible. Garnier saw matters in a different light. His obsession with the Mekong had not abated; for France, and for himself, there could be glory and genuine scientific achievement in tracing the great river to its source, even if hopes for the Mekong as a navigable waterway had been illusory.

Lagrée's choices would have been easier if the information available to the expedition had been less fragmentary. One further major error in planning was now apparent. The party had no truly satisfactory way of communicating with the Chinese officials upon whom they had to rely for advice. Prince Kung's letter produced a readiness to provide assistance, but it could not overcome the lack of a common language. Alévy proved unable to exchange more than the briefest words with the officials they met in Ssu-mao, and another youth brought from the regions near Keng Hung in the express hope that he would be able to aid the Frenchmen in understanding the officials of Yunnan was scarcely better. The result was a painful and often confusing series of exchanges. In audiences with the Governor of Ssu-mao, Lagrée struggled to achieve some grasp of the situation, hindered as much as helped by his interpreters. At the same time Garnier, who possessed the merest smattering of Chinese, tried to work through the intermediacy of the soldier Tei, his Vietnamese companion of the long marches in Thailand and Cambodia. Garnier and Tei could speak together in Vietnamese, and Tei knew sufficient Chinese characters to carry on rudimentary written dialogues with the local population.

If the issues at stake had not been so vital, the situation could have been farcical. One day after their arrival in Ssu-mao, Lagrée had gone to meet the local Governor, who arrived at the audience in a sedan chair borne by eight porters, to the sound of exploding fireworks. He was an impressive figure, who wore a fur cape over his mandarin robes, and he greeted the Frenchmen cordially. But the Governor's amiability was scarcely a sufficient substitute for the exact intelligence the mission sought. Some matters were clear. The Muslim rebellion was far from over. The situation changed from day to day, but at the moment the rebels occupied the important western city of Ta-li, set by a large lake and not far, the explorers believed, from the upper course of the Mekong. Word they had received earlier of dread disease was not confirmed. Large areas of Yunnan were still ravaged by cholera. And to add further worry to the twin dangers of rebellion and epidemic, the general confusion in the province had brought a resurgence of banditry.

Not all was so certain as these basic and discouraging facts. The Governor of Ssu-mao, the Frenchmen now learned, had played some obscure part in the frustrating drama of the past month when they were seeking to enter China. If they understood him correctly, he had been ready to authorize their passage into China but had warned them against the dangerous possibility of traveling to the Muslim stronghold of Ta-li. The suggestion that there had been this guarded authorization for their passage through Keng Hung was made the more puzzling by the news that the Governor's letter had been accompanied by another, written in European "characters," from a famed maker of gunpowder, one Kosuto. Who, they puzzled, was this apparently renowned explosives expert, and how was it that he should have known of their presence in the remote regions of Keng Hung and written to them there? Plainly the answers would not be found in Ssu-mao, and certainly not through the aid of Alévy and the other barely useful interpreter. With an uncertain future before the party, Alévy said he would go no farther, and Lagrée made no effort to retain him. He had served his purpose at Keng Hung, if nowhere else, and there was every reason for dispensing with this servant who was "tolerable if unfaithful." Alévy could be sent back down the Mekong with a message for the French authorities in Saigon, and the other interpreter left to return to the regions near Keng Hung. For the future the mission would have to rely on its own limited linguistic resources.

Beyond the problems of language, the Frenchmen did have some advantages to aid them on their way. So long as poor health did not hinder their progress, the passports they carried, in conjunction with Prince Kung's letter, ensured them an official welcome wherever the power of the Peking government remained unchallenged. In Ssu-mao, and in later resting points along their route, the two medical men in the party aided relations with the local population by treating the sick and injured. Delaporte sketched Joubert engaged in this humanitarian effect. A later engraving made from this sketch is remarkable for the standard, if unconscious, blasphemy of the nineteenth century. In this picture, as in so many others from the same period showing missionaries at work in distant and dangerous lands, the European doctor sits like a latter-day Christ as the maimed, the halt, and the blind stream towards his outstretched arms. All that is lacking are the stigmata to make the iconography perfect.

Dr. Joubert treating the sick.

Less of an advantage was the constant fact of curiosity. Once in China, the explorers found that they were the object of insistent and even dangerous curiosity. For those who had never seen a European, the members of this curious race were a matter for wonder and excitement. Curiosity was not restricted to the city poor who so readily crowded about the Frenchmen, particularly the children, whose sharp observation enabled them to mimic the explorers' military gait and their foreign gestures. A few days after entering Ssu-mao Lagrée was surprised and annoyed when an official with whom they were dealing suddenly attempted to remove Lagrée's hat and to stare at the back of his head. The mandarin had a ready explanation for this curious action. He was searching, he said, for Lagrée's third eye. It was well known in China that one reason for the power exercised by Europeans was that they possessed a third eye, which permitted them to look secretly for riches while apparently gazing in another direction.

Against this background of mingled goodwill, curiosity, and incomprehension, Lagrée still had to make a decision. The reality of the Islamic rebellion was evident all about them; Ssu-mao itself had been occupied by the rebels only a few years earlier, and much damage remained unrepaired. There was a further reason for concern. The Chinese officials of Ssu-mao were well disposed towards the Frenchmen, but could the explorers depend on the capacity of the imperial troops to resist the Muslims? As naval officers the Frenchmen were alternately shocked and amused by the weapons the Chinese troops used. For Garnier, the appropriate comparison was with the period of the Hundred Years War between France and England. The wooden cannon, bound with iron bands, might have done duty at the battle of Crecy or Agincourt, as might the troops' halberds and lances. The primitive long-barreled matchlock guns, fired by a soldier supporting his unwieldy weapon's barrel on a forked stick or staff, belonged, perhaps, to a slightly later age. Armed as they were, the troops seemed barely capable of defending themselves against any serious enemy. As if to add further force to this conclusion, news arrived in Ssu-mao on October 24 that the rebel forces were preparing to attack the next major town to the north, P'uerh.

At this news, Lagrée decided to travel north and east to K'unming, the capital of Yunnan, as quickly as possible. To seek a passage to the west—which Garnier later argued was the desire of the others in the party—would be to risk an almost immediate confrontation with the Muslim rebels. The mission's goal had been to explore the Mekong and to investigate the commercial possibilities of southwestern China. Now was the time to concentrate on the latter aim and so ensure the well-being of the expedition as a whole. If new and more detailed information should be available when the expedition reached P'uerh, a little further to the north, then Lagrée agreed to reconsider Garnier's wish to travel towards the Mekong by way of Ta-li.

In his later discussion of this disputed decision, Garnier suggests that he was not alone in arguing against Lagrée's point of view. Lagrée's order, he recorded, "evoked a degree of discontent in the heart of the expedition. We were all young and enamored of adventures; one is bravest when one does not hold responsibility." This comment was written after the expedition was over and Lagrée was dead. The contrast Garnier makes between bravery and responsibility reflects his own effort to minimize a sharp difference that developed between him and his leader over the goals the expedition should pursue. Yet there is a mystery connected with his description of discontent in the "heart" of the party. Did Garnier wish the readers of his journal to believe that all or most of the others shared his reluctance to turn away from the Mekong? We can be sure from Louis de Carné's account of developments that if he felt any disappointment he was more than ready to follow the orders of a man whom he admired almost passionately, despite the sharp criticisms that Lagrée sometimes directed at him. The attitude of the others is less clear. Possibly, unlike Garnier, they were reluctant, whatever their inner feelings, to show a preference for one route over another.

In the weeks that followed, tensions were barely hidden below the surface of correct relations between the Frenchmen. Ill and exhausted, continually exposed to unexpected dangers and disappointments, they had passed beyond the point where public displays of unity were the answer to their problems. A striking image comes across the years: the members of the party chose to march in isolation from each other during their travels in November and December 1867. There were practical reasons for this choice, not least the need to supervise porters. But this practical concern was only part of the explanation. They had all spent too long in each other's company. When Lagrée sought companionship he turned increasingly to Joubert, not to Garnier, his second-in-command.

This unhappy period following the expedition's entry into China laid the foundation for disputes that persist more than a hundred years later. In part the disputes stem from misunderstandings. To a degree they are linked to genuine and deeply felt disagreements that emerged during and shortly after the expedition. When the mission finally ended, was Garnier to be described as the "leader" or "head" of an expedition that he had commanded for less than six months after Lagrée's death in China? His supporters said yes, and found in the various instances of disagreement between Garnier and Lagrée evidence to show that the second-in-command had made the wiser judgments and pursued the more important goals. Lagrée's supporters, most notably and tragically Louis de Carné, who argued his case at the same time as he battled unsuccessfully against a mortal disease, insisted on Garnier's subordinate role until near the very end of the expedition. In an all too familiar pattern, the arguments grew more bitter after both Lagrée and Garnier were dead. Their partisans, in championing the memories of dead men, readily forgot that whatever disputes occurred in the course of the expedition, the two protagonists tried to act towards each other, and write about each other, with both courtesy and respect.

When the expedition left Ssu-mao on October 30, its members rejoiced in the luxury of once more wearing shoes, Chinese in style but shoes nonetheless. Striking north towards P'uerh, the explorers were gratified by the evidence they initially saw of industry and commerce. Despite the threat of the Islamic rebellion they passed frequent caravans of asses, mules, and oxen bearing goods north and south, and only a little beyond Ssu-mao they found sizable villages devoted to extracting oil and salt from the ground. "With its smoke, its blackened houses, the muffled sound escaping from the extraction wells, we suddenly found ourselves in the middle of civilization," wrote Garnier describing one settlement, "and we could believe that we were in a small European industrial town." Once beyond the salt mines, however, the countryside became desolate. The refining process used in producing salt required constant heat, and the hills and plains to the north of the region had been progressively stripped of their natural cover of pines. Added to this was the destruction caused by the Islamic rebellion. Only the shells of houses remained in what had once been prosperous villages, and previously productive fields lay fallow. The explorers were in a somber mood when they arrived at P'uerh on November 1.

Their reception from the chief official of P'uerh was courteous but distracted. He feared that the Muslim rebels would attack the town within a few days. Despite its administrative importance P'uerh was barely defended. Garnier could find only two cannon on the city walls, ancient and unreliable pieces, and the garrison was clearly inadequate to any real challenge. Given the means at his disposal, the Chinese mandarin with whom the explorers now met had made his plans with one thought in view. If the rebels should attack, he and his staff were ready to flee. Against this background he gave advice and passports to the explorers. They should travel northeast, towards Chien-shui, farther still from the upper reaches of the Mekong that still exercised an insistent fascination for Garnier. This was a bitter blow to his hopes. Lagrée had agreed to review the possibility of a further reconnaissance of the Mekong at P'uerh. The decision was negative, and their route was to take the expedition even farther from Garnier's desired goal.

After three days of rest in P'uerh, and without suffering the feared attack by the rebels, the expedition was marching once again. They had gained at least one piece of information during their brief stopover, even if it had no practical value. Kosuto, they learned, the man who had written to them at Keng Hung and who had such a reputation as a maker of gunpowder, was a missionary. More they could not discover. Although they were now free of the depressing uncertainties that had been so much a part of their slow progress through the northern Laotian and Shan states, as if to replace that difficulty another problem made its appearance. For the first time during the expedition, cold rather than heat became a concern. Not far from P'uerh the path along which they traveled took them higher into the mountains. The party's instruments had shown the town of P'uerh to be some four thousand feet above sea level. During the first day's march after leaving the town the explorers slipped and staggered over muddy paths that took them, shivering, to a height of five and a half thousand feet. The reality of their more northerly position was becoming ever more apparent as they moved through a wild landscape, only sparsely cultivated, with the narrow valleys made insignificant by bare and storm-hung mountain tops looming above. And all the while, to remind them of the rebellion that threatened imperial control of this frontier region, the Frenchmen passed files of soldiers marching towards the west.

Beyond the need to move forward and to match physical endurance to the demands of the path they traveled, there was a new question for the French explorers to consider. Had they moved into a region that was no longer part of the immense drainage and tributary system of the Mekong? The question, both then and for later commentators on the expedition, was much more than academic. Long before the expedition had turned its back on the Mekong at Keng Hung, hopes of using that river as a navigable route to China were dead. With this in mind, and despite Garnier's passion to find the Mekong's source, the possibility of discovering an alternative route to Yunnan became a vital new concern. Did the rivers and streams the group crossed as they moved northeast from P'uerh flow into the Mekong, or were they instead the upper reaches of another system that ran to the east and down to the sea in northern Vietnam, in Tonkin?

In early November 1867 none of the explorers could be certain. Nor did they have any clear information suggesting that a river system running east to Tonkin could offer opportunities for navigation and so, eventually, for French commercial advantage. Later, when both Lagrée and Garnier were dead and the apparent commercial opportunities of the Red River *were* revealed, a sharp controversy developed as to who should be regarded as the discoverer of the Red River's value. The leading adversaries in this public controversy were Joubert, who argued for the expedition's prior claim, and Jean Dupuis, a commercial adventurer who insisted that he deserved the honor. Discussion of Dupuis' claim must wait until later in the story. At the point when the French expedition was traveling towards the Red River, in November 1867, its members were unaware of Dupuis' existence and held hopes, but no more, for what they might find.

Writing to Governor La Grandière in Saigon before they left Ssu-mao, Lagrée had expressed his interest in the Red River and the desirability of reconnoitering its upper reaches. Lagrée's letter seems to place the honor of first considering the Red River's possibilities firmly in the explorers' hands. No one knows if Lagrée's mind had been stimulated by the knowledge that over fifty years earlier French missionaries had traveled up the Red River and into China. The facts of the missionary voyage had been printed, in a missionary journal, but there is no evidence to show that Lagrée had read the account. Nor did the missionaries discuss commercial possibilities. Certainly none of the explorers knew that another Frenchman had already surveyed the extreme lower reaches of the Red River and suggested its commercial possibilities only four years before. In late 1863 Charles Duval, a sergeant in the French army, had made a clandestine reconnaissance of the Red River and reported his findings to the Ministry of War. Perhaps because of departmental jealousies, this report was never passed to the Ministry of the Navy and Colonies, and it lay forgotten in the archives for many years. The explorers knew neither of Duval nor of his secret activities. Theirs was the first serious recognition of the Red River's potentialities for commerce and the first attempt to bring the possibility to the French public's attention.

But who deserved most credit among the members of the expedition? No firm answer seems possible. If Lagrée must receive recognition for insisting on the party's abandoning the Mekong and moving towards the headwaters of the Red River, Garnier, with characteristic enthusiasm, was, despite his continuing interest in the Mekong, the man who embraced the idea of exploring the Red River most ardently. At the end of a long day's travel beyond P'uerh the expedition came to a swift-running river whose muddy waters flowed from the north. In his published journal Garnier insists that he was convinced this was a tributary of the Red River. Lagrée disagreed, arguing that the stream they saw eventually joined with the Mekong near Keng Hung. Unable to discuss the problem with the local population, the matter remained unresolved.

Three days' further travel brought the party to T'ung-kuan, an important settlement in the middle of a broad cultivated valley. Here the Frenchmen saw further evidence of the Chinese government's determination to prosecute the war against the Islamic rebels. Several thousand troops were assembled at T'ung-kuan, and the explorers saw them set off for the west on November 8. They reacted to the contrast between the picturesque vision that unfolded in front of them and the troops' lack of martial discipline. There seemed no order to the army's departure. The colorfully dressed soldiers chose their own routes as they left T'ung-kuan to the sound of exploding firecrackers. Banners waved above them, and each senior officer moved forward to the accompaniment of his personal musicians, men playing guitars and beating on drums of varying sizes. Garnier was sure that "one hundred determined men would have routed this entire army corps." No doubt he had one hundred Frenchmen in mind.

On the same day that the Chinese imperial forces left T'ung-kuan, heading towards the western battlefields, the explorers continued on their own way. Again they crossed a river of some size, and again Lagrée and Garnier disagreed about its destination. "For my part," Garnier notes, "I remained convinced that it

was one of the tributaries that made up the river of Tonkin."
But this watercourse was left behind as they moved on to Mo-chiang, their next major resting place, which they reached
on November 9.

Once more the explorers noted the contrast between the ear-lier months of uncertain relations with local authorities and the
respectful manner in which they were received by Chinese offi-cialdom. Even before they entered Mo-chiang a mandarin had
been sent to greet them. When they took up quarters in a pa-goda outside the city's walls, the Governor came to present his
compliments to Lagrée. He did more; the Frenchmen received a
pig, a goat, three capons, and a sack of rice from the chief offi-cial. His subordinates followed his example, and the expedition
was able to guard its declining funds and eat more freely than
had been possible since leaving Ssu-mao.

In the middle of this comfortable halt there was a disappoint-ment. Soon after their arrival the explorers received a visit from
a Chinese mandarin who had left Peking only a short time be-fore. He was sufficiently accustomed to European ways to greet
them with a handshake. But, despite their entreaties, he could
give them no news of Europe. Why, they asked, did the French
Legation in Peking not think of sending a summary of news by
this man in case he should meet the explorers? This was hardly
a reasonable attitude—how the French Legation was supposed
to foresee where they might be in Yunnan, Garnier does not
say—but tempers were growing shorter as balanced judgment
became another casualty of the prolonged journey.

Throughout their week of rest in Mo-chiang the party was
aware of increasingly cooler weather. As they left the town on
November 16, passing by the freshly severed head of an executed
bandit, they knew that colder days lay ahead. Even so they were
surprised by the sudden fall in temperature during the day of
their departure. In pouring rain, with the mercury little above
freezing, they bivouacked in a village through the whole of the
next day and night. Then, in improved weather, they struck out
for Yüan-chiang. During this day the difficulties of the past
seemed forgotten. The Frenchmen marveled at the energy ex-

pended by generations of farmers in their efforts to use every cultivable foot of land. Terraces succeeded terraces from the narrow plains of the valleys to the heights of the hills they passed. They were marching alongside yet another river, and this time all were convinced that it formed part of the Red River system. This was a cheering thought as their passage took them past convoy after convoy of beasts bearing goods of every description: rice, pottery, spirits, and paper. After an ascent lasting more than an hour, the Frenchmen suddenly saw before them a great vista that brought the party to a halt. Stretching away to the west were endless ranges of dull yellow mountains. At the foot of these towering peaks, and running from northwest to southeast, was the second river to hold such an important place in their minds. There far below them, sparkling in the sun, with the city of Yüan-chiang on its banks, was the Red River, the river of Tonkin.

They descended into a tropical world. After weeks spent at altitudes exceeding four thousand feet, the party dropped down to a city set at a height of little more than fifteen hundred feet. Instead of the terraced hills where men fought to wrest a meager reward from the soil, the plain about Yüan-chiang was kind to its inhabitants. The rice had been harvested for the season, but the stubble remained to add a golden tint to the scene. Palm trees and orange groves mingled with the stands of sugar cane beneath a strikingly blue sky that seemed cleansed by the rain of the previous day. Seen from the heights where the explorers stood, the city, surrounded by this apparent agricultural wealth, was both imposing and mysterious.

They were so distant that they could not see movement in the streets, and the whole city seemed sunk in siesta. Although the explorers knew full well that they were in China, the view of the city with its gray flat-roofed houses, reminded them of Arab or Turkish settlements.

Never before had the explorers experienced such a welcome as they received at Yüan-chiang. When they drew near to the gates of the city, they were met by a reception party of mandarins and an escort of two hundred soldiers and porters, some carrying banners, others bearing placards painted with giant characters proclaiming a welcome to the members of the expedition. As they entered the city cannon boomed and music played.

Later Yüan-chiang's chief mandarin matched his personal generosity to this public welcome, pressing gifts of food upon them. The only immediate concern for the Frenchmen was their inability to offer adequate gifts in return. Yüan-chiang was no place to buy friendship with baubles and shoddy trade goods, not least because European products were well known in this region of Yunnan. Just how well known was a matter for some surprise. In their audience with the chief mandarin he showed them his possessions with pride: a telescope, a watch, and a stereoscope to view hand-coloured photographs that Garnier quaintly described as being "of dubious morality." De Carné, hardly one might think an expert in these matters, was convinced that the "scantily attired courtesans" had to be English because of their fair skin and red hair. Pompously he recorded, "There is no prudery in commerce, even in prudish England."

In the week they spent in Yüan-chiang the explorers found much to interest them. The city had once been the center of another Tai-speaking kingdom and had been conquered by the Chinese less than two hundred years earlier. Its streets were still thronged by a diverse mixture of ethnic groups whose bright costumes, often richly decorated with silver jewelry, contrasted sharply with the somber everyday clothing of the Chinese. The weather was warm and food abundant. And at the edge of the city was the wide river that provided a new basis for hopeful speculation. Here, in front of them, it was more than two hundred and fifty yards wide, shallow and slow-moving. What it might be like as it ran farther east was the question that Garnier repeatedly turned over in his mind.

With K'un-ming still their major goal, the explorers learned that the best route to follow began a little down-stream from Yüan-chiang. On November 26 they boarded a craft that would carry them a short distance down the river. Soon after the party left the hospitable city behind, the country about them changed. In place of the plains that surrounded Yüan-chiang was a valley whose bare sides seemed to draw ever closer about the river. Their destination was a small village on the river's left bank, just above a major rapid that brought a halt to navigation. The journey of three hours took them into a very different world from their quarters during the previous week. The village was inhabited by another Tai-speaking group, the Pa-Y, and the presence of the Chinese Empire seemed minimal. Bandits lived in the hills about the settlement so that guards stood watch on the village walls through the night. The day the party arrived a market gardener who had sold vegetables to the Frenchmen was set upon, beaten, and robbed only a short distance from the village.

This was not a spot in which to linger. While the main party prepared to climb away from the river to travel towards Chien-shui, a city that they believed would bring them within two or three weeks' journey of K'un-ming, Garnier obtained permission from Lagrée to travel farther down the Red River. Bowing to the insistent requests of his second-in-command, Lagrée agreed that a reconnaissance was desirable. The first to arrive in Chien-shui would wait for the other. On November 27 Garnier again set off on an independent survey, accompanied as before by Tei, the Vietnamese orderly.

The river ran through a forbidding landscape, stony and almost totally bare of vegetation except for the faint glimpses of green that could be discerned on the distant heights or rare spots where stunted trees and moss clung precariously to a cliff face less steep than those surrounding it. Soon after leaving the village where the expedition had rested, the cliffs above the river rose to more than three thousand feet. Dwarfed by the landscape, Garnier found little to encourage hopes of easy commercial navigation along the river. He was traveling, it was true, in company with boats carrying merchandise but the boatmen faced problems that were only too familiar. Rapid succeeded rapid, necessitating constant unloading and reloading of the goods the boats carried. And in the period of the year when the river was in flood, Garnier learned, even this slow transportation was impossible.

High hopes once again seemed unjustified, and as night drew

in about the customs post where Garnier and Tei had decided to spend the night, the Frenchman was struck by a terrible headache; simultaneously he developed a racking dry cough that scarcely allowed him to speak. His eyes smarting with pain, Garnier found unexpected help from the Chinese customs official. Motioning the Frenchman to lie down, the customs officer brought opium and a pipe. Carefully drawing a lump of the sticky raw opium from a small pot, he passed it through a flame before dropping it smoking in the bowl of the pipe. Garnier sucked on the stem, drawing the narcotic smoke over his aching throat. Again and again the official prepared a pipe for his guest as Garnier felt the pain in his throat ease and his headache disappear. Like many other Western visitors to eastern Asia, Garnier seems to have experimented, if only briefly, with opium before. "This was," he commented, "the first time that I had smoked opium for such a long period, and this personal experience showed me that correctly used this drug could become a valuable remedy; abuse alone transformed it into a deadly poison." Garnier was in the advance guard of that body of late nineteenth century opinion which was so ready to advocate widespread medicinal use of opium. Abuse, after all, was only likely to be a problem among the less civilized or the undereducated.

The next day, quite recovered from the sudden illness of the previous evening, Garnier determined to continue down the Red River. Reluctantly the small Chinese escort party traveling with Garnier agreed to accompany him, and equally reluctantly some local boatmen agreed to man a craft. The reasons for their hesitation were soon clear. Below the settlement the river ran ever faster before tumbling over a great rapid. Here, with the closely pressing walls of the valley rising a staggering six thousand feet above them, the boatmen would go no further. Neither money nor threats would move them. Garnier's exploration of the Red River had come to an end. The best he could learn was that an undetermined distance downstream, certainly once a traveler was at the Vietnamese settlement of Lao-Cai, navigation of some sort was possible. By midday he was climbing slowly out of the Red River valley, and three and a half hours later, having reached the plateau above, he and Tei were en route for Chien-shui. Turning their backs on the Red River thousands of feet below and the distant vista of sharply rising mountains more than twelve thousand feet high towering to the south, the travelers set off towards the north. In the upland plateau they were crossing, the population was made up of Pa-Y and Lolos, both non-Chinese Tai-speaking groups. They were harvesting as Garnier and Tei, with their Chinese escort, moved quickly towards their rendezvous point with the main party. After the abrupt ascents and descents of the stages before Yüan-chiang, travel over the plateau that stretched north from above the Red River was easy. Their path ran over gently undulating ground rather than across hills and valleys. Only a day and a half after leaving the Red River, as night fell, Garnier's small party entered Chien-shui. Lagrée and the others had not yet arrived.

Once lodged in a pagoda within the city walls, Garnier chose to inspect his surroundings. Away from his lodgings he found himself an object of intense curiosity. Chien-shui was a larger settlement than any other the French explorers had passed through in China, and here without the reassuring presence of his companions Garnier found that curiosity could be threatening. First a few, then scores, and finally several hundreds of the local inhabitants were following him, watching his every move and commenting on every action. There seemed no alternative but to retreat to the pagoda. This he did, with the crowd, now numbering at least a thousand, pressing behind him. When, having retreated inside his lodgings, he found that the curious crowd still struggled to catch a glimpse of his alien features, Garnier recognized that the situation had become precarious:

> Some carefully dressed Chinese, with measured voices and venerable features, came and advised me to satisfy the inhabitants by showing myself outside, in the courtyard where some thousands of persons had pressed in. If I consented to do this, they told me, they guaranteed it would do me no harm. But if, on the contrary, I did not appear, they could not answer for the actions of the crowd.
> I decided I had better follow this apparently sincere advice. I agreed, not without cursing a thousand times at this inopportune demand, to walk up and down between two rows of people who were

close enough to breathe upon me as I passed. So, for more than a quarter of an hour, I paced up and down while with avid and foolishly curious stares the crowd examined and peered at every inch of my person. This concession, despite the cost to my dignity already involved, did not satisfy the inhabitants at all. From every corner of the courtyard, and in twenty different languages the cry went up, "Let him eat. We want to see him eat!" Outraged by this audacity, I announced that I would not eat, and I withdrew without anyone daring to stop me.

If Garnier thought that the matter was ended there, he was soon to be disappointed. As he tossed restlessly on his bunk, near midnight he heard a faint noise. Springing up and grabbing his rifle, he flung open the door to find a group of men quietly mounting the stairs by the light of shaded lanterns, apparently intent on seeing the European stranger. This was too much. Clubbing the interlopers with his rifle butt and kicking out wildly at those who could not retreat quickly enough, Garnier rapidly cleared the stairway. Berating his Chinese escort for allowing such a thing to happen, the French explorer concluded that they might well have played the role of accomplices, allowing the curiosity seekers to enter his lodgings in return for money.

However much his dignity was offended, Garnier recognized the element of danger that was clearly present. He was one and the crowd had numbered in the thousands. In these circumstances, and as the next day dawned, he decided that good sense required him to vacate his lodgings during the daytime hours. The decision seemed wise, and apart from a few children who followed him briefly as he left the city he was able to spend an untroubled day wandering through the nearby countryside. But at sunset he had to return, and he soon found that he was awaited. A crowd followed him to the pagoda where the courtyard was once again filled with curious inhabitants. Even the roofs of the surrounding buildings were being used as vantage points by the population for whom Garnier's exotic appearance was a magnet. Again Garnier was persuaded that the crowd would be satisfied if he should consent to parade before them, and again, red faced and ashamed, he did so.

Finally he could no longer bear the humiliation of this circus display. He withdrew behind the flimsy gate that stood between the courtyard and the passage to his sleeping quarters. Conscious that the mob intended to try to follow, Garnier called on his Chinese escort to assist him in holding the crowd at bay. An ugly situation was at hand. The members of the crowd nearest the light gate hesitated, but those farther back called on them to go forward. Then, with uncertainty hanging over the scene, a group towards the rear started throwing stones. Close as he was to the gate, it was only a moment before Garnier was struck full in the face. There was now no choice but counter action, and Garnier seized the revolver Tei offered him and held it pointing through the gate. As those at the front of the crowd fell back, he fired a single shot. Describing the events later, Garnier captured the surprise of those who had so tormented him:

> I had fired in the air, being very much aware that at the sight of blood the still indecisive crowd would launch itself upon me and tear me to pieces. In a country where match-lock guns still exist, weapons capable of firing two immediately consecutive shots are regarded as marvels. So it was that the crowd thought my one shot had left me quite unarmed, and after the shock of the first shot the hail of stones came again, even more heavily. I fired a second time. The crowd was amazed for no one had seen me reload my revolver. "Bah," said a voice from the crowd, "I have seen double barreled pistols before. There is one at Ta-li brought from Burma. Now it's really over. He is disarmed and we can approach him without fear." I had the good luck to grasp what was said and immediately turned it to my advantage. Three shots, one after another, rang out to terrify the mob, as my weapon still remained unmoving by the gate. Panic set in, and I completed the rout by rushing outside, my weapon in hand, fire in my eyes, and my face bloodied.

With the crowd gone and after the few Chinese who had remained on the scene had given careful attention to his injured face, Garnier received a visit from a local official. The man brought cheering news. Garnier's companions were camped outside the city. They had arrived only shortly before, but because of the uncertain state of the crowd in the city the authorities had asked them to remain beyond the walls. When dawn broke over Chien-shui next morning, Garnier followed his informant along deserted paths to the pagoda housing the main party. At that moment the unanswered questions in Garnier's mind concerning the Red River's future commercial value were submerged beneath his relief and pleasure at being among his own people. Garnier had no lack of physical courage, but his imaginative mind could also clearly picture what might have happened the night before if the crowd had not fallen back.

CHAPTER IX

MISSIONARIES AND MUSLIMS

$\mathcal{T}$he Red River remained a topic of conversation as the entire party rested for a week in Chien-shui, another prolonged halt underlining the physical weakness of the explorers and their escort. For Garnier the river and its possibilities for navigation were to become later obsessions just as demanding as the Mekong once had been. Still without a certain end to the expedition, and with a continuing desire to plot the course of the Mekong's upper reaches, Garnier speculated on the Red River as a future route into China. Proudly patriotic, even chauvinistic, there was no doubt in his mind that France alone should benefit, if his information were correct and commerce could pass up and down the river of Tonkin. He recalled his thoughts in 1870 and put the matter clearly and bluntly. This was "a commercial concern with a great future and an exclusively French affair." Lagrée shared his view and recorded it in the last report he made before he died. For all the Frenchmen in the party the assumed value of the Red River replaced the hopes they could no longer hold of navigation along the Mekong.

By December 9 the expedition was ready to move forward again with K'un-ming, the capital of Yunnan province, the next major goal. Their path took them through an area of ruined tombs, with marble pillars and porticos, which evoked an incongruous sense of the countryside about Rome. Thoughts quickly returned to the reality of China, however, when two galloping horsemen overtook the party bearing news from the Governor of Chien-shui. Not long after Garnier's frightening experience in the city, one of the culprits in the affair had been seized by the local officials. Throughout the explorers' stay in Chien-shui, the stone thrower had been held in a pillory by one of the main gateways into the city. Now, the horsemen told the explorers, he had been executed, his head struck from his body. While still in Chien-shui the Frenchmen had heard rumors that this was to be his fate, but they had not believed it would actually happen. They claimed later they would have tried to prevent the execution if they could.

At midday, with Chien-shui well behind them, the party found welcome relief from the usual weary routine of walking. The first important settlement along their route to K'un-ming was the town of Shih-p'ing and this they could reach by boat, sailing across the lake that lay in their path. Arriving there the same evening, the party rested for a day before heading north once more on December 11. Their route took them over a succession of hills and valleys where stands of cypress trees gave an almost alpine appearance to their surroundings. With the altitude increasing, the party was moving out of the upper basin of the Red River. For a short while, it seems, Lagrée hesitated over the northern route they were following. To have turned east again would have taken the party by land to a point on the Red River where boats could carry them easily to the sea. There was further discussion, even argument. Whatever his interest in the Red River, Garnier still hoped to travel westwards towards the Mekong, and to do this would require passports and advice that could only be found in K'un-ming. Lagrée acquiesced. None of the others was yet as ill as the leader, and he recognized the importance the younger men placed on attempting to discover more about the Mekong. He was still the commander of the party, but this was no time to enforce an unpopular decision at all costs.

So they continued north, to T'ung-hai, where, in the evening of December 14, the whole party found itself the object of unrestrained and potentially dangerous curiosity. The circumstances were similar to those Garnier had experienced. The explorers' arrival in T'ung-hai was the signal for hundreds of townspeople to gather about the pagoda in which the party lodged. Movement in and out of their quarters became impossible, and the posting of a Chinese guard about the walls only increased the interest of the crowd. With the bolder members of the crowd scaling the surrounding walls and roofs to gain entry into the pagoda, the Chinese soldiers standing guard prepared to fire their antique matchlocks. If this sight was insufficient to repel the curious, the view of the expedition's escort drawn up behind had its effect. Fixed to the escort's rifles were long sword-like bayonets, a combination of weapons unknown to the Chinese of T'ung-hai. The party passed an untroubled night. The next day it was Delaporte's turn. Seeking a high spot from which to sketch the town, he suddenly found himself at the center of a brawl as the curious inhabitants fought each other to gain a view of the artist. He extricated himself by waving his revolver threateningly and through the timely arrival of Joubert and de Carné. Months before, as the expedition had moved slowly and monotonously along the Mekong below Vientiane, Garnier had noted that a day without incident was a "disappointment." Incidents were certainly not absent from this stage of the journey, but now more than ever before the emotional cost was high.

It was snowing when the expedition left T'ung-hai on December 16, the first snow Garnier had seen for six years and the first that the Vietnamese in the escort had seen in their lives. Their first reaction was of wonder and delight. This quickly changed to painful distress as their bare feet encountered the snow covering the path. Never previously having worn shoes, the escort's feet had hardened over the years; so they had been unworried by the earlier stages, when the Europeans in the party had found marching barefoot to be such a painful business. But neither the feet nor the hands of the escort were hardened to resist cold, and tears ran down their cheeks at the pain. All in the party suffered. "This day's march both for them and for us was one of the most painful of the journey," Garnier wrote. "Our long beards bristled with icicles, and compass, pencil, and paper slipped from my numbed fingers." The next day was little better. The sun shone but the temperature remained below freezing throughout the day as they hurried on to Chiang-ch'uan. Reaching this town the same day, the explorers took advantage of warmth and hospitality, untroubled by bands of curiosity seekers, to plan ahead.

Delaporte disturbed while sketching.

They still knew little more than the bare essentials of the political and military situation in Yunnan, for, even had they not lacked a proper interpreter, the circumstances changed almost from day to day. K'un-ming remained in the hands of the imperial government, largely because one of the principal Muslim rebels, Ma Ju-lung, a man of great military capacity, had defected to the imperial side in 1860 and, appointed as a general, provided effective leadership against his former comrades in arms. The paradox of such a situation was given further piquancy by the fact that Ma Ju-lung had been joined in his defection by the man who, between 1855 and 1860, had been revered as the spiritual leader of the Islamic rebels. This was Ma Te-hsing, known to his co-religionists and to the French as Lao Papa. As the one man of his people who had made the pilgrimage to Mecca, Lao Papa's religious standing was unchallenged. Why he and Ma Ju-lung changed sides is still unknown.

In late 1867 as the explorers approached K'un-ming the Islamic revolt had many of the elements of a stalemate. To the west, based about Ta-li, the rebels were in largely undisputed control. In the eastern and northern sections of Yunnan, the imperial government's writ ran uncertainly, sustained to a considerable degree by the "reformed" rebel Ma Ju-lung. Yet if stalemate described the situation, from a broad point of view, the threat of sudden changes of control over large regions of the province remained to trouble the French party, and to make discussion of travel to the region near Ta-li pointless until further information was to hand. The wisest decision, it seemed to the men warming themselves in the house of the chief mandarin of Chiang-ch'uan, was to write ahead to K'un-ming to give notice of their intended early arrival. As this information was carried ahead by messengers, the expedition would follow as quickly as possible, spurred on by the disquieting news that the Muslim rebels had achieved new successes within thirty miles of K'un-ming.

Partly restored by the two days of rest, the party set off again on December 20. Even after all their experiences they were quite unprepared for the sight that met their eyes shortly after they had left the town. On a bare untilled plain running gently down to a lake lay hundreds of unburied coffins. The explorers were in one of the regions where the scourge of cholera had followed close upon the heels of war. Local custom called for the bodies of those who died in an epidemic to be left above ground in their coffins for a period, and this requirement had created the macabre landscape through which the party passed. Delaporte's sketch of the scene is evocative. The expedition's route wends through the countless scattered coffins as the men march forward under a gloomy sky. Garnier's brisk commentary barely hides a wealth of graveyard horror. "Chinese coffins," he observed matter of factly, "are, happily, more tightly closed than our own so that only occasionally did foul odors escape from this pile of cadavers." Nonetheless, it was a "genuine relief" to quit the coffin-covered plain and climb into the nearby hills.

The coffin-covered plain outside Chiang-ch'uan.

The next three days were filled with arduous marching. At one point their route took them to a height of seven thousand feet, and along their way they encountered frequent reminders of the war that ravaged the province in the succession of burned-out villages and abandoned fields. By the fourth day after leaving Chiang-ch'uan the countryside's somber aspect had changed. In place of devastation they saw carefully tended fields and irrigation canals. The route they followed became a road rather than a stony path, and they shared its surface with a bewildering confusion of travelers: caravans of beasts bearing merchandise, human porters, and the curtained litters of those who could afford to be carried rather than walk. As they had done before, the Frenchmen reflected sadly on their worn and dirty clothing, which contrasted so sharply with the silken robes of the Chinese officials and merchants who paused to stare at them.

The first view of K'un-ming came at midday on December 23. Under the clear blue sky they saw the great city in the distance, its crenelated walls rising in stark relief. As they halted to look at this ancient city, set six thousand feet above sea level, a horseman rode rapidly out towards them. The rider bore a letter for Lagrée, sent by a missionary and in French! This was more than they had hoped for. They knew there were missionaries in northern Yunnan, but they had no certain information about their nationality. There could be no better greeting to such passionate patriots than the promise of the letter that its writer would see them "à bientôt." With light hearts they passed through the great southern gateway into the city, cheered by the thought of an early meeting with one of their countrymen and joyfully observing the signs they saw all about them of K'un-ming's commercial importance.

This was the biggest city they had seen since they left Saigon. That had been eighteen months ago. Luang Prabang had blended Arcadian surroundings with picturesque buildings, Yüan-chiang had held a special charm in its setting beside the Red River, but K'un-ming was something else again. Despite the damage inflicted during the assaults mounted by the rebels at the beginning of the decade, the city's fortified walls were in good repair.

The streets within were lively with constant streams of passersby. And there seemed every evidence that here in K'un-ming the fabled riches of southwestern China were present in abundance. Shop front succeeded shop front; the merchants' goods were displayed in carefully arranged cases. The uniform color of the buildings was relieved in the commercial quarters of the city by the thousands, as it seemed to Garnier, of golden painted characters hung above the shop fronts proclaiming the nature of the merchandise for sale. Guided through the busy crowd that parted to let them pass, the explorers were brought to their lodgings, a section of the examinations palace. Here, in less troubled days, the young men who sought admission to the imperial bureaucracy submitted to the traditional examinations in the Confucian classics. Set on a hill with a fine view out over the countryside and comfortably furnished, the building offered a happy contrast to the poverty of so many of their recent lodgings.

Father Protteau, for such was the writer of the letter of welcome they had received earlier in the day, soon appeared at the explorers' quarters. This was an emotional moment, their first meeting with a compatriot since the anticlimactic encounter with Duyshart south of Luang Prabang eight months earlier; and he, after all, was not French by birth. But it was a meeting that held a different significance for each of the various members of the expedition. For Lagrée, the missionaries the expedition met at K'un-ming were to be admired for their devotion and respected for their faith. His Jesuit schooling required no less than this, and probably ensured more. The youngest member of the party, Louis de Carné, was a fervent believer, a passionate Catholic who saw in his religion a bastion against the insidious dangers of socialism. To find men of God in the isolated southwestern corner of China was a further testimony to the spiritual power of the creed he held dear.

To Garnier the presence of the priests was another matter altogether. He was, conventionally, a member of the Catholic faith, but in his private letters he revealed that his degree of religious conviction was, at very least, debatable. He could conceive of the existence of a divine spirit, he once observed, but he had no belief in the claims of religion revealed through a savior. If Garnier had a sustaining personal faith it was the worship of his country's glory. He summed up his views of men such as Father Protteau in an uncompromisingly frank observation: "One must make use of missionaries, but not serve them." Like many of his naval compatriots in the East, he had seen the contrast between the missionaries' claims of success in making converts and the reality of meager achievement. If they could serve France, then so much the better. But often, as he made bluntly clear, this was not a role missionaries played.

The man who now stood before them did little to change either de Carné's or Garnier's mind. The young diplomat saw in Father Protteau a living martyr. Here was a man who had sacrificed all his private interests and risked death to convert the heathen in one of the most remote corners of the globe. When, two days later, de Carné attended a midnight Christmas mass and received the Host and took wine from the priest's gnarled hands, he found it a moving religious experience. Garnier was present at the mass, too, as convention required; his real interest in Father Protteau, however, related to the amount of information the missionary could provide. There was much but not enough.

Father Protteau could, at least, solve the mystery surrounding their experience at Keng Hung. The cause of their difficulties in late September, it transpired, had been the inability of the Keng Hung officials to make an accurate translation of a letter sent by the Viceroy of Yunnan. This great official had written on the explorers' behalf, authorizing their entry into China but warning against the dangers they might find on certain routes. The warning in his letter had been mistaken for an interdiction. As for the letter from "Kosuto," this had been sent by Father Fenouil, Protteau's immediate superior and the Deputy Apostolic Vicar in Yunnan. Fenouil had written to confirm all that had been said in the Viceroy's letter. The French party was welcome in the areas controlled by the imperial government. This was partly so, Protteau explained, because of the way Father Fenouil had embraced the imperial cause. He was indeed, as rumor had so often told them, a renowned maker of gunpowder. Unfortunately for the utility of his efforts, his powder magazine had blown up recently, the result, it was thought, of sabotage by the Islamic rebels. The news confirmed Garnier's belief that the missionaries of Yunnan were unwisely set upon a path of excessive identification with the interests of the local government.

Father Fenouil was expected in K'un-ming shortly, but before this meeting the explorers were concerned to present themselves before the local authorities. A visit to the Governor of the province passed quickly and courteously. Then it was time for the French to present themselves before General Ma Ju-lung. Although the Muslims of Yunnan had been prevented for centuries from pursuing their ancient employment as soldiers, Ma Ju-lung had readily captured the spirit of his martial ancestors. He was a large, and to the French a gross figure. As proof of his military prowess he insisted on showing them the wounds that covered his body, pulling open his tunic so they could better see the scars. Although the Frenchmen suspected from Ma Ju-lung's red-rimmed eyes that he had spent the night carousing, their host would not join them in the banquet that he later laid before them.

As the explorers feasted on swallows' nest soup, fishes' entrails, and lacquered duck, the general and his subordinates sat and watched. It was the Muslim month of Ramadan, and as a believer Ma Ju-lung could not eat until the sun had set. But perhaps most striking of all to the explorers was the manner in which the Muslim general surrounded himself with weapons. Unlike the antique guns that had been the equipment of all the Chinese soldiery they had seen so far, much of Ma Ju-lung's armory was stocked with modern equipment. There were ancient blunderbusses, it was true. Besides these, however, were repeating rifles, carbines, and revolvers. Not only that; the evidence was all about them of Ma Ju-lung having tested his weapons. Not a piece of furniture in the general's quarters had escaped use as a target.

Picturesque as he was, Ma Ju-lung was a worrying factor in the explorers' calculations. Could they depend on him? He remained a follower of Islam, so that his enemies were his co-religionists. It was true that when he changed sides he had acted quickly to remove any doubts from the minds of his soldiers as to where their new loyalties should lie. Assembling his troops, he executed twenty among them who had dared to criticize their leader's actions. But that had been years before, and doubts about his intentions remained. Father Protteau, whose spiritual faith waged a constant battle with very earthly fear, wished himself back in the mountain refuge where he had fled on previous occasions when the Muslims threatened K'un-ming. For the French party the best assurance of Ma Ju-lung's goodwill seemed to lie in the fact that Father Fenouil had written on his behalf to the French diplomatic mission in Peking. Whether through his own wish, or because of Ma's threats, as he later himself maintained, Fenouil had written to the French Legation to argue Ma Ju-lung's case to the imperial authorities for increased supplies of men and weapons to prosecute the war against the rebels.

Finally, on January 2, 1868, the expedition's members met Fenouil. Garnier wrote that the French members of the party "loved" this missionary, but Garnier himself soon gives the lie to this description. He may have "loved" Father Fenouil's patriotism, for this feeling was present in abundance. For the rest Garnier's portrait of the Deputy Apostolic Vicar is a cruelly accurate delineation of a man and priest thrust into a role for which he had little talent and less experience. He was a different man altogether from his subordinate. Father Protteau, in the Frenchmen's eyes, had become almost Chinese, a peasant Chinese. His otherworldliness could be amusing and even irritating. Delaporte found this one day as he returned from an expedition on horseback. Crossing a wide and fast-flowing stream by means of a tree trunk serving as an improvised and shaky bridge, he spied Protteau on the other bank. The crossing achieved, Delaporte, still shaking from the experience, was told by the old missionary that there had been no need to be afraid. The priest had accorded him absolution in case he fell into the water and drowned.

Father Fenouil, too, had adapted to his surroundings, but in a very different manner. The treaties exacted from the Chinese government following the Anglo-French occupation of Peking in 1860 had allowed foreign missionaries to assume the titles and privilege of mandarins. Fenouil, a vigorous man in his forties, had hastened to avail himself of these provisions. He dressed in the robes of a mandarin of the appropriate rank, rode in a sedan chair proper to his dignity, and required the proper salutations in return. His decision to become closely involved in the affairs of the province had a cost, however, for Fenouil's name was now well known to the Muslim rebels and he feared for his life should he ever encounter them. Yet, in Garnier's skeptical eyes, this fear had not deprived Fenouil of a secret wish to act as arbiter between the two contending sides in Yunnan. For the moment he was able to render one vital service to the expedition. Acting on the French party's behalf, he negotiated a loan equivalent to five thousand francs from Ma Ju-lung. The expedition's reserves of money had finally been exhausted, and to proceed further without funds was impossible.

How to proceed, and where, remained undecided matters. Lagrée put the question of their future route to his companions, and the opinion was unanimous that they should make a final effort to travel west towards the Mekong and Ta-li. Lagrée's principal biographer doubts that this was Lagrée's personal choice, arguing that the leader now placed the need to preserve a sense of unanimity above his own judgment of what was most desirable. This may well be so, but unwillingly or not Lagrée now worked to gain the information and the papers that might make a visit to Ta-li, and even the Mekong, possible. Ma Ju-lung rejected Lagrée's first proposal: that the expedition should be escorted to the nearest rebel post and left there to fend for themselves. The next plan, however, was accepted as more reasonable. The expedition would first travel north and then turn to the west, hoping in this way to delay their meeting with the rebels until they were close to the seat of Muslim power, the city of Ta-li. To aid in this endeavor, the Frenchmen now looked to the former spiritual leader of the rebels, Lao Papa, the one man among the Yunnanese followers of Islam who had made the *haj* to Mecca.

The French approach to Lao Papa was calculated to play upon his widely known vanity. Many years before, he had studied astronomy in Istanbul. He had even spent a year in Singapore to verify the information that days and nights on the equator were of equal length. Now, alerted to the presence of the Frenchmen, Lao Papa sent them a series of questions indicating his interest and uncertainty over a number of astronomical matters. The rest was easy. The Frenchmen sent messages indicating their admiration for Lao Papa's learning. Then, in actual audience with the old *haji*, Garnier rendered him the best service of all. When he had sojourned in Singapore, Lao Papa had bought a powerful telescope, but on his return the instrument had proved useless. Could the Frenchmen help? Indeed they could, and with the aid of a vise Garnier adjusted the misplaced lenses. For Lao Papa the wishes of the expedition became his own. At their request he furnished a lengthy letter calling on his co-religionists to aid the Frenchmen in their travels towards Ta-li. Despite his association with the imperial forces, the eighty-year-old Lao Papa was still highly regarded by many on the other side, and the French party now seemed well prepared for a passage to the west.

Leaving K'un-ming on January 8, the Frenchmen knew that they were within two weeks' march of the great Yangtze River, which could carry them swiftly towards Shanghai on the China coast. This was a seductive vision but it was counterbalanced by a conviction of the scientific value of exploring the unknown country to the west. Accompanied at this stage of their travels by Father Fenouil, the explorers reached the town of Yang-lin in the afternoon of January 9. Once again there was a potentially dangerous incident. No sooner had the French party occupied quarters for the night in an inn than a party of Chinese soldiers sought to dislodge them from their rooms. The invaders were repulsed by the expedition's escort and, while the Vietnamese militiamen stood guard with fixed bayonets, Garnier called on Father Fenouil to alert the frustrated soldiery to the expedition's status and the nature of the passports its members bore.

When this seemed to have no effect, Garnier told Fenouil to

announce that the French party was ready to fire if there were any further attempts to enter the expedition's quarters. "But," Garnier notes, "the poor priest had completely lost his head before the unheard of audacity of our Vietnamese escort . . . instead of threats he addressed entreaties to the soldiers; he admitted our faults; he suggested that we were ignorant of local customs; he said we begged for pardon." In short, the missionary acted as Garnier would have expected. When, following Fenouil's statements, a Chinese officer rushed in to make himself master of the apparently craven foreigners, he ran against one of the escort's bayonets. An end to the fracas came soon afterward. Lagrée, already suffering acutely from the dysentery that was to bring his death in a matter of weeks, left Garnier and the agitated Fenouil to bring the encounter to a satisfactory conclusion.

The next day Fenouil left the party to travel north and a little east to Ch'ü-ching, his base in the relatively secure eastern regions of the province. Even Garnier seems to have been touched by the prospect that this missionary might never see another of his countrymen again. The party's immediate concern, however, was to travel forward as quickly as possible despite the declining health of the leader and of an increasing number of the escort. On January 14 Lagrée was too ill with a fever to permit the party's further progress. As they continued on the next day, their passage was painfully slow. Although they had horses with them, Lagrée was too ill to remain seated in the saddle, and he took his turn, along with the sick members of the escort, in an improvised litter. The party was traveling over a plateau eight thousand feet high, and to match the cold there was a bare landscape, whipped by a wind that whistled mournfully through the steep valleys running away on either side of their route. Not until January 18 was there any relief. On that day the party completed its travel to Hui-tse by boat, putting behind them for the moment the need to walk. As the early winter evening closed about them, the expedition came to Hui-tse.

With the party halted once more, Lagrée made a supreme effort to carry out his role as leader. For a few days he was able to meet with the local officials and even to consider the possibility that he too would travel to Ta-li. But his indomitable spirit could not overcome the fatigue resulting from the combined effect of three illnesses. By now it was unmistakable that he was suffering from a severe form of dysentery. Like many, perhaps all the others in the party, he had come to look on malaria as an almost routine affair. And finally his throat infection, which in the warmer air of Cambodia had improved if not disappeared, once more troubled him.

The last meeting of the whole expedition was held about Lagrée's sickbed. Again he sought opinions rather than giving an order. The group was in favor of an effort to reach Ta-li, and Lagrée gave his approval. Shortly after, a letter arrived from Father Fenouil telling the explorers that the local mandarins at Hui-tse were disturbed at the expedition's plans and begging them not to attempt a journey to Ta-li. This could only spur Garnier on. There was no way of knowing, he argued, what had inspired the missionary to write in these terms. His opinion was not to be trusted since he was clearly swayed by whatever was the most powerful influence at any given time. The second-in-command now drafted instructions for the party about to attempt the journey to the west. This was the last official document signed by Lagrée. How much he grasped of its import is debatable. In any event, the final paragraph of the instructions seemed as much due to Garnier's inspiration as to thought by the now almost totally incapacitated leader. "If, at any time in the journey," the final paragraph read, "Monsieur Garnier thinks that he might easily reach a point anywhere on the Mekong, he should do so alone and as quickly as possible." As a last instruction from Lagrée, Garnier could not ask for more.

On January 30 the party heading for Ta-li left Lagrée at Hui-tse. Shaking the leader's hand for the last time were Garnier, Thorel, Delaporte, and de Carné. They were to be accompanied by five men from the escort. This time Garnier was not traveling with Tei, whose own illness forced him to remain at the base camp. Left behind with Lagrée were Joubert, the French sailor Mouëllo, and three members of the Vietnamese escort.

CHAPTER X

LAGRÉE COMES HOME

$\mathcal{D}$oudart de Lagrée, the handsome naval officer who could trace his ancestry back to a manor in fifteenth-century Brittany, was a gaunt, dying man when Garnier and his companions left Hui-tse and headed west for Ta-li. The wonder is that he should have survived so long. Why his companions should have thought that the leader they left behind them was likely to recover is uncertain, yet this was the general opinion. Partly this hope seems to have been irrational, a feeling that, having survived so long, Lagrée would not die now; somehow he would overcome disease and be able to reach the Yangtze and travel with the rest of the party down to the sea. More rationally there were other straws of hope to grasp. There could be no doubt that Lagrée was a desperately ill man, but to have triumphed over the illnesses he had already suffered suggested a remarkable constitution. The explorers were well used to sudden death in both Europe and Asia. The fact that Lagrée had survived to this point seemed, therefore, to offer hope. Then, too, there was hope born of medical ignorance. However able they might be, Joubert and Thorel practiced medicine in an age that still knew little about the cause and effective treatment of tropical diseases. They knew the results, all too well, but decades had yet to pass before a thorough knowledge of amoebic dysentery would emerge, and nearly eighty years before a sure remedy would be found.

For it is now certain that Lagrée, lying stricken in Hui-tse, was a victim of advanced amoebic dysentery, racked not only by uncontrollable diarrhoea but suffering also from abscesses on his liver. The disease was in its terminal stages when Lagrée was left in the care of Joubert and Mouëllo. Even before Garnier's group departed, the old problem of his infected throat had come to plague Lagrée again. Adding further to the stricken man's discomfort were undiagnosed pains in his side and shoulder. Joubert, himself seriously weakened as the result of fever, had to treat his patient under severe conditions. In bitter winter weather, Lagrée was lodged in an unheated room. During February and March the temperature in the room never rose above forty-one degrees Fahrenheit; at its coldest, the temperature inside dropped several degrees below freezing. These were trying circumstances even for a healthy man; for someone in Lagrée's condition they were a terrible further drain on his failing strength. Even worse, racked as he was by dysentery, Lagrée's infected throat made normal eating impossible. For a period Joubert had to feed him artificially.

Mentally, too, Lagrée was exhausted. Until the final stages of the expedition's journey he had felt that his role a leader required him to make all decisions of importance without consulting his companions. Once in China, and lacking an interpreter, Lagrée had assumed most of the responsibility for conducting the uncertain exchanges the party had with officialdom along the way. The strain of attempting to make himself understood, and the worry that he might not have been successful in interpreting what was said in return, weighed heavily on his mind. The brief, even deliberately laconic descriptions that remain of the final weeks of Lagrée's life say little of the result of this mental strain, other than noting his exhaustion. But in the reports of his conversations with Joubert, which continually returned to the same subjects, a picture of the dying man's fevered and obsessive thoughts emerges. Tortured by physical pain, Lagrée wondered if he had been right in permitting Garnier and his companions to depart. He repeatedly reviewed the failure of the party to find a navigable route along the Mekong. Turning anxiously to Joubert for reassurance, he expressed conviction that the Red River was navigable, saying again and again, "Should we have no other triumph to bear back to France, our time and our suffering will not have been wasted."

He worried, too, about his family in France. Never having married himself, Lagrée idolized his elder brother's wife and her children. To her he sent his long personal letters, full of brotherly affection and requests for news of the children. Unknown to Lagrée, while he was dying in Hui-tse, news came to Joubert that this woman and one of her sons had died. How the letter reached Hui-tse from the authorities in Saigon who sent on this news is unclear, another minor mystery in the expedition's history. Lagrée, however, was never to learn of the loss. Joubert, fearing for the effect the report might have on his weakening patient, kept the news from him.

As February drew to an end Joubert was faced with a terrible dilemma. Temporarily at least, Lagrée's infected throat had recovered and he was able to take nourishment. But the pain and distress caused by the liver abscesses continued. Joubert decided to operate. This was a decision of last recourse. In barely imaginable conditions, Joubert opened an abscess on Lagrée's liver and drained it, drawing off half a liter of pus mixed with blood. He did not know that there was another abscess, which remained untouched by this desperate surgical intervention. For a brief period the operation appeared to promise success, though pus continued to drain from the opened abscess. If nothing else, Lagrée's pain was eased, and at this point too he was diverted by the presence of another familiar face. Father Fenouil, learning of Lagrée's condition, had traveled from his base at Ch'ü-ching to join the group lodged at Hui-tse. Joubert hoped Fenouil might have communion wine with him that he could use to comfort Lagrée, but the missionary had none. Only after messengers had been sent nearly two hundred miles north to the residence of the French Apostolic Vicar for the region was it possible to obtain a little port wine for Lagrée.

As March began, Joubert allowed himself to hope that his patient might recover. Lagrée was even able to walk about a little. He talked with Joubert and Fenouil, and accepted the devoted assistance of Mouëllo. But Joubert's hopes were false and Lagrée's apparent recovery illusory. On March 6 his condition suddenly deteriorated. The weather changed for the worse, and with the return of chilling cold and fierce winds Lagrée's infected throat once more made eating impossible. At the same time his more serious illness entered its final phase. Lagrée knew that this was the end, and he waited for it with the courage he had shown throughout his life. One final concern weighed on his mind. He was determined that his private papers should be destroyed. When Joubert tried to dissuade him, Lagrée insisted. "A man's work," he maintained repeatedly, "can only be completed by himself." Reluctantly, with inner reservations, Joubert gave his assurance to Lagrée; should the leader die, his private papers, his notes on the expedition, would all be burned. Even in the setting of Lagrée's dying days, his insistence on such destruction appears strange, an almost atavistic embrace of the view that a man's possessions should perish with him.

The end came on March 12. Expected as it was, Lagrée's death was no less moving for the little group that stood about his corpse. In the chill of winter, with his fellow officers an uncertain distance away to the west, Joubert sadly started to arrange for Lagrée's burial. Believing that the body would remain forever in Chinese soil, Joubert removed the dead man's heart and fashioned a leaden box in which to place the organ for return to France. Local craftsmen found the idea repugnant and would not spare Joubert this labor. Mindful of his medical status, he made a post-mortem examination and found the second abscess. Unchecked, the amoebic dysentery had ravaged Lagrée's liver. We can only speculate on the effects of Joubert's operation, performed as it was before men understood the importance of asepsis.

Placing Lagrée's body in a heavy Chinese coffin, Joubert supervised the burial in a corner of the gardens surrounding a pagoda outside Hui-tse's walls. Above the grave he built a small monument, modeled on the one the explorers had raised above Henri Mouhot's grave near Luang Prabang.

There was nothing more to do but wait. Joubert had written to his companions to alert them to Lagrée's increasingly serious illness, and then finally to tell them of his death. He could not know how long it would be before the letters reached Garnier. One thing Joubert could not bring himself to do: burn Lagrée's papers as the dead man had insisted. No less a man of the nineteenth century than his fellow explorers, Joubert was conscious of the sacred character accorded to a dying man's orders. Yet he hesitated. To burn the leader's notebooks would be to destroy vital records. He could not do it, and he waited for the others to return so that the question could be debated. Three weeks passed before Joubert was able to share his account of Lagrée's last days with the other explorers. It was a grim period of waiting in the isolated administrative center whose only active commerce seemed to be in wooden coffins.

It was not until April 3 that Garnier, the first of the party to arrive, returned to Hui-tse. Only on April 2 had he received certain news of Lagrée's death.

On leaving Hui-tse on January 30, Garnier and his companions had struck west; lacking detailed geographical knowledge of the route to Ta-li, and beyond, and with continuing uncertainty about the political situation, they were determined to move as swiftly as possible towards their goal. On their first day they were rewarded by a distant glimpse of the great valley of the Yangtze. The explorers could follow its course as it ran like a deep furrow through the towering mountains. They still could not see the river itself, but that sight came a day later. On the last day of January, standing nineteen hundred feet above the river's banks, they saw the Yangtze for the first time. From this height its waters seemed clear and deep, and the explorers reflected on the fact that they were the first travelers to have seen and charted the Yangtze so far from the sea since the time of Marco Polo.

They could afford little time for reflection, and the party hurried down the steep zigzag path that brought them to a settlement beside the river. Here they returned, briefly, to a subtropical world. After a near-freezing start to their day, the temperature in the river valley was in the middle sixties, and surrounding them was the vegetation of a warmer clime, clumps of banana trees and stands of sugar cane. This was a brief respite. They purchased enough horses to have one for every two men in the party, then crossed the Yangtze and headed west towards

Hui-li. This settlement did not lie on the direct route to Ta-li, but their plan was to travel so as to put off a confrontation with the Muslim forces until the last possible moment.

Four hours of hard climbing brought the explorers back to the plateau above the river and, once more, into a winter world. The road they followed lay across a series of ravines and valleys and took them to even higher altitudes. On February 3 and 4 the party moved through heavy snow; at one stage their route brought them to a height of nearly ten thousand feet above sea level. These were worse conditions than any they had encountered to date, and men and horses suffered as they slipped and stumbled on the icy paths. By February 5 conditions had improved. The route they followed took them down to a well-cultivated valley, and in the evening the party halted at Hui-li, a major market town.

Because of its size and importance, Garnier had hoped to find useful intelligence in Hui-li. But he was disappointed. The local officials were courteous, but there was no way that they and Garnier could exchange information. All that could be done was to wait until the party reached a point even farther west where the presence of a Chinese Catholic priest would permit exchanges in Latin. Two days after their arrival in Hui-li, the party was traveling west again. For the next two days Garnier was in constant pain. A sudden lung infection caused him acute discomfort as the party continued across the high plateau. At times he could scarcely breathe, and he could only move forward with constant assistance. Two men of the escort were needed to hold him on his horse when he rode.

When, late on February 8, the party dropped down rapidly to a settlement at a mere two thousand feet, and not far from the Yangtze, Garnier found immediate relief. In less than ten days and under frequently severe conditions the explorers had covered some one hundred miles as the crow flies—substantially more along the winding and precipitous routes they had followed. They had been as high as ten thousand feet at one stage and down to a little more than two thousand feet at another. Back at this more comfortable altitude, with Garnier in need of rest to recover from his illness and the rest of the party close to exhaustion, a halt of three days was decided.

The hoped-for meeting with Father Lu, the Chinese priest, took place on February 11. This Chinese Catholic had been trained for his vocation at the French missionary college on the island of Penang. He spoke Latin, and the party was able through their conversations with him to learn something of the situation that lay ahead. Trade, the explorers quickly learned, was brisk between the regions of western Yunnan controlled by the Islamic rebels and those parts lying under the authority of the imperial government. In a classically practical Chinese fashion, this was seen as beneficial to all concerned, not least the officials of each side who might have had to look elsewhere for income if the standard arrangements for bribes and gifts were interrupted. But apart from traders, the Muslims were strict in their refusal to allow any other traveler to pass through their lines. Father Lu held little hope for their success. One thing he could, however, tell them. The tiny French missionary post near Ta-li, of which they had previously heard mention, was still in existence. Located only a few days' march from the heart of the Muslim rebel state, a lone French priest, Father Leguilcher, was, in defiance of all logic, allowed by the insurgents to tend his tiny flock. Given Father Fenouil's close identification with the imperial cause, it was strange indeed to think of a missionary left unmolested near the rebel base.

In the face of continuing uncertainty, Garnier decided to push directly towards Ta-li. If there were major difficulties to be overcome, then the sooner these were encountered the better. After three days of further travel, the party crossed the Yangtze on February 16 and headed south and west. They still had not come to a Muslim post and their route now took them again to an altitude of about six thousand feet. As darkness fell about them the party reached a straggling mountain hamlet. The inhabitants fled at their approach, fearing that the explorers were yet another armed band come to loot and pillage. Slowly, however, they were persuaded to return by the Chinese servant who was now attached to the party. Recommended to the explorers by Father

Lu, this former employee of a French missionary bishop provided urbane and knowledgeable assistance.

No sooner had calm returned to the tiny settlement than it was shattered by an outburst of shouting and anger. De Carné was the cause. At the end of the day it was his job to feed the party's horses. Having searched unsuccessfully for mangers in which to place feed, he decided on an improvisation. A large Chinese coffin lay in one corner of a shed; what could be better as a substitute into which to pour the feed? He started to move the coffin's heavy lid, only to be disturbed by an angry woman who shouted and wept at the offense being committed. Coffins here, as elsewhere in China, were revered objects, often the proud possession of a person for many years before death. To contemplate using a coffin as a feeding trough for horses was at best an offense against good manners. But worse was involved here, for the coffin's owner was asleep inside.

This was a rare occasion of humorous relief, an event to be laughed about, to de Carné's embarrassment, after the distressed woman had been pacified and her husband allowed to lie unmolested. There was little that was jovial ahead of them, yet the next few days were pleasant enough.

The explorers found that Father Lu had been right when he spoke of a brisk trade between the Muslim and imperial areas. They passed countless caravans moving east and west along their route, the commercial traffic contrasting with the barely inhabited region they now traversed. The path rose and fell, then rose and fell again. Seldom were the Frenchmen able to see more than three hundred yards in front of them. Despite the cold and their fatigue they could still respond to the natural beauty that lay within view. In apparent defiance of the season the wooded hills dominating the landscape were covered with red and white rhododendron bushes in full flower, while along the fast-running streams there were clusters of camellia trees, their blooms a delicate pink.

On the evening of February 19 they encountered the first Muslim post. The meeting was chilly. With the missionary bishop's former servant acting as his interpreter, Garnier matched his firmness and hauteur to that of the Muslim officer he now met. It was the type of situation that delighted Garnier:

> He told me that there were . . . at Pin-ch'uan, where we would arrive in four days' time, leaders more important than he, and whose decision I would have to accept. "It is to them," I replied, "that I will show my passports." He now more forcefully demanded that I show them to him. I declared that I was too important an official and he too negligible for me to agree to such a show of deference. He threatened to prevent my departure. I laughed in his face and amused myself by showing him our weapons, particularly our revolvers. He was greatly surprised and told me that even in Ta-li there was nothing to match them.

Once again, after long debate, Garnier triumphed. The party left, unimpeded, next morning. Convinced of his own superiority and genuinely unafraid, Garnier, like so many other nineteenth-century Europeans, saw himself as living proof of the capacity of white men to dominate the world.

The scenic pleasures of the previous few days were at an end as the explorers moved into a higher region. Flowers and shrubs disappeared as they marched through a bleak landscape made more forbidding by the evidence of the rebels' justice along the way. Set beside the various crossroads they passed were roughly constructed gallows with the bodies of hanged men twisting slowly in the wind. A grisly audience to watch over the gallows, the heads of other enemies rotted atop tall bamboo poles. And, much more immediately disturbing to the tired explorers, there was snow. The path continued to rise until they once again passed over a ridge more than nine thousand feet high, the second time their route had risen to this height in less than three weeks of hard traveling.

Temporary relief was in sight. Once over the towering pass, the explorers' route lay through less elevated country. On February 21 they reached Pin-ch'uan, an important settlement in a wide valley, and here they found rebel officials who were ready to aid them on their way. A sight of Lao Papa's letter and judicious distribution of presents seemed all that was required. Two days later, after one further tiring climb to more than nine thousand feet, the explorers came to Father Leguilcher's mission station. They were exhausted after eleven consecutive days of the most arduous marching they had undertaken during the entire expedition. Delaporte was ill with fever, and all were in need of rest. Garnier took almost malicious pleasure in recounting the shocked reaction of the missionary who met them. Leguilcher's face betrayed his disbelief that this rough-clad, bearded figure who stood before him, a revolver on his hip and a carbine in his hand, could be Lieutenant Garnier of the French navy. "You will not blame us for our lack of proper clothing?" Garnier asked the astounded priest.

For all their exhaustion, and despite Delaporte's illness, the party did not rest long at Leguilcher's mission station. The end of February was at hand, and the party had still not reached Ta-li, let alone the Mekong lying farther west. On February 25 they left the mission station, accompanied by Father Leguilcher; four days later they saw the great lake on which the city of Ta-li was set. Leguilcher was little help as Garnier planned the next steps of their journey. The missionary priest had managed to remain where he was largely by keeping himself out of sight. Whenever there had been a suggestion that Islamic troops might be in the region of his mission station, he had fled with his few followers deeper into the hills. It was years since he had visited Ta-li, and he could give no useful information on the political situation there.

A few of Leguilcher's fearful converts followed the party as it descended to the plain where the large but narrow lake ran north and south, with Ta-li on its western shore. These worried Christians transmitted the gossip and rumor they gathered to the French priest, who then passed it to Garnier. They told of "sixteen Europeans" who had come to Ta-li with "four Malay" assistants to make bombs for the Islamic rebels. The Europeans, it was said, had been executed and the Malays were in chains. Garnier wisely disregarded it all.

Twenty miles from Ta-li the explorers were brought to a halt. The land between the lake shore and the snow-covered mountains that rose abruptly to the west narrowed at this point, so that a fortress could completely dominate passage north and south. Garnier had already sent ahead a request for permission to enter Ta-li. Seeking a positive response from Tu Wen-hsiu, the Muslim leader who now styled himself Sultan of Ta-li, he had joined to his own letter the words of recommendation written by Lao Papa. The commander of the fortress that barred their way was polite but unyielding. They had to remain until permission to proceed was sent from Ta-li. It came on March 1. The next day, early in the morning, they began their march to the Muslim capital.

Traveling over a paved road, the explorers entered Ta-li in the middle of the afternoon. Their arrival was expected and a large crowd pressed about them, waking memories of the incidents earlier in the expedition's journey when curiosity seekers had become a threat to safety. Followed by the crowd, but escorted by Muslim soldiers, they came to the center of the city. Here they halted in front of the Sultan's palace, a grim fortified building. None of the Frenchmen was ready for the next development. As they stood expectantly below the palace walls, a soldier grasped de Carné's hair, jerking his face upward, apparently seeking to show the European's face to a hidden watcher in the palace. De Carné struck out and the soldier retreated, his face bloodied. For an instant it seemed that the French party might be overwhelmed. The crowd surged forward, only to hesitate before the expedition's escort who stood with their long bayonets fixed to their rifles. Two Muslim officials hastily intervened to bring the incident to a close. It was an unhappy augury for the future.

Lodged in the south of the city, the explorers received a visit from the most senior Muslim official they had yet met. He was courteous but seemed unconvinced of their claims to be explorers, and he was quite unready to believe they were French. Surely, he insisted, they were English. Bridling at this supreme insult, Garnier nonetheless thought that some progress was achieved. Ceremonial for a visit to the Sultan was agreed upon; the Frenchmen could greet the Muslim ruler with a European bow, and it seemed that the party could retain their arms. Yet some uncertainty hung over the exchange, and shortly after two more senior officials called on the French party. They asked much the same questions appearing to take it amiss that Garnier did not claim to have been sent to Ta-li by his ruler for the express purpose of paying respect to the Sultan. They also departed and Garnier began to contemplate his most special desire. If all went well, he would leave his companions to rest in Ta-li and would himself march rapidly to the Mekong. The river which had exercised such a continuous fascination over him was only four days' fast marching further west, and known here as the river "whose waves are vast."

By noon of the next day the hollowness of such hopes was made clear. Early in the morning of March 3 a messenger came requiring Father Leguilcher's presence at the Sultan's palace. The missionary returned three hours later totally discouraged. The Sultan would not receive the explorers, who must leave Ta-li the next day. A follower of Islam he might be, but his message to the French party was couched in the formal and dismissive phrases of the Chinese empire. Did they not know that, only a few days before, he had executed three Malays? "If I choose not to take the lives of those who accompany you," he told Leguilcher, "it is because of my concern for their position as foreigners and respect for the letters of recommendation they carry. But let them hasten to depart." Leguilcher was frightened to the point where he could scarcely speak. But he did try, unsuccessfully, to convince the Sultan and his retinue that these were not Englishmen who lodged within the city. They did not or would not believe him.

There was now no choice but to retreat. The French party was heavily outnumbered, and the city was full of soldiers who, however poorly armed, could readily overcome the small group should they choose. Garnier's growing concern was the possibility that their ordered expulsion might become imprisonment instead. Before first light, at five in the morning, the French party left their lodgings. To avoid traveling through the streets of Ta-li, they passed through the city walls by the south gate, then skirted the city's eastern flank to rejoin the great road leading north. There was no incident. Twenty miles of forced marching later, however, as they reached the great fortress that controlled the road, a confrontation threatened. The Muslim officer who had escorted them this far told them he had orders to retain the party at this point. Garnier refused to stop and the party passed on to take up quarters beyond the fortress, clear of immediate obstructions to their passage east.

After some hours' rest and further unsatisfactory exchanges with local officials, who tried to persuade the Frenchmen to wait for orders from the Sultan, Garnier resolved to place an even greater distance between his party and Ta-li. Despite the twenty miles they had marched earlier in the day, the tired men set off again in the evening and continued to the head of the lake. All had gone well, it seemed, until a major loss was discovered. Along with the rest of his equipment, Delaporte had been carrying a gold bar. It represented half of the party's financial resources, and it was no longer there. They searched in the dark, but without success. The need to speed their return to the east was suddenly made even more urgent than before.

The next night was as worrying as any. Still well within the territory controlled by the Muslim rebels, the French party could not avoid the settlements lying in their paths. On the evening of March 6 the Governor of the town where they had halted demanded the presence of Leguilcher. Garnier would not let the priest go, despite the threats of Muslim soldiers that this refusal would end with the Frenchmen's heads rotting on the gallows in the marketplace. In the morning, with the rest of the party escorting him, Leguilcher learned from the Governor that he had orders to escort the French party through the territory held by the Islamic rebels. Convinced that this was a trap, Garnier refused to comply. They would travel independently, and he made clear their readiness to fight if impeded. They were allowed to go on alone.

If the members of the expedition were retreating in good order, the situation was more acutely dangerous for the missionary. Deeply distressed, he accepted Garnier's argument that to stay at his mission station would be unnecessarily risky. As the party continued on its eastward route, Leguilcher accompanied them.

Eleven days after the dawn departure from Ta-li the party was back in imperial territory. They had failed to gain their dearest wish, the sighting and mapping of the upper Mekong, but their visit to Ta-li was still remarkable. In spite of the speed with which they had traveled and the constant need to be alert against potential dangers, they had mapped and sketched the area through which they passed with care and in astounding detail.

With these problems behind them the explorers hoped for news of their leader. Reaching Hui-li at the beginning of the last week of March, they found news of a sort. Soldiers who had come from Hui-tse gave conflicting reports. Some said Lagrée had already moved on to I-pin, north on the Yangtze; others spoke of his being still in Hui-tse on March 9. On March 25 the anxious travelers had the first world that Lagrée was dead, only to have this denied the next day. Puzzled and deeply worried by these uncertain rumors, they hurried on, sending runners north and east to try to gain certain information. They received it on April 2, when a messenger returned with a letter for Garnier from Joubert. Lagrée, they learned, had been dead for three weeks. Garnier immediately pressed on ahead for Hui-tse.

With the return of Garnier's party and the news of Lagrée's death, the expedition was at its end, symbolically and in fact. Garnier was now the senior member of the party, and automatically the new leader. His first decision, once the rest of the party rejoined him at Hui-tse, may seem strange by twentieth-century standards. By the values of the 1860s it was right and proper. Lagrée's body, which had lain for three weeks in its grave, should be exhumed with ceremony. They gathered for this awful moment on April 5. In its heavy coffin Lagrée's body would be borne by porters into I-pin. In singular testimony to the respect that the dead leader inspired, the men of the expedition's escort volunteered to carry out this task. The labor was, in fact, beyond them, for these almost anonymous men were suffering from disease and exhaustion no less than the Europeans. With the exception of Tei, Garnier's special companion, none in the escort emerges from the records left behind as a personality in his own right. Yet they were essential members of the expedition.

So, too, was the sailor Mouëllo, who was now charged with the duty of destroying Lagrée's papers. Joubert had been reluctant to carry out this charge, but Garnier saw no choice. Under his new leader's eyes Mouëllo carried out his last sad duty to the man he had served so well. Although Lagrée had died in Mouëllo's arms, neither this fact nor his final burning of the papers are described in either Garnier's official or unofficial published accounts of the expedition. For an otherwise generous man, Garnier's omission is surprising, even in the rigid world of rank and discipline that was his own.

When the expedition left Hui-tse on April 7, seven of the fourteen remaining members of the party were ill with fever. The mission's tasks were at an end, but the route to I-pin, on the Yangtze, remained to be covered. With the coming of spring there was frequent rain to plague the exhausted men and hinder the Chinese porters carrying Lagrée's coffin. Only after a week of debilitating stages over mountain paths did the explorers descend to lower altitudes and more temperate conditions. On April 20 they were finally able to embark on a boat that could carry them down one of the Yangtze's tributaries to the great river itself, and so to I-pin. When, on April 26, the mission reached that important commercial center its members were, in Garnier's words, at the end of their energies and resources, but they had "not lost their courage." It was well that they retained some of their courage, for once again at I-pin they had to confront the dangerous results of curiosity that turned to rage when the explorers refused to be treated as some kind of circus exhibit.

The party left I-pin on May 9. Four slow weeks of travel by junk brought them to Hankow and, although Garnier did not realize it at the time, a fateful meeting. Among the French community who fêted the members of the expedition once they reached Hankow was Jean Dupuis. In 1868 he had already spent nearly eight years in the Far East, gradually building a thriving trade in armaments. When he met the members of the French mission he was forty years old, fluent in Chinese and accustomed to dressing in mandarin robes. Later British generations might have called him a rough diamond, for he would have been an entertaining figure in a club, if not necessarily the type of man to be invited home. But for all his Chinese ways, he remained proudly French.

He also possessed a commercial flair, a sense of where money might be made. We may readily believe that he listened attentively when the explorers, particularly Joubert, who came from the same region of France, told Dupuis of their belief that the Red River was navigable to the sea, at the very least from the borders of Tonkin with China. Later Dupuis was to deny bitterly that any such conversation took place, claiming that he had known of the Red River's possibilities for years, indeed since 1861. It is hard to credit this claim. Dupuis was resourceful, not least in lying, but even in his own publications he provides no convincing evidence. Shortly after the expedition left Hankow, however, he started his preparations to visit Yunnan, where the opportunities for an arms salesman seemed unlimited. Garnier and Dupuis were to meet again, five years later.

When, after passing by way of Shanghai, the members of the expedition reached Saigon on June 29, 1868, they had been absent for two years and twenty-four days. Whatever the disappointments they had encountered in their survey of the Mekong, or their hopes for the future use of the Red River, it was the recital of the distances they had traveled that impressed those who greeted them in the French colony. And with good cause, for during their travels the explorers had mapped some four thousand miles that had never been surveyed previously. Garnier alone had mapped more than three thousand one hundred and fifty miles of territory. The course of the Mekong had been established and areas of southwestern China visited that had never previously been seen by a European. All this had been accomplished under conditions a modern traveler finds difficult to imagine.

Garnier had vowed to return Lagrée's body to French soil, and in Saigon it was buried with funerary pomp. The naval shipyard furnished lead for a new coffin, and the Governor of

Cochinchina led the mourners. Lagrée's old missionary friend from the time when they had both been in Cambodia together, Bishop Miche, gave the benediction beside the tomb. Lagrée, it seemed, had come home to his people. In France, however, the news of Lagrée's death and the return of the French expedition passed almost without comment. Going back to Paris before the end of 1868, Garnier was first disillusioned and then angry. Worse, he was in addition the target of a bitter personal denunciation by Louis de Carné as the tension of the expedition flamed into open accusation and counter accusation in France. For a period, at least, success had a bitter taste in Garnier's mouth.

A merchant train in Yunnan

CHAPTER XI

POST-MORTEM IN PARIS

$\mathcal{T}$he explorers returned to the "City of Light," to passing attention, bitterness, and altercations. Paris, at the end of 1868, was poised unknowing before disaster. The Franco-Prussian War was a bare two years away, and the conditions which would hasten that French debacle were, with the wisdom of hindsight, clearly and vividly present. But no one seemed even to guess that Napoleon III's empire had so little time to run. Like a patient afflicted by a terminal disease but unaware of the fact, there was business as usual. Business of all sorts: the Emperor puzzled over ways to gain a revival of electoral approval; the Empress dreamed of young Prince Louis' finally coming into an imperial inheritance; the French armed forces, complacent after years of peace, paraded and postured in their brilliant uniforms; and *le tout-Paris*, the elegant men, the actress-courtesans, the *demimondaines*, danced to waltzes, to polkas, and to cancans before fading into a gaslit darkness for marginally more private pleasures.

This was not Garnier's world, nor that of de Carné, Joubert, Delaporte, and Thorel. Whatever differences there were between them, they had been, and still were, men of action. Unlike most of the splendidly clad army officers who clattered in cavalry troops along the boulevards or gathered at the famous cafés, the members of the expedition had actually known danger and the threat of death. Not that the military fops they now saw proved to be cowards two years later. Lack of leadership rather than cowardice doomed the French forces then. The essential difference between the Mekong's explorers and the society to which they returned was a difference of values. Above all, they had believed in the importance of the painful search for a southern route into China. They found, in general, that their countrymen did not.

Always outspoken, Garnier did not wait long to make his critical views public. He had been invited to visit the imperial court and had spoken with the Emperor. But no new official decoration followed this occasion. The Geographical Society of Paris showed its admiration for both Lagrée and Garnier by awarding them a shared medal in April 1869, yet this could only be recognized as applause from the converted. And, already, the bitter private criticisms had begun. Admiral de La Grandière, the former Governor of Cochinchina, deeply resented any suggestion that Garnier had conceived the exploration project. Whatever honor was to be gained, he argued, some share should be his. In a stormy confrontation, in late January 1869, Garnier's former superior upbraided him for supposedly unwarranted and disloyal behavior. If Garnier's account is correct, La Grandière, in his anger and disappointment, hovered between threats and pleas, begging finally to have the original instructions, which the Admiral had signed, included in the official report on the expedition that Garnier was preparing.

In a mood of growing annoyance and frustration, Garnier fired his first broadside. In a series of articles for the influential *Revue Maritime et Coloniale*, beginning in April 1869, he traced the ironic contrast faced by a man who returned to France from "distant countries" only to find "the profound indifference of opinion towards all that is associated with national grandeur." It was a general problem, but he would testify to a particular example. Virtually nobody, or so it seemed to him, cared about the results of the Mekong expedition:

> A recent voyage of exploration finally made it possible to pull together the few scattered facts that we possessed on this region in a certain fashion. This journey, which has brought a lively response in England, which has had its initial findings published in Germany, is scarcely known in France despite the fact that it was led by a Frenchman, Commander Doudart de Lagrée, who unhappily died near the end of his glorious undertaking.

There was good and immediate reason for Garnier's annoyance and anger, even if he did not choose to detail it in his articles. On top of all the other instances of slight and personal antagonism, there seemed only the most limited interest within the government itself about what the explorers had found in their travels. In January 1869, Garnier's own ministry, Navy and the Colonies, had sent a circular inquiry to the other major government departments. Would they, the circular asked, subscribe to the important publication that was now being prepared on the Mekong expedition's journey from Saigon into China? The replies were an extraordinary mixture of hesitation, shortsightedness, and, rarely, enthusiasm. Within a day, the Ministry of Justice sent its reply: no funds were available. The Quai d'Orsay, conscious that de Carné had been its representative on the expedition, was ready to take five sets of the projected two volumes. But the Ministry of Fine Arts, apparently dubious about "art" outside a European setting, was unready to make any decision before seeing the finished product.

So it went. The Ministry of Education and the Ministry of Agriculture, Commerce, and Public Works seemed to show more interest than most of the other ministries. With their orders for thirty and fifteen sets respectively, they certainly eclipsed the Ministry of War. Two and a half months after the inquiry was originally circulated a reply came back from War to the Navy; the ministry would purchase one copy! A century later, the publication that the ministries treated in such a cavalier fashion is a prized bibliographic rarity.

Worst of all for Garnier's personal peace of mind, the suggestion was bruited about that he was deliberately seeking to diminish the importance of his dead leader, Doudart de Lagrée. This was an essentially unfair charge, but to some extent Garnier was to blame for its being leveled. In the atmosphere of petty backbiting and official parsimony that now existed he set out to publicize the expedition and, unwisely, to emphasize his own role as leader in the final months. On one public occasion he failed to mention the duties carried out by de Carné; in a later discussion of the French party's journey he failed to mention de

Carné at all. Then, in addressing the Paris Geographical Society, he allowed himself to be described as "leader" of the Mekong expedition. This decision should probably be viewed as nothing more than a young man's folly, a case of enthusiasm and pride overcoming good sense. Perhaps, too, his readiness to use the title of leader was Garnier's calculated effort to make clear his major part in bringing the mission's journey to some kind of successful conclusion. Whatever was the case, Garnier found that he had ended by bringing the disputes of the past clearly into the open.

De Carné led the charge, but he spoke for those who resented Garnier's thirst for glory. Whether, his claims notwithstanding, he acted for any other members of the expedition, seems, at best, doubtful. We know, however, that Lagrée's relatives and close friends resented the way the living Garnier was eclipsing the memory of his dead leader. And one needs little imagination to see a gleeful La Grandière reading the accusatory letter de Carné now published in the Paris press. Lieutenant Garnier, de Carné asserted, was willfully misleading the public, though whether he was entirely to blame or was influenced by an ambitious relative was not clear. Whatever the case, the picture being presented to the world was wrong. In de Carné's eyes, Garnier was seeking to create the impression that he had led the Mekong expedition for nearly twelve months rather than merely for the final three. And through all this, de Carné's bitter complaint continued, Garnier denigrated the role of his companions:

> Believe me, Monsieur, it has cost me dearly to alert the public to our disputes. I might not have done so if there were only personal differences between us. But as I have already had the honor to say to you, I am only a spokesman for my traveling companions.
>
> I summarize, Monsieur, by protesting against the omission of my name from the document I have indicated, against the newspaper articles you have written from time to time to draw attention to yourself to the detriment of your traveling companions, and finally against the claims you have made concerning the command of the expedition.

The complaints had a paranoid air. Even if there was some small factual basis for de Carné's attack, there seemed much more direct connection with his now unstable personality and rapidly deteriorating physical health. Of all the personal disputes and antagonisms to emerge in the course of the expedition, none seem to have been sharper than those involving de Carné. Ambitious for success, he had not been able to disguise his intellectual arrogance, which saw little value in opinions other than his own. Yet this arrogance went hand in hand with the ambiguous relationship he had with those he admired. Doudart de Lagrée was such a person, though possibly de Carné's admiration for the expedition's leader was greater after than it was before Lagrée's death. This admiration, however, had to contend with the resentment the young diplomat felt for the treatment Lagrée had accorded him. De Carné had been aware of Lagrée's critical judgments. He seems, nonetheless, to have forgiven them. No such forgiveness was accorded Garnier, the man who had never hidden his view that de Carné was a "parasite."

In the nature of things, de Carné's attack did not have widespread importance, partly because, in the final analysis, only a limited few were interested in the accusations and counter accusations. When he wrote his attack on Garnier, de Carné had little more than a year to live. He had returned to France gravely ill with dysentery. For a brief period there was a remission, but he was dead before the end of the Franco-Prussian War. Although the intensely bitter flavor of de Carné's attacks on Garnier was not matched in the more restrained arguments during the next few years, the expedition's leadership remained an issue. And the argument goes on today.

For Garnier, meanwhile, thoughts for the future became as important as the difficulties of the past and the demands of the present. He worked on his official report of the expedition under irritatingly adverse conditions. His earlier protests about the lack of governmental interest seemed only too justified. By October 1869 his precarious financial position forced him to raise the question of expenses with his superiors. In view of the costs he had met personally for photography, internal travel in France, and translation, could he not, he asked, receive some financial assistance? The dry, dusty tones of the functionary's response echo hollowly more than one hundred years later. A month after Garnier made his request the chief financial inspector at the Ministry of the Navy was still studying the matter and pointing to the problems involved. It was all very well to note that only one hundred francs each month were under discussion, he chided, on November 15, 1869. "Here the question of expenditure is nothing. The danger of precedent is all." A month later Garnier was pursuing another tack. Could the ministry not, at least, deal with another of the explorers' financial claims? None of the naval members of the expedition had yet received their promised compensation for personal equipment lost along the way.

In trying and ungrateful circumstances that persisted throughout 1869, Garnier dreamed of new adventures. He considered resigning from the navy and traveling to China once more. Thoughts of commercial success floated through his mind. If only the Chinese middlemen could be bypassed there was a fortune to be made by purchasing tea and silk in southwestern China and shipping it to Europe. But more than all these things he dreamed of marriage.

His plans and hopes for marriage are revealed in two frank letters from early 1869. Read in a later age, Garnier's discussion and assessment of himself and his need for a wife have a calculating, even cold air. Considered in the context of the late 1860s and in terms of Garnier's personal background, such a judgment must be modified, if not entirely dismissed. Writing to an old school friend, Joseph Perre, Garnier concluded that "I have, for too long, acted contrary to my nature in refusing to give my heart the place it demands in my personality." In terms of a career, he went on, it was difficult indeed to think of embracing a profession in France itself that would require him to act in a dry and purely self-directed fashion. For this reason he still thought of challenges overseas. But to embark on fresh adventures required some new and vital cause for action. Without stating the matter directly in this letter, Garnier had in mind a wife. For, as he now admitted, "there is an affectionate and tender side to my character that I have never entirely succeeded in subduing."

By the end of January 1869, he was able to commit his ideas to paper without hesitation; he wrote as a weary thirty-year-old:

> . . . these days when I return home, my brain tired out from writing and reading tiresome scribbles, I find the house empty indeed. . . . I must have, I feel, another self, a young confidant who will be my mirror, my reflection, who will encourage me to live, lead me to the battle by suggesting to me that her well-being and happiness are my goal. This is the source of energy I must have. I sense it. Without it I find life so terribly lacking and I feel deeply indifferent to everything.

Within six months Garnier had found his mirror. In twelve months he was married. Joseph Perre had summoned him to Avignon to meet Claire Knight. If he had rightly judged that Claire would touch Garnier's heart, Perre may not have properly gauged the difficulties that lay ahead of a proposal of marriage. Claire was the daughter of a Scottish merchant, long resident in Avignon and married to a Frenchwoman. It was she, narrow-mindedly provincial, who raised the obstacles. Claire was the youngest of three daughters and should wait till her sisters were married. Garnier was a Catholic, nominally at least, and Claire was Protestant. And, of course, despite the naval regulation requiring an officer to marry only when a dowry was provided, Claire could not on any account furnish the *dot*.

One by one the difficulties were overcome. A way was found to circumvent the problem of a dowry. A clause allowing for any children to be educated as Protestants were inserted in the marriage contract. Claire's father looked in a kindly fashion on the marriage, even if his fearsomely bourgeois wife did not. The enraptured Garnier married his adoring Claire on January 19, 1870.

Garnier's marriage, despite the calculation and planning involved, was a love match. In the still difficult months ahead, the marriage sustained his spirit. Only twelve days before the wedding, he wrote to Joseph Perre to complain bitterly about the whispering campaign that continued to criticize his readiness to claim credit for the achievements of the Mekong expedition. In terms of personal politics, he wrote, if he was making any progress forward it was with a cripple's gait. His decision to accept the award presented by the Royal Geographical society in London was, in his detractors' eyes, an affront to Lagrée's memory; it did not seem to matter that he had asked for the award to be shared with the dead leader. It was "the same old story: Monsieur Lagrée's name is evoked to bring me down."

Yet when he wrote this chagrined comment, in June 1870, a new dawn did not seem too far distant. He was truly happy with Claire and, just as importantly, he looked forward to leaving France for a journey to China that would combine further exploration with his plans for commercial enterprise. As for publishing the results of the Mekong mission, this enterprise too was now reaching a satisfactory conclusion. He was to bring out a "popular" account of the expedition's journey in the well-known travel magazine *Tour de Monde*, starting in July. The official version, in two volumes, with Delaporte, Joubert, and Thorel each providing contributions, would go to press in November.

The outbreak of the Franco-Prussian War on July 15, 1870, changed everything. Garnier's rapid transfers from post to post in the early months of the war reflected the disorganization reigning in the French ranks. Called back to active duty, he first assumed command of a gunboat on the Rhine. Within a month he had been called away from that post to be aide-de-camp to an admiral commanding a reserve naval squadron at Brest. Only a few weeks later, still before the end of August, his duties changed once more; he was given the command of an armed launch on the Seine. Barely had he assumed this post when he was ordered to another staff position, as aide-de-camp to Admiral Méquet who, as the Prussian siege closed about Paris, commanded one of the defense sectors on the southern perimeter of the city. Soon, temporarily promoted to commander, Garnier became Méquet's chief of staff.

There was little chance of glory for Garnier in the course of the Prussian siege of Paris. He behaved, as might be expected, with courage, but with an increasingly heavy heart. Separated from the now pregnant Claire, even Garnier was forced to real-

Night camp beside the Mekong.

Ethnic groups from South Yunnan province. The explorers were struck by the diversity of races in southwestern China.

View of P'uerh, one of the towns on the explorers' route through southwestern China. See pages 137-40.

Traveling through a ravine near Sop Yong.
See page 121.

Panoramic views of two of the important Chinese
cities the explorers passed through after leaving
the Mekong; Yüan-chiang on the Red River
(above, see page 143) and I-pin on the Yangtze
(below, see pages 180-81).

Ethnic groups of the Ta-li region. See pages 176-80.

The lake at Ta-li, the westernmost point in China reached by the explorers.

*The surviving explorers and their escort
at Hankow in June 1868, two years after
the expedition left Saigon. It was here
that Garnier had his fateful meeting with
Jean Dupuis. See page 181.*

ize that the weakness and ineptitude of France's leaders offered little hope for a successful end to the war. He recorded his views in a journal that he subsequently published anonymously, bitterly noting the incompetence of his superiors and scornfully deriding the military pretensions of the hastily raised Paris militia.

When the end came and Paris surrendered to the Germans, Garnier was outraged by the terms of the armistice — so much so that he took his case to the press, protesting against the terms permitting Prussian forces to seize the remaining French war material intact. He quickly paid for this zeal. Due for promotion to the permanent rank of commander, his name was now removed from the list of officers eligible for advancement. This setback was the beginning of a new series of disappointments. He agreed to stand for election to the National Assembly but did not gain the seat. More importantly, in his own eyes, he failed in his candidature for election to the Institut de France; the honor of membership in that famous body's geographical section was not forthcoming, largely because the feeling still existed that he sought prestige more correctly belonging to Lagrée. Even his property had suffered in the course of the war; the small house he had bought years before in the country was almost destroyed in the battles that had taken place outside Paris. There was only one clear cause for happiness. On the day Paris surrendered, Claire gave birth to a daughter.

Garnier's own description of his position, once the war had come to an end and he had retreated to quarters away from central Paris, made his official position and his state of mind clear. "Whatever happens," he wrote to Perre, "I have withdrawn like Achilles into my tent." Separating himself from the bitter confrontation and then open conflict of the Commune period, he buried himself in his books and in writing. The depth of his disillusion emerges in a comment made in April 1871. With Joseph Perre as his only confidant, apart from Claire, he admitted his readiness to forget the present in favor of studying the history of Asia. "I forget France and Germany and everything else to live in the middle of the unknown past."

Such a retreat scarcely suited the deeper forces of Garnier's personality. His scholarly instincts had to be relieved by action. Of the surviving members of the Mekong party, only he and Delaporte now thought of travel back to Asia. Joubert had left the navy in 1869, and Thorel in 1871. For Garnier and Delaporte, however, there was little continuing attraction to be found in living in France. Once preparations for publishing the official report of the Mekong expedition were in hand again—the war had put an end to all work of this sort—decisions could be made for the future.

Garnier's first concern was to travel back to China. Despite his interest in the Red River, the old question of the Mekong's source remained demandingly in his mind. At the same time, he was conscious of his need for money. The journey he now planned to make through China would have a dual purpose. He would seek geographical information and his fortune. If he could find the commercial source of silk and tea in western China, then wealth would be his. With these plans in mind, Garnier was ready to cede to Delaporte the opportunity to make a scientific survey of the Red River.

This concession was made easier by the knowledge Garnier now had of a journey made by Jean Dupuis. The French merchant the explorers had met in Hankow, in 1868, had not waited long to follow up the information he had gained from them about the Red River. Starting from K'un-ming in January 1871, Dupuis had traveled to the Red River and then down its course to Yen-Bay, a Vietnamese administrative post about halfway between the border with China and the river's entry into the sea. The assumptions of the Mekong explorers had proved correct. Commerce could pass up and down the Red River. But it had been Dupuis, rather than one of the explorers, who had demonstrated it. As Garnier considered his own plans for the future, Dupuis had already returned to France, reported his findings to the Ministry of the Navy and the Colonies, and left France for Vietnam again. He departed without firm, or at least public, assurances that his plans to use the Red River for commerce with Yunnan would have French support. But the Minister was prepared to offer assistance with transport, and a measure of official approval was certainly implied in the ready authorization which Dupuis received to purchase cannon for his Chinese clients. The arrangement fell into that shadowy world where officials give "semi-official" support to risky projects: with success there can be a ringing affirmation of association, while failure brings forth a bland denial of knowledge. Whatever the qualifications involved, this guarded assistance to Dupuis was to have fatal consequences for Garnier little more than a year later.

In late 1872, however, as Garnier prepared to leave for China, the horizon seemed unblemished by a single cloud. There could scarcely have been another time in Garnier's life when reality seemed to accord so well with his own hopes. He had put the disappointments of the past behind him. The navy had granted him leave, and he found backers who were ready to finance his attempts to find the commercial sources of the rich silk and costly tea exported from China. As he prepared to set out for China with Claire, who was now expecting another child, Garnier was gripped by enthusiasm for the future. A friend who saw him just before he left France records the rhapsodic tones in which Garnier spoke of the months ahead. His friends, Garnier observed, could not understand why he wanted to return to Asia. They could not realize the wonder of it all:

> ... it is not at all depressing: Laos is marvelous. But even more so is Yunnan with its great mineral resources; with the high blast furnaces, the hissing machines, the forges, the rolling mills that Europe could install there in abundance, what might it not become? But what of Tibet? And what of the western provinces of China, these provinces which are, up till now, the source of silk, transported in an uncertain fashion, with expensive intermediaries who, from stop to stop, from hand to hand, raise the price ten times before the goods arrive at warehouses on the coast ... ?
>
> For the moment my goal lies between Shanghai and Tibet. There a mystery waits to be unraveled. These Chinese middlemen of whom I have spoken, who gain such a profit from the transport of tea and silk, understandably make a secret of the origin of the goods, so as to maintain a monopoly of their contacts with the unknown producers. Up till now this secret had been maintained because of the difficulties of the routes. But, once the European has overcome this problem,

once he has penetrated into these lands, you will see an economic revolution whose effect will be felt in the old world. We will have tea and silk at half their present price.

It was a happy prospect; exploration through unknown regions with the possibility of personal gain and a triumph for defeated France. Years later Garnier's brother, Léon, suggested that the new journey to the East was undertaken in a melancholy mood, that the weight of accumulated disappointments was such as to rob the enterprise of the hopes more easily held in the past. Garnier's own writings do not seem to bear this out. True, there were setbacks and sadnesses to record along the way. Some were deeply personal. In November Claire gave birth, prematurely, to another daughter. Within a week the child was dead.

Other disappointments mixed personal with public concerns. The brief visit Garnier made to Saigon, en route to China, had left him with mixed feelings. He was glad to return to the region where he had started his administrative career, but in the four years which had passed since he lasted visited the colony so little seemed to have changed. And so many reforms remained to be made. Yet beyond such concerns lay the prospect of the unknown. With a passion akin to that felt by Sir Richard Burton, Charles Doughty, or St. John Philby, Garnier longed for distant unexplored places. When he had left Marseilles, in early October 1872, he looked forward to fulfilling his desire. The hope still remained when he reached Shanghai in mid-November.

The next months were filled for Garnier with almost constant travel. Leaving Claire in Shanghai, he visited Peking, to arrange for the passports he would need during his projected journey towards Tibet. Passports for such distant regions could not be gained quickly. In the interim Garnier set off on a further reconnaissance. His goal was Chungking, the city in western China that he planned to use as a jumping-off point for his projected travel to Tibet. For three months, between early May and the end of July, he traveled alone in central China, without escort or interpreter, his only regular company two spaniels named Ta-li and Lhasa: one named with memory of the past, the other with hope for the future.

There was a possibility that passports for Tibet might overtake him along the way, but nothing of the sort happened. No documents awaited him at Chungking, the most westerly point of his journey, nor at Hankow, when he returned to the east. Instead, when he came joyfully back to Shanghai and Claire, at the beginning of August 1873, there was a brief but important letter waiting for him. It came from the French Governor of Cochinchina, Admiral Dupré, and it asked Garnier to come to Saigon as soon as possible. "I have," Dupré wrote, "some matters of importance to discuss with you."

Garnier needed little urging, yet he set off for Saigon without realizing the true import of Dupré's summons. His newest dream was to be appointed as a French representative in Yunnan, and he was unaware of how fast events were moving in Tonkin. For the "matters of importance" of Dupré's letter were the potentially dangerous developments taking place in northern Vietnam. Since the end of 1872 Dupuis had pursued his aim of taking commercial advantage of the Red River. By mid-1873 Dupuis' activities threatened to spark armed conflict.

This was not known to Garnier and he had not expected a sudden call to duty from Saigon. Nor, it seems fair to say, had Dupré seized on Garnier as his first choice for the delicate program of action he had in mind for Tonkin. Yet it would have been difficult for Dupré not to have had Garnier's name in mind when his thoughts turned to risky new initiatives. The explorer had passed through Saigon only seven months before, and his passion for adventure, combined with a knowledge of the region, was matched by few. Cumbersome theories of historical accident are not necessary to explain the manner in which Garnier was once more moved back to the center of the stage.

For a decade Garnier's life had been sustained by hopes for exploration, adventure and the pursuit of France's imperial glory. The mysteries of the upper Mekong were still unsolved, but in the summons he now had from Dupré there seemed a possibility that his hopes for the Red River might become a reality. Uninformed though he was of Dupuis' activities and difficulties, Garnier's dream of holding a post in Yunnan was linked with an expectation that commerce would be able to pass up and down the Red River, the river that had so fascinated the explorers in November 1867, when they were still pressing north to K'unming. Later, Garnier wrote of his thoughts at that time, recording his firm conviction that the opening of the Red River should be "an exclusively French affair."

As he read Dupré's letter in Shanghai, he found a call that could not be ignored. Duty and glory beckoned irresistibly, and he sailed for Saigon on August 17, a bare week after rejoining Claire at the end of a three-month absence. Garnier was about to embark on the last and most sharply debated episode of his career. There was still one more river to cross.

CHAPTER XII

ONE MORE RIVER

The final act in Garnier's dramatic life had all the qualities of adventure, disputed glory and tragedy appropriate to a heroic figure in the nineteenth century. This is not altogether surprising. Garnier, after all, wrote much of the script himself, but he did so within a web of circumstance which ensured that the drama was played out with apparently unlimited promise of private prestige and public imperial glory. For a brief period Jean Dupuis by himself, and then he and Garnier together, held the hope of transforming the French position in the Far East. With tenuous, or at best ambiguous, official connection these two men for a time defied the Government of Vietnam, intrigued with and against the Chinese imperial authorities, and acted as an advance guard for those Frenchmen who were determined that the tricolor should fly over the whole of Indochina. As a reflection of the imperial spirit at its best, or worst, the final months of Garnier's life are a notable model.

Even today, despite the long searches that have been carried out in official archives and private papers, we do not know exactly what Admiral Dupré told Garnier in August 1873. The official instructions, which Garnier received from Dupré on October 10, 1873, were remarkable more for the caution of their tone than for explicit recommendations matching Garnier's later actions. But there need be no doubt about the basic reasons for the summons Dupré sent to Garnier: first and foremost, the explorer of the Mekong was to bring some sort of order to the muddled and dangerous situation in which Jean Dupuis found himself in Hanoi.

When, more than five years earlier, the ragged and exhausted members of the Mekong mission had met Jean Dupuis in

Hankow, the astute French businessman had recognized the vital commercial significance of their information about the Red River. As an arms merchant, Dupuis did not need to be told that a river route into Yunnan, such as they believed the Red River to be, offered great opportunities. Instead of having to ship weapons by the long and costly way of the Yangtze, and then overland to the Yunnanese capital at K'un-ming, the Red River could be used to transport supplies into the heart of southwestern China. After two visits to the capital of Yunnan, Dupuis had, by early 1871, a major commission to purchase arms for the imperial forces. His plan was to buy these in France, then bring them up the Red River to Yunnan.

In theory, the explorers, and Dupuis, were correct in their belief that the river could be used for commerce. Politically, however, Dupuis' plan brought him face to face with a situation of staggering complexity. It would be hard to draw a map that showed clearly the political situation along the Red River's course in the years between 1868 and 1874. Running in a southeasterly direction through Yunnan, the river traversed this province of China, where imperial and Muslim forces were still joined in unresolved conflict. For the eastern portions of Yunnan to the border of China with Vietnam, superiority, but no more, lay with the imperial forces. Once the border was crossed, however, the complications grew greater.

Vietnam's northern border coincided with the border of the Chinese province of Kwangsi, and in the late 1860s this region was still disturbed in the aftermath of the Taiping rebellion, which had broken out in the 1850s. One important result of that rebellion, and its collapse, was the seepage into northern Vietnam of large groups of Chinese bandits. These were men who had fought, or pillaged, on one side or the other during the course of the rebellion. The two largest groups of bandits to move into the Vietnamese border regions after 1865 were the Black Flag and Yellow Flag bandits—they took their names from the banners they carried into battle.

The border region, where they now established themselves, was a traditionally separate area. To the north, in China, lay the

Jean Dupuis, "Explorer of the Red River."

great southern provinces of Kwangtung and Kwangsi. The southernmost sections of these provinces were, in a fashion similar to Yunnan, at the outer extremity of China's imperial influence. In some areas ethnic Chinese settlers were only a minority among the various hill peoples of the Chinese deep south. Over the border in Vietnam, the Vietnamese Government barely had control of the mountainous northern areas. At the best of times the Tonkinese uplands were a distant and even sinister region in Vietnamese eyes, a land more sympathetic to bandits and freebooters than to agriculture and the orderly pattern of a Confucian administrative system. And in the later 1860s the border lands were not enjoying their best times. Indeed the Black Flags and Yellow Flags controlled large sections of the Red River, so that the first Vietnamese Government outpost was at Yen-Bay, nearly one hundred and forty miles from the point where the river passed from China into Vietnam.

There were further complications, which could be either an obstacle or an opportunity for a man with Dupuis' aims. The Vietnamese of Tonkin were by no means all convinced adherents of the cause of the ruling dynasty in Hue. This dynasty, the Nguyen, had united Vietnam, after more than a century of wars, in 1802. But in Tonkin there were those who still dreamed of the return of an earlier dynasty, the Le. They showed their feelings in periodic rebellion. As for the representatives of the Vietnamese court who were based in Tonkin, many of these mandarins were at least as concerned not to give offense to the Chinese bandits who roamed the region as to follow the directives of their emperor.

The circumstances seemed to offer much to an adventurer, or imperialist, ready to take risks in the hope of gaining advantage from divided, and so weakened, authority. Dupuis was ready to take the commercial risk. Then, later, when Dupuis' position was threatened, Admiral Dupré, Governor of Cochinchina, saw a way to join imperial interest to the businessman's hopes for profit.

Jean Dupuis was far too knowledgeable not to recognize the possibility of danger in his use of the Red River. But danger had to be weighed against the financial returns that might be gained. The affair that began with his visit to France in 1872, when he bought armaments on behalf of Chinese officials in Yunnan, was just such a case. He left France largely content with the semi-official backing of the authorities in Paris for his trading venture up the Red River. To have assurances from the Minister of the Navy that he would receive assistance in the matter of transport was an important step towards success. Once he reached Saigon, in May 1872, there was even more cause for satisfaction. Many of the officials whom he met there were more than ready to render covert assistance to their fellow countryman. He was, after all, about to involve himself in the affairs of Tonkin, an area many of them hoped might eventually pass under French control, despite established French policy, which recognized Vietnamese sovereignty over that region. When Dupuis returned to the China coast to complete his arrangements, he seemed justified in believing that he had, at least, an important measure of support within the French colonial administration.

At the end of 1872 Jean Dupuis entered the Red River at the head of a private flotilla—two gunboats, a steam launch, and a junk, all heavily laden with the seven thousand rifles, thirty artillery pieces, and ammunition Dupuis had bought in France. Money could buy most things in Shanghai and Hong Kong, and Dupuis had found little difficulty in recruiting twenty-seven Europeans and some one hundred and twenty Chinese, and other Asians, to accompany him in his enterprise. They were, European and Asian alike, a cutthroat crew, the scourings of the Eastern Seas. With their gunboats and modern weapons they were ready, if necessary, to fight their way up the Red River. They were certainly well enough armed to override the objections to their passage of the Vietnamese authorities in Hanoi. For Dupuis the fact that he had a commission from the Chinese leaders in Yunnan was more important than his lack of any permission from the Vietnamese Government to proceed up the Red River.

His first encounter with the Vietnamese mandarins suggested that he had his priorities in the right order. Angry though they might be, the mandarins had to let him proceed. Trans-shipping the arms into junks, Dupuis' force moved up the Red River and into Yunnan. Difficulties had to be overcome, but he had demonstrated that the river was navigable for commerce. In mid-March he was in K'un-ming, successfully and profitably concluding his sale.

So far Dupuis' plans had been successful. When he returned to Hanoi, at the beginning of April 1873, he looked to the prospect of continuing operations; and he came accompanied by an escort of troops from Yunnan, about a hundred and fifty men provided by Ma Ju-lung, the general whom the Mekong explorers had met five years before. Dupuis now had enough men at his disposal to prevent the Vietnamese from chasing him from the country. They were not sufficient, however, to overcome a growing Vietnamese determination that the French commercial adventurer should not again use the Red River to his advantage.

From May onwards tension mounted in Hanoi. Dupuis tried to send a cargo of salt up the river, reckoning on an enormous profit by the time he had transported this scarce commodity into Yunnan. The Vietnamese thwarted his plans, ensuring by force and threat that no craft should be available to transport the salt. When, on June 2, Dupuis was threatened with arrest himself, he riposted by assuming a posture of open hostility. Flying the French flag, as if to suggest some official connection, Dupuis defied the Vietnamese authorities, acting with the aid of his troops as if Hanoi was little more than a foreign concession. This was an unsatisfactory situation for all concerned, and both Dupuis and the Vietnamese authorities sent messages to Admiral Dupré in Saigon seeking a resolution.

The historical problem, still not fully resolved, is to know the exact nature of Dupré's reaction to the situation in Hanoi. The evidence strongly suggests that he was ready and willing to use the occasion of Dupuis' difficulties as a basis for a French advance into northern Vietnam. But neither in written instructions nor in public statements was he ready to admit such an intention, which would not only have represented a hostile act at a time when France was at peace with the Vietnamese court but would also have gone against what was, at least in public terms, the policy of the authorities in Paris. It was in these circumstances that he summoned Garnier to Saigon to receive his secret instructions.

Officially, Garnier was asked by Dupré to extricate Dupuis from the complicated Hanoi scene. By the time Garnier reached Saigon, in August 1873, the risks of real conflict had grown greater. Dupuis was in touch with backers of the fallen Le dynasty, who now offered to help him. Adding further to the complexities of the situation was the presence of Bishop Puginier, a French missionary who proclaimed his devotion to spreading the gospel while less than secretly hoping for the advance of France into a region of Vietnam officially hostile to Christianity. While he insisted to the Vietnamese authorities that he could not play any part in their dispute with the beleaguered business-man, Puginier nevertheless hoped that the situation would end with French intervention in aid of Dupuis, to the benefit of the Church and France.

For Garnier's private ears, however, Dupré had a more im-portant brief. The circumstances in Hanoi were ideal for a sud-den initiative that could ensure France's assuming a position in northern Vietnam. It was an old refrain sung to a new tune. Es-tablishing a position in Tonkin would assure France of control of a new route into China, by way of the Red River. In seeking this goal, Garnier was given carte blanche. He was also given instructions that scrupulously avoided identifying Dupré's real aims. If Garnier were to fail, he alone would bear public respon-sibility for aggression against a government with which France officially had no quarrel.

In the twentieth century there is, and need be, little admira-tion for Garnier's conduct. Even in his own time there were Frenchmen, including some friends, who were ready to argue the essential wrongness of his actions. Such judgments would not have made sense to Garnier. In setting forth for Hanoi he was embarked upon the adventure of his life. To be responsible for the seizure of new territory for France would be to match the thoughts he had so often held in the course of the slow jour-ney up the Mekong. He felt no shame, only an overwhelming sense of excitement at the opportunity which was now his. Barely able to hide the true character of Dupré's instructions, his let-ters to Claire and to his friends and relatives in Europe were exultant. Writing to his brother Léon shortly before he left Sai-gon, Garnier's mood was clear: "As for instructions, *carte blanche*! The Admiral is relying on me! Forward then for our beloved France!"

He sailed from Saigon on October 11, at the head of a force of one hundred soldiers. He had hoped to have his old compan-ion Delaporte associated in the venture, but at the last moment

Delaporte was dispatched on a mission to Cambodia. The written instructions Garnier had received form Dupré had spoken of the need to ensure Dupuis' prompt departure from Hanoi; beyond this he was to negotiate the freedom of the Red River to international commerce. Writing to Dupuis ahead of his arrival, Garnier had a different message. The French businessman should not be surprised if, at the start, Garnier did not have close contacts with him. This would not look well. But, he continued, "I can assure you in the most positive fashion that the Admiral does not mean to give up any of the commercial agreements already undertaken. . . . I will soon be in Hanoi and together we can discuss the political situation in the country."

When Garnier reached Hanoi, on November 5, the Vietnamese authorities acted exactly as he would have wished. They received him with ill grace, offered him unsatisfactory quarters, and made clear their view that only one point was open to discussion: the early departure of Dupuis. Ranged against Garnier in the negotiations was Marshal Nguyen Tri Phuong, an old adversary of the French who saw no reason to make concessions to the young naval officer he now faced. The situation had a familiar air for an imperialist in the nineteenth-century world. Garnier, at the head of a combined force of about four hundred men—his own soldiers plus those of Dupuis, not all of whom were fighting men—was ready to risk attack by the much more numerous Vietnamese. The flash point was near.

By November 18 Garnier was ready to proclaim his intentions as "a great mandarin" of France to open the Red River to commerce and to declare that the Vietnamese Government no longer had the right to levy customs duties in Tonkin. The next day he issued an ultimatum. The Vietnamese forces were to render up the Hanoi citadel to his troops. There could be no turning back. The longer he waited, the greater was the chance that his plans might go awry. He and Dupuis were at one in their aims, and Garnier had found in his compatriot a man "full of good sense and patriotism" who would "defer to all my suggestions." Late in the evening of November 19 he wrote to his family in France:

The die is cast! That is to say, the orders are given! I attack tomorrow at the break of day, one hundred and eighty men against the seven thousand behind the walls. If this letter comes to you without a signature, that is without any further addition from me, it is because I have been killed or seriously wounded. In such a case I recommend Claire and my daughter to you. May my friends work together to gain them a suitable pension.

The next morning, in less than an hour, Garnier's small but well-equipped forces gained control of the citadel. As the Vietnamese troops fled into the countryside, leaving the gravely wounded Marshal Nguyen in French hands, Garnier and his curiously mixed band of French soldiers and Dupuis' Chinese auxiliaries extended their presence into the strongholds about Hanoi. Within two weeks he could claim, however temporarily, to be in control of the Red River delta. Continuing to style himself the "great mandarin of France," he issued proclamations promising such mixed blessings as the opening of the Red River to commerce and the removal of the Vietnamese Government's "tyrannical" rule.

It was a fantasy world in which Garnier now worked, though he gave no sign of recognizing the fact. He wrote to friends, instead, of being engaged in the "founding here of either a French protectorate or a new colony, depending on the degree of obstinacy shown by the government at Hue." In his actions, his issuing of proclamations, and his insistence that the Red River should be open to commerce, Garnier proceeded as if his position was beyond challenge. As supporters of the Le, and Vietnamese Christians, spurred on by Puginier and his priests, came to testify to their approval of Garnier's coup, he seemed to have given little thought initially to the possibility of a Vietnamese counterattack. Yet, as he ranged away from Hanoi, directing developments here and there, leading an assault on Nam-Dinh in the southernmost section of the delta, a counterattack was already in preparation, one that was to put an end to this adventure in annexation.

While Garnier had been occupied with developments away from Hanoi, the Vietnamese Government's forces were massing to the west, in the town of Son-Tay, a further thirty miles upstream. Because of the relative ease with which they had established an embryonic French-controlled administration in the Red River delta, Garnier and Dupuis were far too ready to assume that the Vietnamese were incapable of renewing hostilities. By the end of the first week of December, this assumption was very much in question. Not only had the Vietnamese authorities started to mass troops at Son-Tay, but in addition there was the more ominous news that the Vietnamese commander, Hoang Ke Vien, had succeeded in joining to his own forces those of the Black Flag bandits, led by the redoubtable Liu Yung-fu, a battle-tried veteran of the Taiping period. As the days of early December slipped by, the scattered French outposts about Hanoi came under pressure. There were ambushes and brief fire-fights, with neither side gaining a decisive advantage. By mid-December, however, the existence of a real threat to the French position was apparent, and Garnier hurried back to Hanoi to meet it. On December 18 he was in the citadel once more.

His appreciation of the situation was exactly what might have been expected. The attack should be carried to Son-Tay. The next day an unexpected development brought a sudden halt to his plans. The Vietnamese court sent ambassadors to treat with Garnier. It seemed that his goals could be accomplished peacefully. There was agreement that negotiations should open two days later, on Sunday, December 21.

Ever since Garnier's arrival in Hanoi the weather had been ideal for campaigning. The months of November and December are the most attractive of the northern Vietnamese year, fresh, even cold at night, seldom marred by rain during the day. This pattern was maintained on the day the negotiations were to begin; the weather, as one of the participants remarked, was "splendid." Garnier and his officers heard mass celebrated by Bishop Puginier before returning to their duties. With peace seemingly certain, the French soldiers were dismissed after a rifle inspection just before ten o'clock. Only a light guard was posted, as Garnier walked to begin negotiations with the Vietnamese ambassadors.

The alarm was given by Bishop Puginier. Alerted by one of his Vietnamese followers, he rushed to inform Garnier. With the Black Flags forming the advance guard, the Vietnamese army based at Son-Tay was marching on the Hanoi citadel. There was an immediate call to arms, and Garnier deployed his small garrison. For the moment the situation was not desperate. Despite the overwhelming numerical superiority of the forces ranged against them, the French were armed with modern weapons and were solidly protected as long as they remained within the citadel. When Garnier mounted to the western rampart, he and his companions could see that Puginier's informant had been correct. Above the men they could see in the distance, waved, with sinister promise, the great black war flags of the Chinese bandits. There seemed to be five or six hundred men grouped about the flags, with a further two thousand ranged in another force behind them. The presence of an elephant and parasols of office signified to the Frenchmen that a senior Vietnamese was in general charge.

The Black Flags began their attack, moving forward over the broken ground in front of the citadel walls, sheltering behind the clumps of bamboos before dashing forward to fire at the ramparts. In less than twenty minutes the bandit forces were withdrawing, slowly and with discipline, but withdrawing nonetheless. They do not seem to have reckoned on the presence within the citadel of French light artillery, which Garnier used to telling effect.

The initial French success was not a decisive victory, and Garnier was the first to recognize the fact. If the Black Flags and the Vietnamese troops chose to besiege the citadel, the position of those within would soon become perilous. Even more immediately dangerous was the possibility of a concerted attack on all sides of the citadel. Given the small number of men within, such an attack could well succeed. The Black Flags, moreover, had already shown their capacity to fight with discipline. As Garnier saw the matter, there was little choice before him or his men. "The enemy now attacking us," he told his officers, speaking of the Black Flags, "is the only one I fear in Tonkin. We must make a sortie; we cannot leave such an enemy a thousand yards away." Neither he nor the others present seem to have considered the dangerous possibilities of such a decision.

Garnier took command of one of the small bands that set off in pursuit of the Black Flags. He had only a dozen men to accompany him, but with their light field artillery piece they had no reason to doubt that they could better the enemy. Less than half a mile from the citadel, Garnier split his party into two, leaving the artillery piece on a path while he and nine others continued their pursuit across the rice fields. They were nearing the enemy when Garnier further deployed his small group into units of three so they could better engage the Chinese bandits hidden behind the scattered clumps of bamboo.

Perhaps, as a naval officer, he had no sense of the dangers in such an infantry tactic. Possibly there is no better explanation for his decision than his courageous but foolhardy character. Whatever the case, this manner of using his small force was Garnier's fatal error. By the time he was three-quarters of a mile from the citadel, accompanied by only three French sailors, he had reached the area where the Black Flags were waiting in ambush. As he ran to scale a small dike, calling on his men to follow him with fixed bayonets, his foot caught in a depression and he fell—with all the shots in his revolver expended. The sailor nearest to him was killed at almost the same moment as a bullet struck him in the chest, while the remaining two Frenchmen fell back. With Garnier lying helpless, the Black Flags launched themselves at him, hacking and stabbing with swords and lances. In minutes he was dead, his body left on the ground as the bandits bore away his head as a trophy.

While the Black Flags continued to withdraw, the French rallied to collect their dead. Four others had been killed besides Garnier, but for the moment only two of the other bodies were found, to be borne back with the leader's headless corpse. Dupuis' description of Garnier's body lying within the citadel mixed nineteenth-century sentiment with the horror felt in the French ranks at the outcome of the engagement.

. . . I went in to see Garnier's body. He lay between the two sailors. Nothing is more dreadful than these bodies without heads. There
they were, stretched out on the straw, just as they had been carried in
the evening before. Garnier's right arm was stretched out, his left lay
alongside his body. His right foot was still in its boot, the other was
clad only in a white sock. His clothing was in tatters, his body covered with the wounds made by the swords and lances. His stomach
was open, his heart had been torn out . . . his two hands were clenched.
. . . I grasped his hand for the last time, holding his poor, cold right
hand tightly as I swore vengeance.

This was the end of a life and of a dream. When Garnier and
his men fought their short battle on December 21 they did not
know that Dupré, in Saigon, had already decided to undercut
Garnier's initiative. Despite the bitter polemics that followed
Garnier's death, the available records make two things clear.
Dupré's initial inclination was to allow Garnier a free hand. Once
he saw the difficulties resulting from the advantage Garnier had
taken of this leeway, however, and particularly when his superiors in Paris made clear their unreadiness to give any formal approval to a French advance into Tonkin, Dupré was ready to
disavow Garnier's actions. In deciding to send Lieutenant Paul
Philastre to Hanoi as his agent, he signaled his readiness to withdraw from Tonkin. Philastre had already made known his opposition to Garnier's actions. There could be no expectation that
he would compromise Dupré's instructions that French forces
should withdraw from Hanoi.

This was a bitter business. Garnier's companions, with Dupuis
and Bishop Puginier the most vociferous among them, were opposed to withdrawal, but in the end there was nothing they could
do to prevent the course of action Philastre insisted was necessary. The grim reversal of circumstances led to criticism of
Garnier's role even among his companions in Tonkin. One of
them, Jules Harmand, later to be a French proconsul in the East,
had been ecstatic as the tiny force had moved from success to
success. With Garnier's death and the expedition's evident failure, Harmand allowed a harsh note to creep into his view of
developments. Writing to his mother a week after the debacle
outside the Hanoi citadel, he commented sharply on the dead

leader's actions. The expedition's sorry position was the result of Garnier's determination to be its commander. "If, instead of sacrificing everything to his ambition . . . Garnier had asked for six hundred men, Tonkin would today be taken and almost pacified." His leader's insistence on a force of only some one hundred men had been dictated, Harmand observed petulantly, by Garnier's awareness that a larger number would have required a more senior commander. Now France would conclude a treaty with the Vietnamese Government ensuring that no other power had the right to interfere in Vietnam's internal affairs, protecting Catholic missionaries from persecution, and opening Vietnamese ports to commerce; but the central hope of both Garnier and Dupuis was not met—a clause of the treaty explicitly stated that the Red River was closed to foreign navigation. In the eyes of the disappointed supporters of Garnier's efforts, the developments since his death seemed exemplified by the "odious proclamation" pasted up on the walls of Hanoi by Vietnamese officials:

> A certain Garnier was sent to Tonkin for matters connected with commerce, but knowing nothing of business matters he spread disorder in the country and seized four citadels, the capitals of provinces; this is why the ambassador Nguyen and Philastre have come to re-establish the order which had been compromised.

In the long term the treaty Philastre negotiated was to form the basis for further French advance, but in early 1874 the immediate consequences seemed more important. The French, their martyrs unavenged, were to withdraw from Tonkin. Garnier was a hero to his men in Hanoi and in the scattered military posts elsewhere in the Red River delta. His death, in contrast, made him an embarrassment to Dupré. The report the latter sent to his minister called for Garnier's posthumous promotion, but it also strove to separate the dead man's actions from any intentions that Dupré might have held. The Governor was only "imperfectly informed" of developments after Garnier had seized the Hanoi citadel, he insisted. Garnier, he went on, had been imprudent, he had possibly made "mistakes," but then he had paid the ultimate price in expiation. To Claire, Dupré was ready to write of Francis Garnier's "indomitable courage" and "ardent patriotism," but this was a private rather than a public testimonial.

Worse was yet to come. The Government in Paris was unready to honor Garnier's memory as Dupré had suggested. The request that he should receive posthumous promotion to the rank of commander was rejected, as too was the request for authorization to open a national subscription that would raise funds for a statue in Garnier's honor. For the dead man's friends, increasingly angered by the readiness with which officialdom was prepared to forget or condemn Garnier's actions, the rewards accorded Philastre were, perhaps, the unkindest cut of all. When the promotions within the Legion of Honor were announced in August 1874, Philastre's name figured among them. He was named to be an officer of the order, "for exceptional services in Cochinchina and Tonkin." Even Philastre's most vehement critics would not have denied his right to official recognition for services in Cochinchina, but to link his name with Tonkin was too much. It was only too easy to remember that this was a man who had always been ready to defend Vietnamese rights against those of France; indeed, he had gone even further and *married* a Vietnamese.

Throughout this period of sorrowful recrimination Garnier's body still lay in a Hanoi grave. Claire and her late husband's family wished the body to be buried in Saigon; like Lagrée, Garnier should rest in French soil. But when arrangements for the removal of Garnier's corpse began, it was in a very different climate of feeling from that extended to the Mekong expedition's leader. Dupré was no longer Governor of Cochinchina. Instead the chief French official was another admiral, an austere autocrat, the Baron Victor Duperré. For Garnier's partisans, little could be said that was more damaging than that he relied upon Philastre for advice.

As the efforts to bring Garnier's body to Saigon commenced in 1875, Duperré gave blunt notice of his unreadiness to join in official testimonies to the young officer's memory. To an officer acting on Claire Garnier's behalf he refused to sell the lead she sought from the Saigon naval shipyard for an outer coffin; it had to be bought in Singapore. Then to emphasize his view that Garnier was disgraced, Duperré issued further orders. When the body, its head now returned to lie with the trunk, arrived in Saigon, at the beginning of 1876, the governor forbade any general mourning as the coffin was drawn to the cemetery. Only those officers who could justify their presence on the basis of personal friendship had Duperré's permission to take part in the funeral procession. Fewer than half a dozen mourners walked behind the hearse including, to the outrage of Garnier's strongest partisans, Philastre. They would have been even more outraged if they had known that their hero's death was already the subject of a satirical Vietnamese poem, a mock funeral oration that heaped scorn on Garnier's actions in Tonkin.

Dupuis, meanwhile, faced financial disaster. Prevented from using the Red River for commerce, he had, in addition, to contend with the seizure of his goods and small flotilla while the French Government debated the proper course of action to be taken towards him. Still full of fight, he returned to France with two goals: his financial re-establishment and a renewed French advance into Tonkin. For decades he was vigorously engaged in both these tasks. He was growing a little plumper, but above his sweeping mustache his eyes still sparkled with belief in future possibilities. As he besieged the French Government and the Chamber of Deputies with petitions insisting on his right to financial restitution, his unflagging energy led him to write a series of books and pamphlets. In the best nineteenth-century tradition the author's name, on the title page of these works, is followed by the proud affirmation, "Explorer of the Red River."

This Dupuis insisted upon, and it led to yet another sharp exchange with those who cherished the memory of either Garnier or Lagrée. Whatever others might argue, Dupuis declared, the right to be known as both the explorer and the discoverer of the Red River's possibilities belonged to him alone. No matter that Louis Delaporte argued the contrary case, telling of how he and the other members of the Mekong mission had alerted Dupuis to the potentiality of the Red River in 1868 during their halt at

Hankow. The commercial adventurer rejected their position. Again and again he insisted that his own awareness of the river's possibilities dated from as early as 1861. What evidence there is does little to support Dupuis' contention, but it was one he held throughout his life, until his death in obscurity in 1912.

As with so much of the history of the Mekong expedition, the debate as to who first discovered the Red River's commercial possibilities ended with a final twist of irony. Just as the Mekong was found to be impossible for long-distance navigation by craft of any size, so eventually did the Red River prove to have little commercial value. It was, as Dupuis had found, navigable, with some difficulty, from the Gulf of Tonkin into China, but his experience did not represent any general indication of the river's possibilities. Dupuis' arms sales to the imperial forces in Yunnan had been a special case. He had, for a brief period, stood ready to supply the one commodity which the officials in Yunnan required. When, more than a decade later, France did occupy Tonkin, the last thing the new colonial administration wished to see was the use of the Red River as a conduit for arms. In later years the upper waters of the Red River were important for local commerce, but little more.

With Dupuis asserting his right to be regarded as the "discoverer" of the Red River's reputed possibilities, the old dispute between Garnier's and Lagrée's supporters did not end with the death of the two principals. The issue was fought out, in generally restrained terms, with Léon Garnier defending his brother's claims and two of Lagrée's closest friends, Félix Julien and Captain de Villemereuil, acting on his behalf. For the rest, the surviving French explorers faded into the background. Delaporte's failure to join Garnier in the latter's final exploits had a happy consequence for the Mekong expedition's artist. He went, instead, to survey the great Cambodian ruins of Angkor and to use his artistic talents to record the state of the temples before they were cleared of the jungle's embrace. This was the start of a new career, which lasted until Delaporte's death, fifty-two years later at the age of eighty-three. The violin-playing naval officer of the exploration party was transformed into one of France's most eminent authorities on the ruins of Cambodia.

Delaporte outlived all his companions of the Mekong party. Thorel, who remained in contact with Delaporte and introduced him to his future wife, died in 1911. Joubert, who practiced medicine in the provinces after leaving the navy, died in 1893, in his sixty-first year. Mouëllo, Lagrée's faithful orderly, did not survive so long. He died, still serving in the navy, in 1880.

As for Claire, she remained the widow Garnier all her life, never remarrying before her death in 1923. In the fifty long years between the loss of her husband and the end of her own life she did not join in the sharp controversies over the events in Hanoi, nor in the arguments as to who should gain most kudos for the leadership of the Mekong expedition. This was the province of her brother-in-law, Léon. Hers was an obscure life, even including a period when she worked as a secretary to supplement her tiny income. For herself, her daughter, and posterity, she guarded Garnier's letters to remind later generations of the brief period of halcyon joy that she and the young explorer had known.

Yet, as the first explorers slowly slipped out of sight, the idea of the rivers of Indochina offering a route into southwestern China remained alive. Decade after decade, French planners pored over maps still convinced that it ought to be possible to use the Mekong as a link to China; if only the rapids could be conquered, this great river would offer a way to the country that had been so very much in French minds from the earliest days of their colonial presence in Vietnam. In the eighties and nineties, and even into the early twentieth century, plans were made and, more rarely, put into action. All to no avail. Highly powered steam launches could master some of the rapids, but the Khone falls remained a major obstacle to passage from Cambodia into Laos. In Laos itself, navigation above Vientiane was made tortuous and slow by the rapids that had cost the French expedition so much effort. The best that could be done was to link the navigable stretches of river by other, land-based forms of transport. When British naval intelligence produced a handbook on the Indochinese region during the Second World War, the information provided on the Mekong as a navigable route was succinct and to the point. At the end of the 1930s it still took longer to travel by river from Saigon to Luang Prabang than by sea from Saigon to Marseilles. The golden route to China did not lie along the Mekong.

Nor did it lie up the Red River—not, in any event, along the river itself. Despite the major arms sale Dupuis made in 1873, using the river to transport his goods, the Red River remained a commercial backwater. When France did officially follow the policy Garnier embraced in Tonkin, eleven years after his death, the thought of access to China was firmly in the minds of those who both made and executed policy. This access was finally gained with the construction of the Yunnan railway in the early years of the twentieth century. Built on a line roughly parallel with the Red River as far as the Chinese border, the Yunnan railway was a testimony to engineering ingenuity and human greed. To push the track through the staggeringly difficult physical obstacles required an immense expenditure in money and lives. During the seven years required for construction, more than twenty-five thousand coolies died working on the railway, some from accidents but most from malaria. And when it was completed the line proved to be of only the most limited commercial importance. Apart from the profits gained by speculators in Paris, the Yunnan railway was a financial failure. The riches of Yunnan that Garnier so readily conjured up in his mind were, in the final analysis, illusory.

History and historians play strange tricks with men's reputations. The English-speaking world, and beyond, has remembered David Livingstone: Livingstone of Africa, the missionary, the explorer. Few today, however, will remember that he and Garnier shared a special award at the geographical congress held in Antwerp in 1871. Few, even fewer, have heard of Doudart de Lagrée. Yet the expedition he led for so much of its slow and painful progress was seen as a mighty triumph of discovery and endurance one hundred years ago. No greater accolade could be bestowed than that given by Sir Roland Murchison, president of the Royal Geographical Society of London, in 1870. He spoke as the foremost authority on exploration of his day; the man whose judgment was appealed to when questions of priority were in dispute; the arbiter who had declared that John Speke had indeed discovered the source of the Nile. When Murchison assessed the achievement of the Mekong expedition, he called it "the happiest and most complete of the nineteenth century." "Happiness" for a man such as Murchison was, of course, no simple hedonistic value. What he spoke of was the happiness of duty done and a task achieved.

Perhaps it should not be too surprising that Garnier, Lagrée, and the others are unremembered. Their lives and deaths were linked with Asia, and Asia has always occupied a more ambivalent place than Africa in the European mind. Then, too, they were French. Their achievements and their failures have remained, essentially, the preserve of French writers addressing a French audience. Yet the aim of the Mekong River expedition was far more universal in character than its French membership suggests. The French explorers were seeking a way into China, a goal harking back to Marco Polo and stretching into the present when the political route to China is still uncertain for the Western world.

To write of the Mekong explorers, and of Garnier's fatal search for another way into China, is not to celebrate their imperial values. In the long course of Indochinese history they played their small part in the tragedy of French advance and withdrawal, when the flame of the colonial spirit passed to other hands. The interest of the explorers' story lies in more fundamental matters than concern for imperial glory or even the age-old preoccupation with trade routes to China. The real interest of their story stems from their enduring courage in the face of hardships, their resilience after the experience of many bitter failures and all too few successes. In the past, French secular hagiography has often replaced a simple account of the facts of these men's lives and their actions. The facts, in themselves, are eloquent enough.

Yet if hagiography has left its mark, there is always other evidence to remind us that human frailty lurks not far distant, even when heroes pass in review. Among the yellowing papers carefully preserved in the Paris archives that relate to the expedition is correspondence dating from the years 1874–75. The letters deal with requests from Father Fenouil in Yunnan, couched in almost despairing terms as he wrote on behalf of the Governor of Yunnan province. Fenouil wanted to know when some effort would be made to repay the five thousand francs the explorers had, with his assistance, borrowed over seven years before in K'un-ming. It is far from clear that he ever received a reply.

CHAPTER XIII

EPILOGUE–A HUNDRED YEARS LATER

$\mathcal{A}$ century after Lagrée, Garnier, and the other members of
the French party left Saigon on their mission of exploration, much
of the great river over which they traveled remain unchanged.
There have been physical alterations in the passage of more than
one hundred years, but these are dwarfed by the political trans-
formations. The French colony of Cochinchina, where they began their travels, is now in 1975 part of an independent if fragmented Vietnam. Cambodia, which had only recently been placed
under French "protection" when they journeyed through it in
1866, has passed from independence to near disintegration as
the result of a savage civil war.

Further north, in Laos and upstream towards China, the political changes have been, if anything, greater. There was no single state of Laos as the explorers moved slowly towards their
Chinese goal over the dark waters of the Mekong. Even Thailand, in some ways the most resilient of the nineteenth-century
Southeast Asian states, was a very different country, with different boundaries and circumscribed power, one hundred years
ago from the state existing today. The French party traveled
with Thai passports, but some of these were for use in dealing
with petty "kings" whose partly independent domains had
not then passed firmly under the control of the central power
of Bangkok.

As for those northerly regions where the Burmese court un-
easily confronted Chinese power, and where the party experienced one of the most dispiriting and exhausting stages of their
journey, change here has been remarkable but in some ways ex-
traordinarily limited. The fabled Sip Song Panna, still an important entity in late 1867, has ceased to exist. A solitary southeast-

ern segment has passed into the territory of modern Laos, but the remainder is now firmly within the confines of the Chinese state. This represents change indeed. But an observer conscious of history might very well ask skeptical questions about the extent to which real change has taken place outside the borders of China. Maps mark the border regions of China, Thailand, Burma, and Laos with clearly defined lines, as if there were geographical and political order in these still out-of-the-way regions. The confident delineations of the cartographer are an illusion. The question of who rules what and where in this area remains a matter for continuing debate, at times a cause for conflict. Separatist groups of Shans oppose attempts to incorporate them into the Burmese state, and maintain their own armies and a framework of government. In the region where Thai territories join with Burma, the rump of a Chinese Nationalist Army maintains a tenuous existence, more concerned now with the profits to be made from opium trading than with any military goal of confronting the Peking government's forces, which drove the Nationalists south in the late 1940s. Despite the modern weapons used by the competing forces in this "Golden Triangle" area, despite the political aims that have linked opium trading with the American attempt to find allies in the Second Indochinese War, something of the character of the past is retained here. Lagrée and his party encountered a fragmented political structure, open to pressure and manipulation by stronger powers. The same general description is valid today.

Within China itself change has been the most remarkable, by comparison with all the other areas traversed by Lagrée and his companions. The People's Republic of China controls its southwestern province of Yunnan in a manner never achieved by the Chinese imperial dynasties. This is still a distinct region, with its identity marked by the presence of large numbers of non-Chinese inhabitants. But there is no doubt concerning the province's firm links with the government in Peking.

Of all the political changes that have occurred, France's disappearance from the region as a power would surely have been the least expected by the men who suffered so much in the hope of advancing their country's interests. For Garnier the advance of France into the countries of Indochina was a cause to dream about, to work for, and finally to die for. Lagrée and most of the other members of the expedition held the same views, though they expressed them with less passion and eloquence. Here, as in other ways, Louis de Carné was the exception. His passion matched Garnier's, as his public denunciation of the second-in-command revealed. He was never so eloquent a writer, despite almost painful efforts to find a telling phrase. Yet in the final pages of his account of the expedition, written shortly before his death, he revealed a skepticism about France's future in the Indochinese region that was more accurate than Garnier's enthusiastic expectations. He hoped France would succeed, but he also saw the distant possibility that his country might lose its colonies and be regarded as no more than "a school for political casuists."

Later French imperial triumphs in the half-century after the Mekong mission, and the early attempts to capitalize on the Red River, brought profound change to the region. The French position in Vietnam ended with the bitterest possible form of failure, the defeat at Dien-Bien-Phu, but aspects of the French position lingered on after 1954 and the evidence of the French impact is still clear today despite the overlay of the later American influence. The explorers' ghosts drifting through Saigon in the 1960s, one hundred years after they had set forth with such high hopes and cheerful hearts, would still have been able to see buildings dating from their own era. But not many, and few that remained were linked with their original purpose. The Denis Frères building would have been one of the exceptions to the general rule of disappearance and transformation. As important and remarkable in its own way as the better-known British Far Eastern commercial firms, such as Jardine Matheson, Denis Frères grew with French power in Indochina and survived its fall. The original offices still stand by the Saigon waterfront. The shadowed interior, with dark wood furnishings and the decorative presence of great Shanghai jars, strikes the visitor as a curiously unsurprising mixture of southern France and the East.

And the language of the French explorers still remains important, from Saigon to the distant northern provinces of Laos. If the ghosts had passed directly across the street from the Denis Frères building to the ugly Hotel Majestic, as I did in 1966, they might have witnessed a businessmen's banquet where French still reigned supreme among the Vietnamese who met in this transplanted French provincial hotel. Set beside the Saigon River and long known for the view from its upper floors, the Majestic was a place where, in happier times, a diner could look out over seemingly endless green rice fields stretching to the horizon and observe the incongruous sight of large ships "sailing" through the flat land. In this low-lying region, the difference between land and water level is so limited that one quickly loses sight of the river's course as it coils through the green of the rice fields. One hundred years and one month after the Mekong expedition left Saigon was not, however, a happy time, and the view from the Hotel Majestic was not as peaceful as it had been in the past. The river was crowded with the shipping that fueled a war, with the ships, the black water, and the shadowy land beyond bathed in the blue-white beam of a searchlight probing in irregular sweeps to guard against sabotage. This was the surreal background for a banquet complete with inferior French wine and caustic if witty speeches about port congestion, something that was seen as the fault of *les touristes* — the Americans. The evening was a triumph for the power of presumed French values and the French language. These Vietnamese Francophiles were the descendants and the survivors of those among their countrymen whom Garnier thought could be recreated in the image of their colonial masters.

If the explorers' ghosts turned from contemplating men and were granted, instead, the opportunity to see the Mekong delta one hundred years after they tried to journey to the river's source, they could not be other than surprised. Here, if nowhere else, the river and the land about it have been dramatically transformed. When the French first began to establish themselves in Saigon, in the early 1860s, they had many hopes for the region's agricultural possibilities but little concrete evidence that their hopes could be realized. Garnier himself had painted an enthusiastic, if visionary, picture of what might be grown or produced for export in the lands to the west of Saigon. There could be tobacco, cotton, sugar, silk, indigo, building wood, salt, plants for oil and dyes, spices and herbs. All this, he suggested in 1864, could be added to the most fundamental product of all, rice. The equally fundamental problem, which Garnier did not discuss, was that much of the vast delta plain could not be used for agriculture until it had been drained. The enormous amount of dredging and draining required to make the Mekong delta productive was to occupy many decades and still is not complete today. In the process an agricultural transformation has been achieved, at great and continuing human cost. The newly cultivable land did not pass into the hands of a prosperous peasantry, but rather under the exploitative control of rack-renting landlords.

To fly at a low altitude across the Mekong delta is to be rewarded with an extraordinary vision of agricultural richness. From horizon to horizon the dead flat land stretches beneath an observer, the rice a vivid green directly below the aircraft, paling to a smokier tint in the far distance. The scattered points where there is any variation from the standard flatness—the Seven Mountains region far away to the west and the sacred Black Virgin Mountain to the north near Tay-Ninh—only serve to emphasize the vastness of the delta plain.

Although the flatness and the green of the plain provide the first dominant impression, it is not long before one is struck by that other tribute to man's capacity to alter his environment, the canals. Varying greatly in size, these are beyond number. Some are merely local affairs, serving a hamlet and its fields. Others are scores of yards wide and run, straight and uninterrupted, for more than forty miles at a stretch. Nowadays, there are other signs of human activity beyond those provided by the spreading rice plains and the angular pattern of intersecting canals. Great craters mark the path of B-52 carpet-bombing strikes, and distant pillars of smoke are a guide by day to show where, in 1975, artillery is engaged in still unceasing war. An altitude of two thousand feet turns war into an enormous diorama.

The explorers traveled across the delta, along one of the canals built years before the arrival of the French, to join the Mekong and set off on the first stage of their voyage of exploration. If a modern traveler had followed their path one hundred years later, he would have found that their first major stopping place along the way, Phnom Penh, still held something of the royal character so evident in 1866. A new palace had replaced the wooden structures where King Norodom ruled, and a king no longer sat on the Cambodian throne. But the royal ballet troupe still performed its dances beside the river; the dancers posturing with slow, sinuous precision, timing their movements to the music of flutes and gongs that rippled like water passing over stones in a gently falling stream. The music, the dancers' movements, and the shimmering clothes they wore, had scarcely changed in a century; and the ballet was still performed in an open pavilion, which allowed the soft breeze of a tropic night to carry with it the smells and sounds of the river city.

If there was no king, there was a prince who had been king. Prince Norodom Sihanouk, a direct descendant of King Norodom I, was a ruler who, if he inherited nothing else from his great-grandfather, shared that earlier monarch's passionate belief in the need to try and preserve his country's identity. Sihanouk shared other passions with old King Norodom, though a love for "good brandy" was not one of them. As a man who had been king, Sihanouk was no more willing than his great-grandfather had been to brook argument with his decisions; nor was he ready to accept less than regal treatment. His ministers and officials, the diplomats accredited to his government, and any visiting foreign dignitaries were assimilated within his style of life and government to become members of his court. By 1966 the court lacked cohesion, and Sihanouk's power was still slipping, but the sense of majesty remained in part. And the memory was still strong of the last great royal event the kingdom had witnessed; a mere six years earlier, the last Cambodian king had died and had been cremated to the accompaniment of ancient ceremonies, in an extraordinary blending of pomp and gaiety, processions of shaven-headed women and royal elephants, the beating of funeral gongs and the shimmering light of rockets and fireworks.

Apart from the great stupa at the center of the city, Phnom Penh in the 1960s bore little resemblance to the straggling if busy settlement to which the explorers came in 1866. At that time it had a population of less than forty thousand. A hundred years later Phnom Penh's population was perhaps five hundred thousand: Cambodian, Chinese, and Vietnamese, with a scattering of Indians and Europeans. This was a cosmopolitan descendant of the town where Lagrée and his companions made their last purchases of supplies and trade goods. Electric light and modern vehicles had not driven the peddlers from the streets or stilled their cries. The soup seller, his steaming containers hung at either end of a shoulder pole, hawked his wares to the accompaniment of clacking bamboo sticks, the task of a young assistant who walked ahead. The charcoal dealer alternated his long drawn-out cry with the resonant thumping of a hand drum, a tambourine-like instrument with a "clapper" reminiscent of a hand bell. Poverty, disease, and inequities of all sorts lay beneath the surface, yet Phnom Penh seemed a happy city when I lived there in the 1960s. And, in contrast to Saigon, it was.

By 1974, only eight years later, there may have been a million and a half persons crowded into a war-ravaged capital. Phnom Penh had become a city under seige, subject to attack by rockets and artillery. The charm of the tree-lined boulevards, in the center of the city, was marred by the construction of fortified defense points about ministries and residences: sandbags, concrete, and barbed wire have an infinite capacity to diminish the appearance of a city. The greatest transformation, however, lay not so much in the city's center, where foreigners still shielded their minds from reality in the bars and French-style restaurants, as on the edges, where the tragic cost was was reflected in the hundreds of thousands of refugees who had flocked into Phnom Penh. They huddled, family crowded upon family, in shanty towns lacking the most basic services and placed in such a way that they often bore the brunt of random shelling from the city's besiegers.

Beyond Phnom Penh, the Mekong and the land through which it runs were little changed one hundred years after the Frenchmen steamed north and east in their gunboat towards Kratie. Despite the presence of crowded river ferries, fueled by diesel oil or wood, which in the 1960s supplied the readily navigable reaches running up to the Sambor rapids, much of the river's traffic had changed little in the course of a century. Great barges drifted downstream, barely making way in advance of the current under the loose sails rigged to aid their progress. Lateen-rigged fishing boats clawed against the wind, and gondola-like sampans, rowed from the stern by a single oar with skill equal to any found in Venice, crept up and down the river's margins. The villages came down to the banks, the houses partly hidden behind the dark foliage of fruit trees. Pagodas were everywhere, with high peaked roofs of glistening ceramic tiles in patterns of yellow, red, and blue. From the distance these centers of Buddhist worship have an exotic, fantastic air, a promise of richness without and within. Closer inspection is, for an outsider, almost always disappointing. Distantly perceived carved pillars supporting the roof become crudely decorated concrete when viewed near at hand. The colors that appeared mellow and harmonious from afar too often resolve themselves into sharp and conflicting primary shades, roughly daubed on concrete and stucco, lacking harmony with either European or traditional Cambodian esthetics. Inside the pagodas the gilded images of the Buddhas are usually artistically crude, however vital to the devoted villagers who pray before them.

The land along the river from Phnom Penh to beyond Kompong Cham was full of life a century after Lagrée's party passed by. In the 1970s, in sharp contrast, most of the Mekong's course through Cambodia north of Phnom Penh is as far outside our knowledge as it was for the French explorers. As a terrible war has engulfed Cambodia, so have large areas of the country become blanks on the map. A modern cartographer might do little better than seek some twentieth-century equivalent for the device used by his predecessors of a long-distant age. The empty spaces could be filled with the warning "Here be dragons." Farther up the river from Kompong Cham, which had been little more than a minor fishing settlement in 1866, a traveler in the middle 1960s entered another world. This region, too, has been lost to view since 1970, but even before that date few Western travelers passed through Kratie and Stung Treng. As for Cambodians, those not born in this separate area of the northeast seldom traveled there by choice.

Beyond the red cliffs of Krauchmar, north of Kompong Cham, the river enters a region distinct in character and separate from the geographical pattern of central Cambodia. The farther one penetrates, the greater is the lack of reassuring familiarity. Garnier was filled with a sense of depression when he came to Kratie, seeing in the settlement a condemnation of Cambodia's weak king and government. While it was still possible to visit Kratie, and Stung Treng farther north again, the same sense of depression was not far distant. Even if one escaped depression, it was difficult not to be gripped by an awareness of decay in these upcountry river towns.

Kratie, Stung Treng, and the river towns along the Mekong farther north into Laos are all of a pattern. Stuccoed shopfronts line the river bank, built a little above the high-water mark, offering for sale what sometimes seemed the most uninteresting merchandise in the world. Who, I always wondered, was going to buy the rusting hardware, the cheap enamel dishes, the heaped sacks of grain, and the great coils of tarred rope? There must have been customers, for the Chinese merchants, sitting calmly in their singlets, reading out-of-date newspapers sent up from Phnom Penh, would not have remained otherwise.

Back some distance from the river and the shopfronts would be the market, an area with a little more life but lacking the animation of the markets nearer to Phnom Penh. Occasionally, providing a special sense of the strange and the unknown, a tribesman from the hills would appear at the edge of the market, visibly uncomfortable in the trousers he wore only for his rare visits to the town. Such a visitor would stare and be stared at before making his purchases and slipping back to the east, where in the 1960s the forests still offered some hope of sanctuary from the encroaching world. One needed little imagination to see fear in his eyes. Much less than a century had passed since the lowland Cambodians regularly struck out from Kratie and Sambor for slaving raids on the hill peoples.

With a pattern of life dominated by the seasons and the river, these forgotten towns always summoned up for me images from Conrad. Not the images of Conrad's Lord Jim, for no white man ever came to Kratie or Stung Treng or, farther to the north, Savannakhet, with the hope of preserving an ideal against the savage onset of civilization. Instead the semi-fictional world inhabited by some of Conrad's other characters had a semi-factual existence along the Mekong. While the French still held some sway over Indochina, men with no past and less future sat in these little settlements where nothing ever happened. Almayer would have recognized the setting. So, too, would Marlow — but he would have been passing through, pausing only briefly at the bungalow where damp, peeling plaster on the walls had looked old from the day it was first spread over the rough local brick, and where the rough Algerian wine was served diluted over dubiously clean ice, brought up river, wrapped in straw. Not even the brilliant sunshine of the dry season could drive away the sense of hopelessness that cloaked so many of those whose duties called them to a lonely existence on the periphery of the colonial world.

The French in colonial times had their own literature that described and dwelled on the regions distant from Saigon, Hanoi, Hue, or Phnom Penh. Little of this writing is of Conrad's towering quality, but the themes of distance, expatriation, and slow acceptance of local values, are present in the same fashion. There is one major difference: opium played a central part in the French dream of the exotic. The evening pipes were romanticized as if only in the grip of narcotic fumes were it possible to bear with the boredom and monotony of isolation.

When I first visited Kratie, in the early 1960s, changes seemed to be on the way; there was some hope that the town would become the base for a mighty river-development plan, a dam to be built as part of the Mekong River Project. For a period, foreign engineers bustled about. Landrovers, splattered with red mud, roared off each day towards drilling sites being explored by an Australian engineering survey team. When I revisited the area in September 1966, all this seemed forgotten; the character of the town had slipped back towards the past. The pilot survey for the dam had been completed, but there was no intention to take action in the immediate future. Life in Kratie had resumed its usual somnolent pace.

The Cambodian officials in these regions in the middle 1960s were affected by their surroundings, unconsciously adopting the ways and attitudes of those half-forgotten Frenchmen whom they had replaced. They looked at the Mekong rushing in flood past their town, the river's waters the color of strong tea with the barest splash of milk, and found it as threatening as did any Frenchman fresh from the Ecole Coloniale on the Avenue de l'Observatoire in Paris. To spend an evening with them in Kratie—with the province's Governor, the army doctor, and the chief forestry official—was to be reminded that expatriation takes many guises. There was some talk of Phnom Penh and current politics. But there was much more of Paris and "that little café just off the Boul' Mich'." I did not know whether to be saddened or amused by the matchbox holder to which the visitors' attention was carefully drawn. There, as we sat in the greenish glow of a gas lantern, with the river in flood clearly audible in the background and mosquitoes pasturing on our ankles, out host kept his grip on the past through a treasured souvenir matchbox holder from the Café de la Paix.

The matchbox holder was a reminder of the way reality and illusion, and past and present, often blended. At Sambor, just to the north of Kratie, the last resting spot for the French explorers before they began the first of their countless passages through rapids, it was not a continuing sense of the colonial world that impressed us in 1966. That we had left behind when we drove northward out of Kratie and took to the river, to sit at the bow of a large sampan while the powerful outboard motor struggled to overcome the current, no easy task even along the calmer waters of the bank. Rather, at the village of Sambor, the past that was important was more distant than the period of the late nineteenth and early twentieth centuries when French officials had presided over the building of "modern" Kratie.

For the inhabitants of Sambor the present was blended with a past as far off as the ninth century, in the great stones that lay about their village, the debris of ancient temples built a thousand years ago. These stones, in the villagers' view, had been left by the "gods," since gods alone would have had the capacity to move them. A more recent past was evoked by the memory of terrible raids in the 1830s, when the Thai armies leveled their forebears' houses, cut down the fruit trees, and carried off some of the inhabitants into slavery. These events were not forgotten; nor was the miraculous discovery of the unharmed body of the princess taken by a crocodile in 1834. The stupa raised above her ashes was maintained at Prince Sihanouk's orders. As late as the 1960s it was no paradox, in Cambodian minds, that the spirit of the princess, when summoned through the proper medium, gave valuable advice on questions of foreign policy.

Monuments from the past lie along the banks of the Mekong far to the north of Sambor. The ruins of Wat Phu, near Bassac in southern Laos, offered the French explorers a subject for study and a cause for reflection. De Carné had found in them evidence of the incompetence of the ancient artists responsible for decorating the temples. They did not, he insisted, "know how to copy the human body. Without requiring them to attain our ideal, realized in Greek art, we might ask that they should have tried to imitate the forms under their eyes." Such critical remarks, however, are only a footnote to the history of growing appreciation of Khmer art, an appreciation fostered by the surveys carried out by Lagrée's exploration mission and furthered by Delaporte's later work at Angkor. Today the ruins of Wat Phu remain slumbering at the base of their mountain; war and its aftermath make archeological work difficult, if not impossible.

The "facts" of the scholarly world have little importance to the people who live with the monuments as a familiar backdrop to their daily existence. Across the Mekong from the town of Stung Treng is a decaying red brick tower, a minor ruin in comparison with the great temples to be found elsewhere in Cambodia and Laos but interesting for specialists, who gain knowledge of the past from the clues given by the style and type of construction. Very different was the appreciation of the local villager who left his cattle to come and explain the monument to three Western visitors who had made their way there in 1966. It was a temple to the great gods, as we would probably guess, but there was more to be known than this. There, high above the lintel where one could see a suggestion of a pattern; there, in ancient times, had been a sparkling decoration of diamonds. The past, however distant, lived for this man. The diamonds had gone, but he had no difficulty in visualizing their legendary fire.

Beyond the great waterfalls at Khone, no less formidable one hundred years after the explorers paused below them and were forced to admit that there was no easy passage, the Mekong runs through Laos. Here the descendants of the rulers the Frenchmen met still hold some sway over the population. There are no longer any "kings" of Bassac like the one Lagrée and his companions watched so critically as he joyfully and drunkenly celebrated the arrival of a new son. But a modern traveler might well see a family resemblance between the explorers' "king" and Prince Boun Oum of Champassak, the amiable descendant of earlier rulers, who was prominent briefly when the politics of Laos took on an international character in the 1960s. This prince has lost any claim to temporal power in southern Laos, but he retains his importance for his countrymen. His presence is necessary at the major festivals, which are still celebrated with the consumption of huge drafts of rice spirit. For some observers Boun Oum is a figure of mirth, a fat, gray-haired old man, fond of wine and spirits, seldom far from the comforting presence of his household of young women. A more perceptive assessment might be that he is a saddened man, bypassed by time. He can no longer believe in the importance of the festivals at which he must preside, but the population still sees him as a semi-divine prince and believes in these rites of propitiation, and so he must participate. Despite the war, despite the blood that has been shed, some of the old ways continue, and the pirogues still race down the Mekong to welcome the coming of the dry season.

Farther north again, beyond Vientiane, the administrative capital of modern Laos, is the royal capital, Luang Prabang, possibly the settlement that has changed least since the explorers traveled along the Mekong. The French impact on this region of Indochina was never as peaceful or as unchallenged as the histories published in Paris have suggested. But neither the French, nor the contending forces who continued to wage war in Laos after the French left, have succeeded in robbing this city of its Arcadian charm. Where the Mekong mission found a Prince of Luang Prabang, there is now a King of Laos, a paradoxical change since the King has less power than his princely ancestor. Larger now than when the explorers saw it, Luang Prabang continues to lie nestled beneath the hills which in this area of northern Laos dominate the Mekong. Memories of a greater past are still brought forth by the great ceremonies of the passing year. Laos was once, the inhabitants of Luang Prabang remember, the "Kingdom of a Million Elephants," and each New Year the King's elephants parade before the palace and attend and "listen to" a sermon preached by a Buddhist monk for their special benefit.

This would please de Carné's shade. He was fascinated by elephants, reacting to the skills displayed by the trained beasts on which the explorers traveled from time to time; and to the aura of primitive power and majesty attached to the herds of wild elephants seen in the forest of southeastern Laos. In his descriptions de Carné gave the elephants he observed almost human qualities. His own mount "discharged her duties as a mother with tenderness." The males were something else again, and de Carné's comment suggests the prurience that lay beneath much coy nineteenth-century writing: "As to the males they are lavishly gallant. They hide their mysterious amours in the depths of the woods; but they do nevertheless, on the march, use their trunks for the most immodest sport."

Beyond Luang Prabang, when the French explorers finally abandoned the Mekong, at Keng Hung, they traveled through an area of China at the very limits of imperial influence. The war against the Muslim rebels, which raged in the 1860s, was only the latest evidence of long-term resistance to central control. One hundred years later Yunnan province still retained its separate character. This is the most complex region of all China in terms of ethnic composition, with nearly a third of its inhabitants belonging to non-Chinese-speaking groups. Nothing gives Yunnan's distinctive character greater affirmation than the fact that the government in Peking administers large sections of this southern province through "autonomous regions." Despite the firm grip the central authorities have over the territory of Yunnan, and the extent to which the introduction of social programs has changed the life of the population, not all of the past has vanished. Old styles of dress and manners of behavior still survive, if uncertainly. As for economic change, this too has come; but Garnier's dream of Yunnan as an industrial region, with China's own version of Europe's "Dark Satanic mills," has not materialized.

It is temptingly easy to dwell on the exotic in any passing glance at the Mekong River and the lands through which it flows. Visions of dark foliage and a flooded river, of festivals, colorful clothing, and lumbering elephants are more agreeable to contemplate than the facts of war. Yet war, however tragic, is not the only threat to life along the course of the mighty river. Just as deadly is the still pervasive presence of endemic disease. The French explorers and successive generations of outside observers have marveled at the apparent bounty bestowed by nature on those who live along the Mekong. Enjoying a topical climate and a seeming abundance of food, the peasants who dwell by the river might have coined the Cambodian proverb, "If it grows, why plant it?"

The picture was and is an illusion. All along the Mekong the peasant's life involves risk and the possibility of insufficient food. A plentiful supply of tropical fruits is not a replacement for the necessary staple of rice if the crop should fail. Beyond the demands of farming, and the hardship that can follow a crop failure, the Mekong's peasantry suffers a terrible toll from disease. The fevers which were such a frequent and debilitating experience for the members of the French expedition may be better identified today, but they have not been eliminated. A century later we can be certain that some of the physical cost exacted from the explorers was the result of malaria; and malaria remains endemic. The scale of the disease is still staggering. More than ninety percent of the population of the lower Mekong basin live in high-risk malaria regions. At times the incidence of the disease comes close to one hundred per cent in some areas.

The catalogue of endemic diseases is a rollcall of poverty and deprivation: malaria, dysentery, yaws, and intestinal diseases are common over a wide area; tuberculosis and trachoma exact their toll in many regions. The incidence of venereal disease is high. For an outside observer the cost in infant deaths sometimes seems the deepest of the many personal tragedies that afflict Vietnamese, Cambodians, Thais, and Laotians along the Mekong. There are areas of Cambodia where only about fifty percent of the children born survive the first five years of life. Even those who do survive can look forward to an average life expectancy of only something less than fifty years. Outside the ranks of the elite, men and women alike look old, decades beyond their actual years, by the time they reach their fortieth year.

These medical facts would have been less disturbing to the French explorers a century ago than they are today. Medicine in Europe in the 1860s was only beginning its progress down a path of expanding discovery and scientific understanding. Compared with the cost of waging the war that has raged near and about the Mekong almost ceaselessly for nearly thirty years, the price of an effective program against disease along the course of the Mekong would be small indeed. Governments' priorities are, however, a tragedy of their own; and the peasants along the Mekong still await deliverance from disease.

One pale ray of hope may be discernible, which could ultimately pierce through the dark clouds of war, neglect, and disregard for human suffering: in the Mekong Project. Since 1957, under United Nations sponsorship, four of the countries whose borders lie along or about the Mekong River have joined, with external assistance, to plan the transformation of the river system. Despite the political fragmentation, the threat and fact of war, and the major uncertainties as to what program should be followed, some progress has been made.

The fact that no projects have yet been undertaken on the main stream of the Mekong is a reflection of the size of the problems to be solved. There are plans for the future and hopes of as many as ten dams along the river's course to control flooding, facilitate navigation, and produce countless kilowatts of hydroelectricity. Such an enormous program of building and damming would have far-reaching effects, by no means all of which have been fully evaluated. On the negative side there is need for caution about the social costs involved. And research into the likely changes in the ecology, into the possible public health problems that might be associated with such a massive transformation, has, in a long-term perspective, only just begun. On the positive side, there is the hope that this giant project might provide the basis for real social and economic advance. It only needs to be recalled that the scheme is on a scale that dwarfs the achievements of the Tennessee Valley Authority or the Aswan High Dam in Egypt, and that the cooperation of not only the countries of the area themselves but also of the world's major powers will be required for its execution, to suggest that the explorers' ghosts would have little difficulty in recognizing the Mekong for some time to come.

At the heart of all discussion, after all of the other factors have been reviewed, there is still the great river, the twelfth largest in the world when measured by length, the sixth largest when measured by the amount of water discharged into the sea. It still retains its mystery. We believe it is about 2,800 miles in length, but even today this is an assumption rather than a geographic certainty. Knowledge is certainly greater today than it was three centuries ago when Father Giovanni Filippo de Marini published his *New and Curious History of the Kingdoms of Tunquing and Laos* in Italian and French editions. His account of the river's origin was as follows:

This great river, which has been incorrectly situated by geographers ancient and modern, has its source in a very deep marsh, shaped like a lake, that lies to the north on high mountains in the province of Yunnan, on the frontiers of China; falling from thence it rushes headlong from this valley and, forcing its passage through sheer violence, small and narrow though it be, it does not tarry there long. . . .*

Yet, while we know that this Jesuit priest was wrong in detail, many of Garnier's questions about the river's origins remain unanswered, even in the late twentieth century, as official publications of the Mekong Project clearly indicate:

The biggest problem is of course the river itself. The Mekong is believed to be about 4,500 kilometers [2,812 miles] in length, but nobody can be sure, for no man, as far as is known, has ever set eyes on its source, or followed it through all the fantastic ravines of its upper course. It is believed to rise at a height of about 5,100 meters [nearly 16,600 feet] in the Thang Hla mountains in China, probably only a few kilometers from the equally unpinpointable source of the Salween. It tumbles down about 2,100 meters [more than 6,500 feet] to Chamdo, on the main (yak) road from Kanting in China to Lhasa, where it is called the Dza Chu. It then disappears into more virtually unexplored gorges until it emerges at Paoshan on the Burma Road.

The Mekong has not become the route into China that Lagrée, Garnier, and their companions hoped it might be. But it has remained a mighty river. Whatever changes the Mekong Project may achieve, however much the river is transformed by dams and reservoirs, it will dominate its surroundings as it has always done. At low water the Mekong's surface will still be dark and calm, a study in placidity. In flood, particularly at the countless rapids, or most dramatically of all at the Khone Falls, the river will continue to overwhelm the observer with its elemental force. In flood it will threaten; as the river waters drop during the dry season, they will leave behind their great deposits of silt and be a

* The English rendering of Father de Marini's account is taken from *Kingdom of Laos* (Limoges, 1959), p. 60, a translation of *Présence du Royaume Lao*, edited by René de Berval (a special issue of *France-Asie*).

source of vast supplies of fish.

No river so large and important can be without a personality, and this is as true one hundred years later as when Francis Garnier gave his own descriptions of the Mekong's many moods. He was fascinated by the animal life along the banks, by the kingfishers diving for prey in the swirling waters, by the tropical forests running back from the river's edge. His marveling accounts dwelled on the contrast between the emergence of great sandbanks at low water and the thundering torrents at flood time. But he knew, too, the disappointments that awaited a traveler pressing north towards China, as the banks crept in and the countryside along the river rose to enclose the Mekong in towering gorges. In a brief and unemotional comment, he said all that is necessary as a final word: "Without doubt, no other river, over such a length, has a more singular or remarkable character."

AUTHOR'S POSTSCRIPT

$\mathcal{T}$wenty years after I wrote the Epilogue chapter of my book, the changes that have taken place along the course of the Mekong River have been just as momentous, perhaps even more so, than those I charted as having occurred in the century that had passed since the explorers made their way towards China. When the book was completed in 1974, Vietnam was still a divided country in which war raged, as it did also in neighboring Cambodia and Laos. China was still led by Mao Zedong, and although the shockwaves of the Great Proletarian Cultural Revolution were beginning to subside the rulers of Asia's largest country still rejected Western concepts of a market economy. Burma, now called Myanmar, in many ways the least accessible of all Southeast Asian countries, remained a state with its face turned away from the outside world.

For the countries that had once formed French Indochina, 1975 was a year of high drama. In Cambodia, 1975 saw the triumph of the Khmer Rouge forces and the subsequent descent of that country into a terrifying period of state-sponsored brutality against its own population. In Vietnam, the same year saw the end of the war that had pitched the communist forces linked to the government in Hanoi against its Saigon-based opponents and their American backers. And in Laos, too, though in an idiosyncratic and gentler Laotian fashion, a communist government finally came to power after years of war.

Now, twenty years on, there has been further change to the politics of the countries that border the Mekong. In the broadest sense, the passage of time has had the least effect in Burma, where a central government dominated by ethnic Burmans continues to hold sway and seeks by all means, including through its armed forces, to exercise control over the minority ethnic groups spread around the country's borders. These were the same ethnic groups the explorers confronted and which caused them so many painful delays.

Dramatic change has come to China in the past two decades. The death of the 'great Helsman' in 1976 signaled the beginning of a shift from communist economic orthodoxy to an embrace of market economics, with accompanying political consequences that still cannot be fully assessed. Then, with the end of the Cold War and the disintegration of the Soviet Union, China finds itself in the final decade of the twentieth century the last major power to order its political affairs through the apparatus of an entrenched communist party.

Communist parties still control the politics of Vietnam, and Laos, but these countries, too, are wrestling with the dilemma that faces the Chinese leadership. How, in a post-Cold War world, with an increasing reliance on market economics and openings to the outside world, can the authority of the party be maintained?

Of all the political changes that have taken place over the twenty years since my book was completed, none have been more dramatic, or more terrible, than those affecting Cambodia. For more than three awful years, a leadership espousing a bizarrely primitive version of Marxism pursued policies that caused the death of upwards of one million Cambodians, through executions, exhaustion and starvation. Only after a Vietnamese invasion and then an agonizingly protracted civil war has Cambodia been able to attain a measure of peace in the 1990s.

Yet if political change along the course of the Mekong has been considerable, the landscape through which the great river flows has altered remarkably little. In Vietnam the settlement from which the explorers began their journey is now called Ho Chi Minh city rather than Saigon and in the nearly twenty years that have passed since the communist forces gained control of the city many of the old landmarks have been demolished. But not all, for the Customs House that dominated the waterfront when they set off is still there. No longer linked to the business of the port, it has become the Ho Chi Minh Museum.

The other capitals that sit beside the river - Phnom Penh, Vientiane and Luang Prabang - have changed remarkably little over the past twenty years. Both Phnom Penh and Vientiane have grown in size, with 'modernity' doing little to enhance their charm. Luang Prabang continues to escape the worst ravages of contemporary development. For the rest, while there has been some change to the river towns that dot the Mekong's banks as it wends its way from Tibet to the South China Sea, these changes have not been of a striking kind.

There is one notable exception to this generalisation. For the first time the Mekong has been bridged. Opened in 1994, a bridge more than one kilometre in length now links Thailand and Laos, from Nong Khay on the Thai side of the river to a location on the Laotian left bank, a little to the south of Vientiane. The construction of this bridge represents change indeed and may be a sign of greater changes still to come. There is talk of a second bridge and discussion continues to take place of future dams, either along the Mekong's tributaries, or even on the river itself.

One thing has not changed in any important fashion over the past two decades. The hopes that were so central to the French explorers' mission of the Mekong becoming a trade route into China remain unrealized. So the Mekong is still what it has always been. It provides opportunities for relatively limited local water-borne traffic. But more importantly it is an essential element in the life of the men and women along its course whose lives are linked to agriculture and to fishing. When the Mekong floods it deposits rich layers of silt along that runs back from its bank. Far to the south from its source, in the Mekong Delta, the river spreads to form a region of rich fecundity that is once again being exploited in an atmosphere of political calm. Through the enormous volume of water that flows down the Mekong, Cambodia's Tonle Sap river is turned around to flow backwards into the Great Lake, where vast numbers of fish breed. When the waters reverse once again, the fish are harvested in huge quantities to form an essential part of Cambodian peasants' diet.

The Mekong is still the 'Great River' that so fascinated Lagrée, Garnier and their companions. With its origins only finally discovered in 1995 in the high plateaus of eastern Tibet, it still embodies mystery as well as bringing life to the lands through which it flows. Still known by many names at different points along its length, the passage of another score of years will leave it what it has always been - the great and dominating physical feature of the Indochinese world.

Milton Osborne,

April 1996

SOURCES

$\mathcal{A}$nyone who seeks a more detailed account of the events and individuals described in this book must turn to the writings of the explorers themselves and to the rich and fascinating holdings of the French Archives. In the course of intermittent research in Paris, over a period of nearly ten years, I have come upon information of interest and importance for the Mekong expedition and the abortive episode in Tonkin of 1873 in the following *dépots:* Archives Nationales de France; Archives Nationales de France, Section Outre-Mer; Archives du Ministère des Affaires Etrangères (Quai d'Orsay); Archives de la Marine; Service Historique de l'Armée de Terre, Section Outre-Mer.

The listing of printed sources below is far from exhaustive. It does, however, provide some suggestion of the most important, if not always readily available, Western language sources. There is no need, perhaps, to emphasize the fact that modern Vietnamese historians hold a very different view of the efforts mounted by Garnier and Dupuis to seize Tonkin, in 1873, from that offered by French writers of the nineteenth century.

Aymonier, E. *Voyage dans le Laos.* 2 vols. Paris, 1895–97.

Beauvais, R. de. *Louis Delaporte, Explorateur (1842–1925).* Paris, 1929.

Berval, R. de. *Kingdom of Laos.* Limoges, 1959.

Cady, J. F. *The Roots of French Imperialism in Eastern Asia.* Ithaca, N. Y., 1954.

Carné, L. de. *Travels in Indo-China and the Chinese Empire.* London, 1872.

Clifford, H. *Further India.* London, 1904.

Colquhoun, A. R. *Amongst the Shans.* London, 1885.

Conder, J. *The Modern Traveller.* London, 1830.

Delaporte, L. *Voyage au Cambodge.* Paris, 1880.

Dupuis, J. *Les Origines de la question du Tong-Kin.* Paris 1896.

——, *Le Tong-kin et l'intervention Française (Francis Garnier et Philastre).* Paris, 1898.

——, *Le Tonkin de 1872 à 1886.* Paris, 1910.

Dutreb, M. *L'Amiral Dupré et la conquête du Tonkin.* Paris 1923.

FitzGerald, C. P. *The southern Expansion of the Chinese People.* New York, 1972.

Francis, G. (Francis Garnier). *La Cochinchine française en 1864.* Paris, 1864.

Garnier, F. *Voyage de'exploration en Indo-Chine, effectué pendant les années 1866, 1867 à 1868*. 2 vols. Paris, 1873.

——, *De Paris au Tibet*. Paris, 1882.

——, *Voyage de'exploration en Indo-Chine*. Paris, 1885.

Gautier, H. *Les Français au Tonkin (1787–1883)*. Paris 1883.

Julien, F. *Lettres d'un précurseur: Doudart de Lagrée au Cambodge et en Indo-Chine*. Paris, 1886.

Laffey, E. "The Frenchman as an old China hand: Jean Dupuis and the Garnier Affair," *Journal of Southeast Asian Studies*, Vol 6. No 1. 1975.

Levy, P. "Le Voyage de Van Wuysthoff au Laos (1641–1642) d'après son Journal (Inédit en Français)," *Cahiers de l'Ecole Française d'Extrême-Orient*, 1944.

Lintingre, P. "Permanence d'une structure monarchique en Asie: Le royaume de Champassak," *Revue Française d'Historie d'Outre-Mer*, 1972.

McAleavy, H. *Black Flags in Vietnam: The Story of a Chinese Intervention, the Tonkin War of 1884–85*. London, 1968.

Mallaret, L. "Aspects inconnus de Francis Garnier," *Bulletin de la Société des Etudes Indochinoises*, 1952.

Mouhot, H. *Travels in the Central Parts of Indo-China (Siam), Cambodia and Laos*. 2 vols. London, 1864.

Moura, J. *Le Royaume du Cambodge*. 2 vols. Paris, 1883.

Petit, E. *Francis Garnier: Sa vie, ses voyages, ses oeuvres, d'après une correspondence inédite*. Paris, 1894.

Pouvourville, A. de. *Francis Garnier*. Paris, 1931.

Reinach, L. de. *Le Laos*. Paris, 1911.

Romanet du Caillaud, F. *Histoire de l'intervention française au Tonkin, de 1872 à 1874*. Paris, 1880.

Taboulet, G. *La Geste française en Indochine*. 2 vols. Paris, 1955–56.

——, "Le Voyage d'exploration du Mékong (1866–1868): Doudart de Lagrée et Francis Garnier," *Revue Française d'Histoire d'Outre-Mer*, 1970.

Thorel, C. *Notes médicales du voyage d'exploration du Mékong et de Cochinchine*. Paris, 1870.

Truong Buu Lam. *Patterns of Vietnamese Response to Foreign Intervention: 1858–1900*. New Haven, Conn., 1967.

Valette, J. "Origines et enseignements de l'expédition du Mékong," *Bulletin de la Société d'Histoire Moderne*, 1968.

——, "L'Expédition du Mékong (1866–1868) à travers les témoinages de quelques-uns de ses membres," *Revue Historique*, 1972.

Vercel, R. *Francis Garnier à l'assaut des fleuves*. Paris, 1952.

Villemereuil, A. B. de. *Explorations et missions de Doudart de Lagrée*. Paris, 1883.

INDEX

Note: This index does not provide entries for the Mekong River. In the case of the six principal French explorers, and Jean Dupuis, initial index entries are followed only by entries to specific events.

BIOGRAPHICAL NOTE

Milton Osborne is an internationally acclaimed expert on Southeast Asia. After graduating from the University of Sydney with first-class honors in history, he joined the Australian Embassy in Phnom Penh, Cambodia, between 1959 and 1961. This experience inspired him to undertake postgraduate study at Cornell University where he received his Ph.D in Southeast Asian history. During this time he carried out extended research in Vietnam, Cambodia and France.

Dr. Osborne has since held academic appointments in Australia, England and the United States, and he was the first Director of the British Institute in Southeast Asia, based in Singapore. An advisor to the United Nations on the Cambodian refugee problem between 1980 and 1981, he then became Head of the Asia Branch of the Australian government's Office of National Assessments in 1982. He is the author of seven books on Asian issues, and since 1993 has been a full-time writer and consultant on the region.